Taming the Beast

Taming the Beast

Human–Animal Encounters in the Bible

YOSSI FEINTUCH

WIPF & STOCK · Eugene, Oregon

The worst sin towards our fellow creatures is . . . to be indifferent to them. That's the essence of inhumanity.—George Bernard Shaw

Contents

Abbreviations

'Abot	Avot
Ag. Ap.	Josephus, *Against Apion*
ALT	Alter, Robert. *The Five Books of Moses: A Translation with Commentary*. New York: Norton, 2004.
b.	Babylonian
Baal HaTurim	Jacob ben Asher
B. Bat.	Bava Batra
Ber.	Berakhot
Ber. Rab.	Bereshit Rabbah
B. Met.	Bava Metzi'a
Chizkuni	Hezekiah ben Manoah
DAV	Davis, Menachem, ed. *The Latter Prophets with a Commentary*. New York: Mesorah, 2014.
Dev. Rab.	Devarim Rabbah
'Erub.	Eruvin
Hul.	Hullin
JPS	Jewish Publication Society
J.W.	Josephus, *The Wars of the Jews*
KH	Kol Haneshamah. *Prayerbook for the Days of Awe*. Reconstructionist, 1999.
Kli Yakar	Shlomo Ephraim ben Aaron Luntschitz

KRAUS	*The Book of Job*. Translated by Donald Kraus. Woodstock, VT: Jewish Light, 2012.
M.	Mishnah
Maimonides	Moshe Ben Maimon
Malbim	Meir Leibush Weisser
Mech. Shem.	Mechilta Shemot
Midr.	Midrash
NOAB	*The New Oxford Annotated Bible*. 3rd ed. Edited by Micahel D. Coogan et al. Oxford: Oxford University Press, 2001.
Noda BiYehudah	Ezekiel Landau
Ohr HaChaim	Chaim Ibn Attar
Pesaḥ.	Pesahim
Pirqe R. El.	Pirqe Rabbi Eliezer
PLAUT	*The Torah: A Modern Commentary*. Edited by W. Gunther Plaut. New York: URJ, 2006.
Qidd.	Qiddushin
Qod.	Qodashim
Radak	David Kimhi
Ralbag	Levi ben Gershon
Ramban	Moses ben Nachman (Nachmanides)
Rashar	Rav Samson Raphael Hirsch
Rashbam	Samuel ben Meir
Rashi	Shlomo Yitzchaki
Sanh.	Sanhedrin
Šabb.	Shabbat

SB	*The Schocken Bible, Vol. 1: The Five Books of Moses*. Translated by Everett Fox. New York: Schocken Books, 1995.
Shadal	Samuel David Luzzatto
SON	*Soncino Chumash*. Edited by A. Cohen. London Soncino, 1947.
Sotah	Sotah
Shem. Rab.	Shemot Rabbah
STONE	Scherman, Nosson, et al. *The Chumash*. The Stone Edition. New York: Mesorah, 1994.
Ta'an.	Ta'anit
Tanḥ. Ber.	Tanhuma, Bereshit
Tanḥ	Tanhuma
Vaik. Rab.	Vaikra Rabbah
Yal.	Yalqut
Yebam.	Yevamot
Yoma	Yoma (Kippurim)

Preface

Man was created as a bloody animal, and I think he will always thirst for blood and will manage to have it. I think he is far and away the worst animal that exists and the only untamable one.—Mark Twain

"Beast": The Word Masking Human Evil

"An evil animal";
"a beast that looks like a horse";
"a dog within dogs";
"a large-boned ass";
"a mouse";
"a hyena";
"a monkey frog";
"a wild ox";
"a rooster."

The vastly popular Yiddish writer Shalom Aleichem—known as "the other Mark Twain"—recalls in his autobiographical book *The Life of a Person* (*Chayei Adam* in Hebrew) the many curses that his stepmother cast at him when he was growing up in nineteenth-century Russia, as though by using such aliases the person so named would utterly be mocked and diminished.[1]

1. Aleichem, *Chayei Adam*, 2:104–7.

In the same spirit, the word "beast" has been used most widely by Bible translators as the primary English (or *bestia* in Spanish) moniker for the various Hebrew references to "animal" therein. The word "beast" quickly evokes negative connotations such as stupidity, loutishness, and cruelty. In her endorsement of Stephen G. Michaud's and Roy Hazelwood's *The Evil That Men Do*, which is about sadistic sexual offenders, Manhattan's sex crimes prosecution unit's chief, Linda A. Fairstein, betrayed (if only subliminally) her associations of mind-depraved criminals with animals. In the book, she writes, "Hazelwood takes us into the belly of the beast . . . [and] the mind of the beast."[2] No predatory animal comes even close to exhibiting the human ferocity and villainy described in that book, the exclusive acts of human beings.

The Nazi "Beasts"

When, in December 1942, the United States, Great Britain, the Soviet Union, and eight other Allied powers issued a joint statement, they condemned "in the strongest possible terms the [Nazi] bestial policy of cold-blooded extermination" of European Jews.[3] Likewise, Moshe Bahir, a survivor of Sobibor, a Nazi-operated death camp in Poland during the Shoah (Holocaust), described Gustav Franz Wagner, the deputy commandant of the camp, as a diabolical "wild beast" whose lust to murder knew no bounds as he would snatch babies from their mothers' arms and tear them to pieces in his hands, alongside other heinous actions.[4] Due to his virulent ruthlessness, Gustav Wagner's other moniker was "wolf."[5]

Even the twentieth-century, eminent rabbi Mordechai Kaplan, the founder of the liberal movement of Reconstructionist Judaism, described man as having "evolved from an animal ancestry and [ergo] is still largely dominated by beastly urges and impulses that are a part of his natural heritage"; hence, the Shoah was a case of "human bestiality," and by contrast, "whatever goodness exists in human nature and human society is evidence of man's ascent from the beast."[6]

2. Fairstein, Endorsement.
3. "11 Allies Condemn."
4. Wikipedia, "Gustav Wagner."
5. Wikipedia, "Gustav Wagner."
6. Kaplan, *Questions*, 131, 256.

When Humans Behave Like "Animals"

An Israeli digital news outlet that reported about the funeral of the young Fogel family of five, slain by a lone terrorist in March 2011 when they were asleep in their beds in the town of Itamar, quoted the eulogizing speakers. The eminent rabbi Yisrael Meir Lau referred to the "predatory animals" who committed the massacre, as did another speaker, by referring to those "animals who walk on two."[7] The fact is that, unlike human predators, a carnivore animal does not kill more individual prey than the single quarry it manages to successfully hunt and consume, as there is no mass ravening committed by predaceous animals (or for that matter by carnivorous fish and insects); Why waste energy and efforts on killing another prey that would not be consumed any time soon? Nor are predators driven to kill by emotions of rancor or plain hatred. Even on a rare occasion when a predator kills a human, it would not typically engage in multiple assaults on other individuals who may be at the scene.

US president Donald Trump also used this endemic stereotyping of animals while calling for stronger immigration laws by defining "people coming into the country or trying to come in"—namely, Mexican gang members—as "bad people" who "aren't people. These are animals."[8] Trump repeated such comments on April 2, 2024, while speaking in Grand Rapids, Michigan, calling immigrants illegally in the United States "not humans, they're animals."[9]

The Imperiled Life of Animals' Mates

In September 2020, Benny Gantz, at the time Israel's "alternate prime minister," posted on Facebook about a woman, Shirah Iskov, who miraculously survived her husband's ruthless and violent murder attempt that left her critically wounded in front of their toddler. Gantz wrote, "Shira survived heroically the animal-like villainous murder attempt by her husband."[10] Such a comparison ignored the truth about animals.

7. *Kikar HaShabbat*, "B'ma'amad kore'a lev."

8. Korte and Gomez, "Trump Ramps Up Rhetoric."

9. Liles, "Trump's 'Animals' Remark."

10. Gantz, בני גנץ—Gantz's Post."

Yes, females of some spider species kill after mating and eat their smaller male partners, although male black widows may also eat their female mates. Sea slugs are carnivores that sometimes feed on each other after mating. The much larger female praying mantis might, if hungry, behead its male counterpart immediately after mating. The mating of two Labord's chameleons might be lethal for both partners. Male octopuses risk an accidental death in mating, like the male anacondas sometimes do after mating with their much larger females. Also, female sagebrush crickets feed on their male partners during mating. But that's it!

In his Facebook post, was Gantz thinking specifically of these very animals that pose a lethal menace to their mates when he compared a heinous assault by a husband on his wife with a normative animalistic behavior? Indeed, no other animals but those critters attempt to slay their female counterparts.

Exclusively Human: Misogynistic Cruelties

While "approximately 231 million" human beings, mostly civilians, were "killed or allowed to die by human decision" in wars and conflicts during the twentieth century,[11] women have been subjected to the most horrific monstrosities by conquering armies in essentially every scene of hostilities from antiquity to this day. It has been manifested in preying on girls and women with mass rapes, often supplemented by additional acts of torture. To be sure, such horrendous assaults are absent from the ways of "brutes," namely, wild or feral animals; they are exclusively human.

It is wrong, therefore, on all accounts to compare deliberate and vile human conduct with an animal that kills a single prey at a point of hunger (or a serious threat), merely with its fangs, tapers, and claws as fast as it can and while risking itself a critical injury if not death. Predatory animals, as a rule, do not attempt to prolong the ordeal of their prey for the sake of deriving pleasure from the act, especially "sexual" pleasure—as the word "sadistic" connotes. Some of the most luridly atrocious actions of humans towards other humans, especially against women—most from recent centuries—are as follows:

11. Center for International and Security Studies, "Death in Wars."

- The mid-thirteenth century invasion of Austria by the Mongols was also manifested in gang raping of young girls and women to death or cutting their breasts off before eating these and the rest of their bodies.[12]
- The Timurid invasion of Syria between 1400 and 1401 exhibited itself in mass and gang rape of native women (even in mosques) while forcing the women's brothers and fathers to watch.[13]
- In 1877, the Russian Empire conducted a genocide of the Muslim Circassians during its war against the Ottomans. The perpetrators, Russian General Grigory Zass's troops, impaled and ripped open pregnant women's bellies, and mass raped women and children.[14]
- The 1937–1938 Nanjing (Nanking, the capital of China at the time) Massacre, which involved the murder of anywhere between one hundred thousand and three hundred thousand residents by Imperial Japanese troops, was accompanied by the widespread rape of scores of Chinese women.[15]
- World War II is so notorious for its atrocities that no apex predators could come even close to resembling. Nazi Germany (and its allied, willing, murderous collaborators) were on a mission to methodically obliterate ethnicities whom they considered ideologically inferior and subhuman. When a predatory animal hunts to eat, its action is rational. When the Nazis liquidated their victims out of sheer demonization, they gained nothing beneficial for their essential interests or national well-being; had the Nazis acted like animals there would have been no Holocaust or genocide.
- In 1945, as the Nazi German army was retreating on all fronts, the advancing Soviet troops committed mass rapes (half of which were gang rapes) of Polish, Romanian, Hungarian, Lithuanian, Estonian, Latvian, Yugoslav, Austrian, and German women and girls from the ages eight to eighty; it was an army of rapists. This included more than two million German women being raped—in many cases women were the victims of repeated rapes, some as many as sixty to seventy

12. Wikipedia, "Mongol Incursions."
13. Wikipedia, "Sack of Aleppo (1400)."
14. Gender Security Project, "CRSV."
15. Britannica Online, "Nanjing Massacre."

times, many in public as well as in front of their husbands, before both were murdered.[16] Writer Alexander Solzhenitsyn, a Red Army veteran, wrote a poem about "the little daughter on the mattress, dead. How many have been on it? A platoon, a company perhaps? A girl's been turned into a woman, a woman turned into a corpse"[17]

- During the Bosnian War (1992–1995) that followed the breakup of Yugoslavia, anywhere from twenty thousand to fifty thousand Bosnian Muslim girls (from age twelve) and women were mostly mass (i.e., 80 percent) or systemically, (i.e., happening over a prolonged period of imprisonment) raped, mainly by Christian Bosnian and Serb (and to a lesser extent Croat) forces in their homes in front of family members and in the streets in front of villagers and neighbors. At times, rape was also committed with objects such as broken glass bottles, guns, and truncheons.[18]
- During the 1994 genocide in Rwanda, perpetrated in just one hundred days, members of the Hutu militia, commonly using machetes, murdered more than eight hundred thousand civilians of the Tutsi ethnic tribe. It is estimated that between two hundred fifty thousand and five hundred thousand Tutsi women and girls were systematically raped—also with objects such as sharpened sticks, machete knives, boiling water, and acid, with the intent of destroying their reproductive capabilities—including the mutilation of breasts or buttocks perpetrated during or following rape, not excluding pregnant women, and frequently perpetrated in plain view of others at sites such as schools, churches, roadblocks, government buildings, or in the bush.[19]
- The 2014–2017 Yazidi genocide perpetrated by the Islamic State in Iraq and Syria (the self-dubbed "Caliphate") was characterized by massacres of thousands of Yazidi men through beheadings, crucifixions, beatings, mutilation and dismemberment, the stoning of both children and adults, and the live burning of people. Between seven thousand and ten thousand eight hundred Yazidi (and Christian minority) girls (some as young as ten yeas old) and women were subjected to organized genocidal mass rape and sexual slavery. By 2015,

16. Staff Writer, "In Pictures"; Wikipedia, "Soviet War Crimes."

17. Solzhenitsyn, *Prussian Nights*, 154.

18. Wikipedia, "Bosnian War."

19. Britannica Online, "Rwanda Genocide of 1994."

upwards of 71 percent of the global Yazidi population was displaced by the genocide.[20]

- During the first two decades of the twenty-first century, thousands of elderly women in Tanzania had been strangled, beaten, or knifed to death, after which their bodies were burned, while others were burned alive after being denounced as witches by vigilante mobs.[21] (Around 2,500 people—mostly women—were executed in Scotland between 1563 and 1736 under the country's Witchcraft Act.[22])
- In the Russian war on Ukraine that began in 2022, Russian soldiers in Kherson and Bucha raped and gang-raped at gunpoint as a component of their war strategy. Rapes were frequently committed in front of children or other family members, kept in an adjacent room, and coerced thereby to hear the violations taking place. Mutilation of Ukrainian prisoners of war was also committed.[23]
- Abject horrors were committed by Hamas terrorists from the Gaza Strip, attacking numerous Israeli border farm settlements and towns on October 7, 2023. These "numerous war crimes and crimes against humanity"[24] included "rape and gang rape"[25] as well as "mutilation [of] and despoiling bodies"[26] perpetrated "against women and men."[27]

Our Knee-Jerk Comparisons to Animals

Israel's president, Yitzhak Herzog, called the vicious terrorists "human animals" who perpetrated "nonhuman cruelty."[28] Like him, the Israeli premier, Benjamin Netanyahu, used the same words to describe Hamas terrorists, adding that they were "predatory animals" because they "celebrat[ed] the

20. Human Rights Watch, "Iraq."
21. Migiro, "Despite Murderous Attacks."
22. Recker, "Scotland Issues Formal Apology."
23. Noone et al., "Russian Use of Rape"; Wikipedia, "War Crimes."
24. Human Rights Watch, "October 7 Crimes."
25. Human Rights Watch, "I Can't Erase."
26. Human Rights Watch, "October 7 Crimes."
27. Human Rights Watch, "I Can't Erase."
28. JDN News, "Nesi hamedinah."

murder of women, children and the elderly."[29] US senator of Florida Marco Rubio, now Secretary of State, spoke similarly in the wake of the massacre: "These people are vicious animals who did horrifying crimes."[30] White House National Security Council spokesman John Kirby told reporters in June 2024 that "a beast" like Hamas leader Yahya Sinwar "takes glee" in the bloodshed on the Israeli side and among Gaza's Palestinians.[31] To be sure, predatory animals don't show elation over a successful kill of prey. Gang rape, torture by mutilation, or "just" murder in front of other members of the family, whose turn quickly arrives as well, is an exclusive human handiwork. And it is what Sinwar and his fellow terrorists perpetrated, like those who had come before them, in committing atrocities for no other goal than to shame, humiliate, mock, and abuse their human prey.

A principal investigator in the Israeli police Lahav Unit 433 that had been collecting testimonies from captured Hamas terrorists told a radio interviewer that by murdering children and abusing women and dead bodies, Hamas was "a more nefarious organization than ISIS in that everyone there is a bad dog."[32] Avigdor Liberman, a former Israeli government senior minister and a veteran parliamentarian, tweeted "Every dog has its day"[33] following the killing of Hamas military leader Sinwar in mid-October 2024.

Needless to say, to compare arch-terrorists to dogs goes beyond the pale of absurdity. While no animal, let alone a dog of any breed, would be able to come even close to matching the cruelty of ISIS or Hamas terrorists, such words were nonetheless conveniently chosen to describe the dog as an archetype of unparalleled ferocity.

A Deceptive Comparison

That the Torah does not view carnivorous animals as agents of malevolence or ferocity can be inferred from its hundreds of prohibitions, none of which forbids acting "like an animal," not even "like a predator." On the flip side, the Torah forbids emulating the ways of the Egyptians or the

29. Eichner, "Netanyahu."
30. Faguy, "America's New Secretary."
31. Lillis and Marquardt, "US Intelligence."
32. Hakmon, "O-nes v'hit'aleloot achzarit."
33. Ashkenazi, "Netanyahu."

Canaanites—"by their laws, you are not to walk" (Lev 18:3 SB). Unlike people, the Bible never defines a wicked person as one who imitates "an evil animal."

The spontaneous choice of deprecating words such as "acted like an animal," "in a beastly fashion," or "inhuman brutalities" points to carnivorous animals as examples of heinous actions that are human handiwork. We similarly seek, if only subliminally, to comfort ourselves with the idea that it is uncharacteristic of humans to follow the modus operandi of predatory animals. So, to elevate the concept that animal predation of prey is incomparably crueler than what humans inflict on their fellows, whether human or nonhuman, we invoke an idiom such as "the laws of the jungle." In doing so, we intend to compare humans who acted viciously to animal predators.

In this vein, the term "jungle justice" is used today, especially in Cameroon and Nigeria, to describe a mob that takes with impunity the law into its hands to barbarically execute, usually by public stoning or burning, unfortunate individuals, most of whom are falsely accused of their alleged crimes.[34] Yet predatory animals in the jungle do not act likewise.

Unlike humans who are gunned down or stabbed and consequently have no realistic chance to escape their lethal predicament, prey animals have considerable chances to run away for their lives even when chased by a predator. Tigers concede anywhere between 50 to 95 percent of their would-be prey being unable to execute a kill, and polar bears, albeit crown predators in the Arctic, have only 10 to 28 percent successful kills. Wolves have a 20 percent success rate. Leopards see anywhere between 62 and 86 percent of their intended prey escape, even as the super-fast cheetah must concede a would-be prey in the course of 50 to 60 percent of its charges.[35]

Lions—also top predators—bring down prey only at a success rate of 27 to 34 percent. In short, the success rate in hunting for most mammal predators is below 50 percent.[36] Even then, after it devours a single animal, the lion becomes lazy and sleepy, and it would not get up from its crouch until it has digested its food fully. Indeed, the grazing animals in its immediate proximity do not fear it any longer at such times of satiation. By contrast, human terrorists and mass shooters seek to murder with malice, rather than for food, as many victims as they can manage.

34. Wikipedia, "Jungle Justice."

35. Wikipedia, "Hunting Success."

36. Wikipedia, "Hunting Success."

In a 2024 interview with *The Economist*, President Zelensky of Ukraine likened Russian president Vladimir Putin to "an animal" who "likes the feeling of blood."[37] What President Zelensky did not know about animals is that the great majority of the sixty-four hundred mammals on earth today are non-predatory; ergo, they do not like the feeling of blood, let alone of their species. Only a very low percentage of mammals are obligate carnivores, of whom only a very few would dispatch their very kind as numerous humans do without batting an eye.[38]

The meerkat is one such mammal, as is the marmot, and certain breeds of lemurs. Lions, wolves, hyenas, Hanuman Langur monkeys, hippos, and Komodo dragons may also kill members of their species. However, apes in general rarely kill a fellow adult; their victims are babies, a phenomenon that is known with lions and hippos, too, when one alpha male, who enjoys exclusive breeding rights with many a female, is dethroned and replaced by another. The latter might resort to the killing of the deposed ruler's offspring.[39]

The Ruthlessness of Biblical Rulers

The Bible shows us, however, in some five stomach-churning episodes that the murder of would-be heirs, or potential successors of an overthrown ruler, was normative even as it was gruesome, thus leaving humans, morally speaking, with no leg up over the small number of animal species that do so as well. Abimelech, one of the seventy sons born to the chieftain Gideon by his multiple women, desired to succeed his father and reign over Israel (Gideon's induction into leadership as a chieftain was via a divine revelation and personal commission and it was not his to bequeath to an heir [Judg 6:14, 21–23]). To proclaim himself as his father's successor, Abimelech had his sixty-nine brothers executed—their hands were tied as they were slain by hired assassins "upon one stone" (Judg 9:5 JPS).

Likewise, King David resorts to subterfuge by eliminating all potential heirs from King Saul's bloodline who one day might challenge his royal line (see Judg 20). The last Judean king of the house of David, Zedekiah, who had rebelled against Babylon in 586 BCE, saw his sons butchered by the

37. Beddoes, "Volodymyr Zelensky."

38. Answers, "What Percentage"; Bradford, "Carnivores"; Connor, "How Many Species."

39. Answers, "What Percentage"; Wellbank, "Hippos."

Babylonian king Nebuchadnezzar (2 Kgs 24:20, 25:6–7; 2 Chr 36:13; Ezek 17:15–18), thus ensuring the end of the Davidic royal bloodline and with it any future restoration, as his actions reneged on the vassal status of Judea.

About three centuries earlier in the northern kingdom of Israel, Ba'asha, the chief officer of King Nadav's army, struck him dead and replaced him on the throne. He promptly proceeded to slay and wipe out all family members of his predecessor to secure his kingship so no one from the previous royal line would ever be able to reclaim the crown. When Elah succeeded his father Ba'asha, Zimri, a high-ranking military officer who served the new king of Israel, rebelled by slaying him (when Elah was intoxicated), and then proceeded to liquidate the whole royal household including Elah's siblings, paternal uncles and their sons who were eligible for carrying out blood revenge, and friends of the crown to boot (1 Kgs 15:29, 16:11–12).

This massive purge went on for seven days, the total number of days that Zimri would reign as king before he, too, was deposed by Omri, another military chief. Several decades later (around mid-ninth century BCE), Jehu, the commander of the Israelite army—believing that he was fulfilling God's will after the prophet Elisha facilitated his anointing as king of Israel—orchestrated a military coup against the Israelite king Yoram (who had succeeded his slain father Ahab) and struck him dead with an arrow. Moreover, Jehu also orchestrated the killing of Ahab's grandson, Ahaziah, king of Judah, and a wholesale butchering of his forty-two nephews, potential heirs to the Judean (Davidic) crown (2 Kgs 10:14).

In line with Elisha's instruction to "strike down the house of . . . Ahab . . . for all of Ahab's household shall perish; I will cut off from Ahab every male, bond or free, in Israel" (2 Kgs 9:7–8 NOAB), Jehu saw to the beheading of "seventy" offspring of Ahab's bloodline (plus other loyalists). This is possibly an inflated and round number that the Bible employs to call attention to the atrocious act perpetrated by their spineless guardians and tutors. He thus left "no survivor" (i.e., not even babies) of the "house of Ahab in Jezreel" (the location of Ahab's winter palace). Jehu then had the decapitated heads that were put in baskets by the perfidious slayers displayed publicly at the gate of Jezreel (2 Kgs 10:6–8, 11, 17 NOAB) to instill fright in people, and in so doing he violated another biblical statute that bans the desecration of a corpse, an offence to God (Deut 21:23).

But the Bible also ascribes the liquidation of Ahaziah's young sons to their grandmother Ataliyah (King Omri's daughter who married Yehoram, king of Judah; upon his coronation, Yehoram himself slew all his younger brothers). Ataliyah obsessively desiring to succeed Ahaziah, her slain son, on the throne wanted no threat to her reign even from her grandsons. Hence, "she arose and destroyed all the seed of the royal house of Judah," Joash being the sole survivor (2 Kgs 11:1–3; 2 Chr 21:4, 22:10 JPS). Ataliyah thus managed to reign for six years.

To be sure, filicide, the murder of children by a parent, is not foreign to the Bible. Abraham was prepared to sacrifice his son Isaac to God on Mount Moriah, but he ceased the act just in time when a divine messenger commanded him to stop. Similarly, King Saul insisted on executing his son Jonathan, the crown prince, after discovering that he violated (albeit unknowingly) the king's curse against anyone among his troops who would not fast until the evening on the day on which his army pursued the Philistines. It was only the king's warriors who coerced him not to carry out his son's execution (1 Sam 14:39, 44–45). However, the daughter of the chieftain Jephthah was not as lucky; her father offered her up "for a burnt offering" (Judg 11:31, 39 JPS). Also, the Moabite king Mesha "took his firstborn son who was to succeed him and offered him as a burnt offering on the wall" (2 Kgs 3:27 NOAB). Jeremiah references a common practice by Israelite fathers of murdering their children by burning them alive in idolatrous sacrifices to Baal outside the walls of Jerusalem (Jer 7:31; 19:5).

Samson: A Mega-Terminator of Animals

One iconic episode of a grisly dispatch of animals by the chieftain Samson (the "Ironman") took place soon after he had already ripped apart a young lion with his bare hands, rather than disengage from the scene. Seeking to avenge his botched romantic liaison with a Philistine woman, Samson resorted to a ruthless way of revenge by entrapping three hundred foxes whose tails he tied in pairs, tethering a fiery torch in between. He then sent them off to frantically incinerate the fields of grain, the harvested crop, and olive trees, namely, the entire agricultural yield in the woman's town of Timna (Judg 14:5–6, 15:4–5).

Samson's horrid action is an anathema to the future rabbinic code of Jewish law predicated on Torah laws and values that he must have known—the prohibition against causing pain or sorrow to any animal and the obligation to deliver from distress any animal, even if it is ownerless or abandoned.[40] Nonetheless, the Bible sounds no word of compassion or sympathy for the tortured animals, nor does it admonish the vindictive Samson for violating several other prohibitions, either against taking revenge, resorting to a collective punishment that imputes guilt by association, damaging or destroying fruit trees (even of an enemy in wartime), or ruining anything else that is beneficial to others (even a mere one seed of mustard as the rabbis explained).[41]

But like the Bible, the rabbis, too, remained silent concerning Samson's scandalous zoocidal action and its destructive outcome. The Roman Stoic philosopher Seneca said, "All cruelty springs from weakness."[42] It might explain why research studies have shown that lacking compassion for animals, let alone cruelty directed at them, is linked to aggressive tendencies, indifference toward people's suffering, and a disconnect from the natural world. Samson's case is a fitting case study that authenticates these findings.[43]

Who Is Ravening Whom?

For thousands of years, humans played a key role in the zoocide and disappearance of many large mammals from all habitable continents, like the giant armadillo and giant ground sloths or elephants, rhinos, lions, and mammoths from Europe. Thanks to methods of mass hunting, the gradual disappearance of the Persian deer from the landscape of the ancient Middle East began as early as five thousand years ago.[44]

Within two hundred years of the Polynesian settlement in New Zealand in 1300 BCE, humans drove to extinction numerous species like the Tasmanian tiger or the moa—nine species of ostrich-like birds that were endemic to these islands where they evolved over millions of years.[45] When Lewis and Clark's Corps of Discovery crossed the West from 1804 to 1806, the vast and "wild" northern country was devoid of adverse human impact. By 1880, just eight decades later, bison were nearly extinct, with grizzlies

40. Gonzfried, *Kitzur Shulchan Arukh*, siman 191.

41. Sefer HaChinukh, 529; Bal, Ach.

42. Philosiblog, "All Cruelty."

43. American Humane Society, "Facts."

44. Gammelby, "Evidence"; Nitnaware, "Ancient"; Zoological Gardens in Jerusalem, "Persian Fallow Deer."

45. Wilmshurst, "Human Effects"; Grosser, "Invader or Resident?"

losing much of their natural habitat. Concurrently, the jaguars also disappeared from the American landscape and spirit.[46]

Around the globe, nearly five hundred animal species have become extinct in the last one hundred years.[47] Wolves in the continental United States now occupy less than 10 percent of their historic range.[48] The lion, an apex predator, has seen its numbers decline precipitously in the wild. The reliably estimated hundreds of thousands of lions, who had roamed Africa, the Middle East, and India a century ago, now count fewer than twenty-three thousand remaining in the wild in Africa. Lions now occupy just 8 percent of their historic habitat in Africa.[49]

As for other animals, humans kill sharks at the rate of approximately one hundred thousand per year,[50] resulting in numerous breeds of sharks that are nearing extinction. Hippos, too, are a vulnerable species, and their numbers are decreasing due to habitat loss and illegal hunting as they are targeted for their meat and ivory canine teeth. Trophy hunters in the United States kill hundreds of thousands of America's carnivores (black bears, coyotes, foxes, mountain lions, bobcats, and wolves) each year, exclusively for their body parts or for bragging rights to hang on the wall. Moreover, they do so by gunning them down from aircraft, ATV chases, explosives, trapping (even by choking snares), and poisoning. In the state of Florida alone, some eight thousand "nuisance" alligators are killed annually to make room for new development.[51]

The truth is that since its emergence on the face of the globe, humanity has caused the loss of 83 percent of all wild mammals. Hence, it has been aptly said that "humans hit this planet like an asteroid, and the dust is still settling as wildlife continues to decline."[52] Sören Faurby, a zoologist, thus suggested that "without humans, Earth would largely resemble the modern-day Serengeti, an African ecosystem teeming with life."[53]

46. National Park Service, "What Happened"; Western Wildlife Outreach, "Grizzly Bear History"; Saligumba, "Jaguars' Disappearing Lands."

47. Enviroliteracy Team, "How Many Species."

48. World Population Review, "Wolf Population."

49. Enviroliteracy Team, "Could Lions Go Extinct?"

50. Matthews, "100 Million Sharks."

51. Pearce, "Poaching"; Grazing Facts, "Wildlife Killing"; Associated Press, "Thousands"; Cohen, "Thousands"; Florida Fish and Wildlife Conservation Commission, "Statewide Nuisance Alligator Program."

52. Pester, "How Would Earth Be."

53. Pester, "How Would Earth Be."

The Rabbinical Assembly prayer book for the Day of Atonement, *Mahzor Lev Shalem*, invites sin-confessors to add modern cases of wrongdoing they perpetrated unto God besides traditional ones: "For the sin whereby we destroyed for eternity wonderful animals that You saved from the waters of the flood, and for the sin of cutting down tree forests that sustain the souls of all ensouled livings."[54] Indeed, this is a rabbinic attestation of humans' immoral activities against God's works like nature and wildlife. Emblematic of such decried acts are the words of the American Ornithological Society's president Charles B. Cory who, when invited to attend an Audubon Society meeting in 1902, replied, "I do not protect birds. I kill them."[55]

Lessons from the Coronavirus Pandemic Lockdowns

Although humans dread animals, this primal fear is "false evidence appearing real" (FEAR). In general, animals fear and shun humans. That became evident during the first months of the Coronavirus pandemic lockdowns early in May 2020 with the outdoor disappearance of people and vehicles from cities to national parks and beaches, a time when travel by air, sea, and land came nearly to a complete halt. With carbon emissions plummeting due to almost total quarantines worldwide, wildlife everywhere suddenly suspended its hiding in fear from humans for the first time in extant memory. Animals such as coyotes, deer, bobcats, and black bears were spotted congregating fearlessly in parts of California's Death Valley and Yosemite National Park, which are typically teeming with visitors. Coyotes also ventured to appear on the streets of San Francisco.[56]

Other national parks in the western United States, like gardens, castles, and waterways, along with city and car parks across Britain, also reported similar sightings of emboldened diverse wildlife exploring and foraging for food in areas where they were never before observed. Descending from the mountains near Barcelona, wild boars were seen in the city center. With the human- and dog-deserted landscape, nature began to venture into city streets from Thailand and Japan to Italy and the Americas.[57] The pandemic closures and their immediate propitious effect on many animals

54. Feld, *Day of Atonement*, 267.

55. Gallagher, "Fellow Ornithologists."

56. Sweetney, "Coyotes Prowl."

57. BBC, "Coronavirus."

demonstrated who is afraid of whom; it attested cogently to the adverse radical impact humans have had on the well-being of the animal kingdom.

Animals thrive when people leave

Cal Flyn's book *Islands of Abandonment: Life in the Post-Human Landscape* presents a vision of the future (which is already here) characterized by the worldwide pattern of rural population declines (e.g., Scotland, Cyprus, Estonia's Harju County) that invite wildlife to prowl throughout and rebound. Japan is another country showing this trend of *akiya*—namely, ghost homes (with one in every eight rural homes lying empty), old fields, and neglected gardens presently reclaimed by wildlife such as the Asian black bear. In Europe, lynx, wolverines, brown bears, and wolves (including the Iberian species in Spain) have all grown their populations over the last decade, with skyrocketing numbers of wild boar and roe deer to boot.[58] Also, when humans are forced to leave conflict zones, areas such as the Korean Demilitarized Zone (DMZ), the UN Buffer Zone in Cyprus, Chernobyl's Exclusion Zone, and Israel's northern border with Lebanon (2023–2024), animals often venture back in, turning deserted communities and farmland into their new habitats.[59]

The Media Instills Fear

The numerous popular heads-up online stories about the "most dangerous" animals in North America provide information about wildlife, which we might encounter one day in the open outdoors. But once you begin to read such reports, you also realize how wide the gap was between the eye-catching, alarming title and the actual concern-allaying details that followed.[60] Looking at a picture of a cougar ready to lunge at me with exposed sharp fangs, I immediately calmed down upon reading that cougars typically avoid human contact and attacks on humans are extremely rare.

Such attacks can be fatal, though, especially if the animal is cornered or the human whom the cougar encounters either flees or stands still—thus

58. Flyn, *Islands*, 253–59.

59. Kraus, "Toshavey"; Sadiq, "What Happens"; Wikipedia, "Passive Rewilding."

60. Ahmed, "12 Most Dangerous Creatures"; Eberhardt, "15 Most Dangerous Animals."

imitating the typical reactions of quarry animals upon spotting a predator—instead of backing slowly away without turning their back to the animal.

Furthermore, I kept reading that the American bison would pose no threat of charging if one kept enough space from the animal, akin to what we must do while driving behind another car. The same applies to the moose, an animal that isn't generally prone to attack humans unless provoked. Moreover, the article noted that the American alligator or crocodile typically avoids humans, so fatal, unprovoked attacks are rare, or about 0.39 fatalities per year in Florida. It stands to reason that the best way to live harmoniously with alligators is to stay away from their territory.

Venomous snakes, the article went on, are shy and offish, preferring to avoid humans who do not provoke them; indeed, outdoors enthusiasts who walk the trails probably pass by dozens of hiding and camouflaged snakes even without knowing it. Only when they sense vulnerability and are frightened, the non-combative rattlesnakes would shake their tails' tip with a distinctive sound to warn whoever is perceived as a threat to keep a distance; it is a defensive mechanism, rather than an offensive one. Biting would only happen in self-defense, even as about 20 to 33 percent of such bites do not deliver venom (i.e., "dry bites").

Also, gray wolves, I continued to read, opt to avoid humans; they can become dangerous if humans encroach on their territory, thus posing a threat (don't people avoid visiting certain cities, areas, or countries they deem as risky?). Still, such wolf attacks are extremely rare. The actual risks associated with a wolf attacking a human are above zero, but far too low to calculate; between 2002 and 2020, twenty-six fatal attacks were reported throughout the world, with more than half of them being due to rabies.[61] The article I read also listed the arctic fox as another perilous animal, although it poses no direct threat to humans; I wondered why this species was even included in a story about deadly animals, just like the inclusion in the article of the Canadian lynx and bobcat. These two species are unlikely to interact with humans unless provoked.

The wild boar was also listed as a dangerous animal, though only four fatal wild boar attacks have ever been reported in the United States; three resulted from attacks by wounded animals during hunting circumstances, with the most recent charge occurring in Texas in 1996. The probability of such an attack would be less than one in a million. This being the case,

61. International Wolf Center, "Are Wolves Dangerous."

why even list it in an article focusing on life-endangering animals in North America?

Black and grizzly bears were also named among the twenty-one species that made the list of North America's potentially deadly animals, although bears, the story admitted, are typically reclusive animals. Human–bear encounters are mostly (59 percent) initiated by humans or their unleashed dogs, even as bears are more likely to flee than attack when confronted with a group of people. All in all, bear attack statistics reveal that such incidents are rare because bears, who are more afraid of humans than the other way around, would go to great lengths to avoid contact with them if given plenty of space to disappear. Adverse encounters with brown bears are rare and mainly non-fatal. Most interactions, however, result in a quick parting of ways, although two fatal attacks per year take place across North America (as in 2020–2024).[62]

All in all, the media tends to unnecessarily alarm the public about a phenomenon that is in essence very rare. Thus, it abets the consternation from such encounters and buttresses the "beastly" stereotype of such animals. Indeed, the *Scientific Reports* journal conceded that "the media often overplay large carnivore attacks on humans" by overestimating "the risk of such attacks on humans"; in so doing it "irrationally" enhances "human fear and negative attitudes towards coexisting with and conserving these species."[63] Or as USA Today has it, "With animals like the great white shark in 'Jaws,' gigantic alligators in 'Crawl' or Leonard DiCaprio's intense fight with a bear in 'The Revenant,' cinema has perhaps provided a lot more fear than is necessary."[64] *The Independent* similarly observes, "Reptiles prevalent in [the US] southeastern states [are] much feared but rarely attack humans."[65] Generally speaking, humans need not be afraid of big wild animals, carnivores included, as long as they do not travel alone and earnestly avoid surprising and provoking, let alone cornering and threatening them, especially when their young are present. Being scared of wildlife is gratuitous when these general caveats of caution are adhered to.

62. Wikipedia, "List of Fatal Bear."

63. Penteriani, "Human Behaviour."

64. Mendoza, "Here Are the Deadliest."

65. Sommerlad, "How Many People."

A "Dangerous" Porcupine

Human immanent fear of animals is vividly demonstrated in the following episode published in 2021 in *Maariv*, a major Israeli daily: "Something ran on the road. That something was the size of a cat; noticing me at the corner of its eye, it swelled. It spread its giant needles and ran into the small garden of an apartment building. . . . 'Mom, what is it?' a small child asked his mother as she hastened to reply: 'It's a porcupine. It is dangerous. Don't get closer to it.'"[66] Needless to say, porcupines are not dangerous unless one wants to catch them by hand.

Human-Killing Animals

Despite not having the fangs of a lion or the venom of a rattlesnake, mosquitoes have earned the title "earth's most lethal animal" (after the crown and ultimate predator, the human being). The Anopheles mosquito, which carries malaria, is considered the deadliest animal in the world, claiming "more than 608,000 deaths every year" (the majority of victims being children under the age of five, predominantly in sub-Saharan Africa).[67] Moreover, other mosquitoes or flies (e.g., the tsetse fly, *Aedes* mosquito, *Culex* mosquito) contribute to many more deaths—approximately 92,000 annually—by transmitting diseases such as West Nile virus, Zika, Japanese Encephalitis, dengue fever, and yellow fever.[68]

Snake bites are the next cause of most deaths, killing between 81,000 and 138,000 people around the world (about one half of them in India alone), while scorpion stings kill another 3,500 humans every year. African lions and tigers are the most lethal among the big cats, killing every year, altogether, three hundred humans worldwide. The herbivorous hippos kill annually in Africa about five hundred people who invade their territorial waters to boat, swim, or fish therein. Also, the herbivorous elephants claim human lives—some 500 people each year—in conflicts over space.[69] Lethal shark attacks on humans are rare, with fewer than ten deaths globally each

66. Vaaitz, "Nihyeh tovim el hateva."

67. Enviroliteracy Team, "Deadliest Mosquito."

68. World Health Organization, "Vector-Borne Diseases."

69. Handwerk, "Elephants Attack"; Learish, "20 Deadliest Animals"; Wikipedia, "List of Animals."

year.[70] Alligators kill fewer than 1 person annually throughout the United States, with a total of 26 human fatalities from alligator attacks between 1948 and 2021.[71]

In his *Unstoppable Us: How Humans Took All Over the World*, a children's book based on his magnum opus *Sapiens*, the internationally famed historian Yuval Noah Harari writes that humans are "the deadliest animals on earth, far more than any lion or any sixteen-foot snake."[72] Indeed, animal attacks on humans that end in fatalities are incomparably smaller than what people inflict on them or on other fellow humans. Hence, Mark Twain's ribbing observation: "There are no wild animals until man makes them so."[73]

While animal attacks and parasitic diseases are serious, statistics show that by an incredibly wide margin—and it is not even close—humans are more likely to be wounded or killed at the hands of members of their race than by all other animal species combined. "Deaths in wars and conflicts—[both military personnel and civilians]—'killed or allowed to die by human decision' [are assessed at] 231 million for the 100 years of the 20th Century."[74] Homicides result in approximately 475,000 fatalities worldwide (a global rate of 6.2 per 100,000).[75] Furthermore, deadly work-related incidents and vehicular crashes—which humans, rather than force majeure, cause—contribute to approximately 1.19 million fatalities worldwide each year.[76] Clearly, humans are the most lethal mammals of their kind all over the planet.

"The King of Beasts"

As the following chapters will demonstrate by delving into the depth of the Bible, animals are not evil (unlike man's built-in proclivity to perpetrate evil, as God attests to). Nor do predatory animals normatively see people as their prey, for they usually try to dodge encountering them. Invariably, the Bible's animals lose out in ordinary encounters with man who is their

70. Keeley, "Shark Attacks."

71. Sommerlad, "How Many People."

72. Harari, *Unstoppable Us*, 179.

73. AZ Quotes, "Mark Twain."

74. Center for International and Security Studies, "Deaths in Wars."

75. World Health Organization, "Homicide."

76. World Health Organization, "Global Status Report."

unsurpassed "beast," or they become inexorably collateral victims when God punishes humanity.

As a matter of course, to compare human atrocities perpetrated against other humans as "beastly behavior" is to wittingly overlook and deny the reality that humans are the top crown predator everywhere on the face of the planet, even as other animals fear and dread them. The blood-shedding hand of man makes "red tooth and claw" animals pale by comparison. Indeed, a recent study in *Current Biology* suggests that lions, the primary apex predator on the African prairie, do not strike as much fear in other animals as humans do.[77]

The rabbis of yore taught that the Torah has seventy "faces"; namely, as the creator God is infinite, so is the Torah or the ways to understand it. This book embodies one of these symbolic seventy faces. Whether one reads the Bible as God's verbatim word or as spiritual and inspiring human literature par excellence, the Bible, writes Andrew Linzey, "needs to be read, studied, and reclaimed for the animals."[78]

This book you are now reading embodies a veritable attempt to comprehensively cover the Bible's animal kingdom, especially as it comes into contact—physical or literary—with humanity. Hence, my quest to examine the full biblical record and determine what the Bible thinks of animals, and whether it ascribes a low image to them as people have axiomatically been wont to believe. Let us start then and excavate the ample evidence that the Bible stores in its pages, beginning with creation and through Isaiah's vision of the end of days.

I have done my best in this book—or at my blogging, teaching, and public talks on the subject—to live up to Albert Camus's double challenge to any writer: the "refusal to lie about what we know"[79] and the insistence to "always go too far because that's where you'll find the truth." Indeed, "by urging us to go too far, Camus challenges us to step outside of our comfort zones and embrace the unknown . . . [because] the truth is not always found in the safe and familiar, but rather in the unexplored and uncertain."[80] Similarly, the Hebrew word for a book is *sefer*, a word that shares its etymological root with the word that means "a boundary"; I hope this book will take you to the very far frontier, to places where you have not been before in

77. Shrader, "Ecology."

78. Citatis, "Andrew Linzey."

79. AZ Quotes, "Albert Camus."

80. Blinkist Magazine, "Top 10."

understanding the Bible as it pertains to animals and their encounters with humans. And as you begin delving into reading, remember Mr. Okamoto's words from *Life of Pi*: "Yes, the story with animals is the better story."[81]

81. Martel, *Life of Pi*, 317.

CHAPTER 1

From Cosmic Dust to Us

If having a soul means being able to feel love and loyalty and gratitude, then animals are better off than a lot of humans"
—James Herriot, *All Creatures Great and Small*

More than 4.5 billion years ago, future living beings on Earth began to evolve from bits of cosmic debris in the primordial waters that covered the face of the planet. The creaturely species—either extinct now or extant—start their evolution when the creator God sets conducive conditions for life on Earth, such as sunlight, greenhouse gases (to trap the sun's heat and insulate the earth), the accumulation of oxygen in the atmosphere and the appearance of trees and grass.

Hence, some 2.7 billion years ago, a new kind of life, the oxygen-generating photosynthetic microbe (cyanobacteria), established itself in shallow seas where it was protected from full exposure to the sun's harmful radiation. This organism became so abundant that by 2.4 billion years ago, whole forms of life—indeed, more complex ones—continued to emerge. Though the Torah ascribes to the entire evolution of blooded species merely two "days," Ps 90 metaphorically likens a day to "a thousand years" in God's "eyes." It thus advances the poetical element rather than that of science (e.g., the Permian, Triassic, Jurassic, and Cretaceous periods), which imbues this timeline of evolution with a symbolic allusion to six different and distinctive times or periods represented by these allegorical days when material creation happened.

The Fifth and Sixth Days

The Torah defines each of the species that God "created" on the fifth day as "the great sea monsters and every living creature [literally 'ensouled animal'] that crawls, which the water had swarmed forth of each kind and the winged fowl of each kind" (Gen 1:21 ALT). On the sixth day, God made according to his spoken proclamation a living soul (*nefesh khayah*) of every kind: herd animals and the earth's wildlife of every kind (v. 24). Significantly, the word *khayah* ("animal") is a derivative of *khayim* ("living" or "life"), the word describing God's essence as in *Elohim khayim* (e.g., Deut 5:23, 1 Sam 17:26, 36), thus linking the two closely together.

Notably, when the process of creation continues its evolutionary course from the fifth to the sixth day (or from one evolutionary age to the next), the Torah switches the verb that describes the earlier creation of animals from "And God created" to "And God made." This is a momentous shift from the primal creation of life to other evolving species that emerged from already-existing "ensouled animals." The creator God observes twice on each of these days that the creation of animals was "good" (with no strings attached), while neither species was seen as "bad" or "wicked." Nor does the creator God regard any animal as a means to aid or sustain the life, well-being, or comfort of the yet-to-be-formed human species; still, such a divine statement is forthcoming.

Is There a Difference Between an Animal and a Human Soul?

The basic parity between a human and an animal soul may also be learned from Abraham, who substitutes the offering of his son Isaac to God with a random ram he found entangled in a thicket (Gen 22:13); clearly, only an ensouled creature could be designated as a proxy for a human. Based on the same concept is another iconic biblical narrative, that of the Yom Kippur (the Day of Atonement) mystifying ritual that centers on the "scapegoat" ram; it "receives" the people's sins and carries them into the wilderness of the Judean desert. This narrative attests to the ram's ability to become a vicarious "recipient" of humans' transgressions.

Indeed, it may seem like a compatible human "organ donation"—albeit of human sins—that the animal gets and retains, like a fellow creature that relates closely to humanity. It is reminiscent of the transference of human sins in Christianity to Jesus, who takes on the burden of human transgressions and atones for them through his sacrifice on the cross. To impute such a task to an animal testifies to the essential equality between a human and an animal soul. In the same spirit, stock animals are held equal to humans in biblical law, even as the Decalogue (or the "Ten Commandments") commands rest from all types of labor on the Sabbath Day for humans and farm animals alike, a full day of respite from work. The Decalogue does not only decree what *not* to do but also what "to do [on] the Sabbath day"; hence, according to the rabbis, equines should not only be used for mere riding but also be taken from their stable to the outdoors to frolic and enjoy the pasture to allow them an enjoyable rest (Rashi on Exod 23:12).

The concept that animals possess a soul that is not essentially distinguishable from the human soul is mirrored in the idea that God would only enact covenants with ensouled individuals. It is attested in the aftermath of the flood by the eternal rainbow covenant between humanity and every ensouled animal [in other translations, 'living being'] among all flesh (Gen 9:15). Such is the case in the end-of-war covenant between God "with the animal of the field and the bird of the heavens and the creeping thing of the ground" (Hos 2:20 DAV).

Poignantly, when the Torah discusses the laws of tit for tat (or *lex talionis*, the Greek translation for the law of "retribution-in-kind" or "eye for an eye"), it is decreed that a human who murders "any human being [literally, 'a human soul'] shall be put to death." Also, a person striking dead "the life of an animal [literally, its 'soul']" will indemnify the owner for its market value (Lev 24:17–18).[1] While the penalties are very different, the Torah invokes equally the term "soul" to describe both the life of a human and an animal, even doing so in one heartbeat without dithering.

The unambiguous conclusion is that an animal's soul is not inherently lesser than a human soul, even when the rulings in both cases are not identical. To be sure, different laws in the Torah distinguish between Israelites and non-Israelites (like those on slaves and lending money for interest), between priests and non-priests, or between physically non-blemished priests and priests with bodily defects (Lev 21:1–7, 18–23; 25:39–46; Deut 23:20–21).

Another testimonial for the equality of animal and human life is observed in the Torah's insistence that a person who slaughters an animal either "in the camp" or "outside the camp," but apart from the sacrificial

1. Author's translation.

system, should be considered a murderer—"he has spilled blood, and that man shall be cut off from the midst of his people" (Lev 17:4 ALT). Such a grave consequence—most likely an untimely death—is also relegated to those who perpetrate the other two cardinal sins of idolatry and carnal turpitude (e.g., adultery and incest); one must surrender his life to avoid them, the rabbis posit.[2]

Isaiah's assertion that "the animals of the field" honor God, even "the jackals and ostriches," in gratitude for being given "waters in the wilderness, and rivers in the desert" (Isa 43:20),[3] further makes the case for animals possessing a veritable soul. Joel similarly expresses the same idea when describing the devastation of the land due to environmental plagues such as drought and fire. He says, "Also the animals of the field desperately cry to You, for the springs of water have dried up and fire has consumed the pastures of the wilderness" (1:20).[4] The medieval Torah commentator Abarbanel posits that those wild animals symbolize the other nations besides Judea that the Babylonian king Nebuchadnezzar will also conquer. This resemblance of people to animals evinces how facile it was for the prophets to personify them allegorically.[5]

God, in his dialogue with Job, refers to the raven's hungry chicks who implore him for food (Job 38:41), a point that the psalmist also makes (Ps 147:9). To express their feelings in such a way, those sentient animals must possess a soul. Similarly, the psalmist's call for "every living, breathing creature [to] praise God" (Ps 150:6 MSG), namely, "you wild animals, and every livestock, you creeping thing, and bird of wing" (Ps 148:10 KH), is answered when these creatures "all give thanks to You" (Ps 145:10 KH).

The book of Proverbs likewise confirms the presence of "a soul" in animals that a righteous person recognizes and sees in their provisions and proper work conditions (12:10). But this expectation of a righteous person does not materialize in the iconic Talmudic story—discussed lengthily in chapter 31—about a calf that was led to slaughter. Sensing its imminent doom, it fled to the preeminent Rabbi Yehudah to sound a silent "SOS" or at least solicit empathy. But the highly learned scholar failed to observe in the calf's tearing eyes the soul of an animal begging mercifully for its life.

2. b. Sanh. 74a–b.

3. Author's translation.

4. Author's translation.

5. Davis, *Latter Prophets with Commentary*, 123.

Indeed, it hung its head on the corner of the rabbi's garment and wept in sorrow for its imminent demise.

Moreover, animals like humans are also subject to heavenly reward or punishment as we find in the solemn liturgical ode for High Holy Days called *Unetaneh Tokef* ("Now, we declare"). It relates to "the souls of all that live" who pass before God who "decide[s] for each creature its cycles of life . . . [by writing] down its destined decree"; "for none can be exempt from justice's eyes!"[6] Rabbi Loew, the sixteenth-century giant of Torah and Talmud scholarship known as the Maharal of Prague, elevates animals above the average person who fails to experience the presence of the divine in his daily life. As such, animals instinctively commune with God, even as they intuitively know that God provides their sustenance; thus, they naturally sense God's presence in the physical world.[7] This concept reverberates clearly in the early morning Jewish liturgy, which praises God as "the master of all souls, in whose possession is the soul of every living thing, and the spirit of all flesh."[8]

Postscript

Chris Klimek, in "Are Wild Animals Really Just Like Us?" posits that the "shared characteristics" between humans and other animals are not only found "with big-brained animals," but with birds and insects too. Indeed, scientists assert that mammals and humans are only different versions of each other; all have "emotions, memories, and culture." They also admit that, akin to humans, bees do not only experience changing moods but also demonstrate abilities to play with toys, learn, and remember. Cockroaches have personalities to the extent that they recognize their kin and assemble for decision-making, even as flies experience fear.[9] Charles Darwin wrote similarly about insects that express "anger, terror, jealousy, and love by their stridulation."[10] Britain, notably, has recognized lobsters, crabs, and octopuses as "sentient" or species sensing pain.[11]

6. Kol Haneshamah, *Prayerbook*, 349–50.
7. Breier, "Between the Bible."
8. Kol Haneshamah, *Prayerbook*, 173–74.
9. Klimek, "Wild Animals."
10. Libquotes, "Charles Darwin Quote."
11. Department for Environment, Food, and Rural Affairs, "Lobsters."

To Love as a Bird

I read on Facebook a short post affirming the acute basic feelings that only ensouled creatures can possess, as the Bible recognizes and Charles Darwin confirms by saying, "the lower animals, like man, feel pleasure and pain, happiness and misery."[12] The Facebook post read as follows:

> Yesterday, I witnessed something that took my breath away. I heard a sound at the window of the cottage. When I looked, a cedar waxwing had hit the window and fallen to the deck. Its mate stood beside it. It was clear that the fallen bird was dead. I turned away for a moment, and when I looked again, its mate had hopped over. It lay down beside its partner, their heads touching. It closed its eyes and passed over to the spirit with its mate. The sadness and beauty of the moment were such a privilege to witness. If anyone has ever doubted that animals feel emotion and love, this moment, I felt, was absolute proof of both. Nature truly has much to teach us."[13]

A Whale of Gratitude

On December 11, 2005, a crab fisherman off the coast of San Francisco spotted "a female humpback whale," entrapped and twisted tightly in a mass of nylon strings, striving "to stay afloat." Recognizing her precarious state, he "radioed an environmental group for help." A rescue team that arrived at the scene dove in and took hours to slice the ropes cautiously, a most perilous task. When they freed the leviathan, it swam in "what seemed like joyous circles," as if celebrating her newfound freedom. Then, remarkably, she approached each diver one by one, nudging them gently—apparently, her way of expressing gratitude. Some of the rescuers described it as the most moving and "beautiful experience of their lives."[14]

A Whale of a Mother

A mother orca named Tahlequah gained renown in 2018 when she carried her stillborn calf for seventeen days around the one thousand miles of the

12. Richards, "Charles Darwin."
13. What's Up New Brunswick, "From Janis Mirynech."
14. Mikkelson, "Does This Photograph Show."

Salish Sea, just off Washington state and British Columbia, as "a sign of grief," if not an attempt to revive it. Hauling her dead calf meant that she gave up eating, unable to hunt for food for many days.[15] The news of her behavior, widely covered in news media, mirrored the strong bond between a leviathan mother and her child, pointing out the general complexity of animals' emotions, particularly in sorrow.

Breaking a myth: sentient animals possess a soul like humans do.

15. Richards, "Mother Orca."

CHAPTER 2

The Making of Humanity: An Ordinary Day in Creation

It is incumbent on us, humans, to see significance in the acts of animals, and not as creatures akin to robots who operate automatically.
—RABBI AVRAHAM STAV

Are Humans Superior to Animals?

With the animal kingdom already in existence, God dedicates the "sixth day" to making new animal species before turning to creating humankind. The emergence of the two humans within one evolutionary continuum did not merit an exclusive day to distinguish this creation from those living beings who had preceded them. After all, since animals are called *nefesh khayah*—"a living soul"—even before humanity came into being, it is apparent that humans merely "catch up" with what the animals already possessed. Since all animals (in Gen 1) were created before humanity, God blesses them with fecundity, a blessing that he would also reiterate for the newest creatures, the humans, to multiply and increase.

Genesis 2, which features the second of the two creation narratives, does not relegate specific days for its coming into being. Rather, it begins with God's formation of man, even from the "dust of the ground," and on to similar formations of "every animal of the field, and every fowl of the air"; all endowed with "a living soul" and predating God's making of the woman, the last act of creation.

The descriptions of these creations, which employ intermittently the same verbs "made/make" and "formed"/"created" for both man and animal (while the verbs "fashion" or "built" are used for the making of the woman), points to the great similarity of all species. The intrinsic value of the animal in the order of creation is similarly attested to by the very similar Hebrew word for a human, *adam* ("an earthling"), and the word for blood, *dam*, that runs in the veins and arteries of all animals, human and non-human alike. Notably, it is only the first letter that distinguishes between the two words.

This keen etymological similarity attests to the closeness of all blooded species and humans, intimating the interconnection between the building blocks of humans and their other ensouled fellows, which preceded (or followed) the appearance of humankind as in the first and second chapters of Genesis respectively. Indeed, Charles Darwin notes in *The Descent of Man* that "there is no fundamental difference between man and the higher mammals in their mental faculties. . . . The difference in mind between man and the higher animals, great as it is, certainly is one of degree and not of kind."[1]

More Than a Similar Anatomy

Numerous studies show that pigs are similar "to humans in anatomical size and structure, physiology, immunology, and genome."[2] Pigs are, therefore, considered ideal donors for human organ transplants. Due to the remarkable similitude of pig tissues and organs to those of humans, their skin has been used in human skin grafts, and their other organs infused into human recipients ("xenotransplantation").

Are We Similar to Octopuses?

Humans shared a last common ancestor even with the truly intelligent octopus more than five hundred million years ago. And though we don't look like the boneless octopus with tentacles, the idea of a common ancestor may look credulous when we consider the animal's curiosity and cleverness. Such characteristics may "remind us of our thirst for knowledge" or "astonishing cognitive abilities," suggests neuroethologist Lisa Poncet.[3]

1. Richards, "Charles Darwin."
2. Lunney et al., "Importance of the Pig."
3. Poncet, "Suckers for Learning."

Vive la petite différence

God, however, distinguishes humans, the last phase in the evolutionary order of species (as in the first narrative of creation), from all that preceded them by creating the male and the female "in God's image," a unique characteristic that may point out to both the ability to understand and act on God's commanding voice and the idea of death (Gen 2:16–17). Rashar, a nineteenth-century Torah scholar, admits that animals and humans are close to each other but not equal. Rashar draws a sharp line between the two by viewing man's soul as of a higher status because God breathed it into him.[4]

Indeed, when it comes to the commencement of breath in Adam, the text, though only in the second account of creation, informs us that the creator turned on Adam's breath "personally"—a divine act that is unique to the man himself—while the animal's soul originated from the earth just like the human body but not the human soul. This distinction, however, cannot hold water because God's blowing into Adam's "nostrils the soul of life" (Gen 2:7 STONE) was not replicated with the imminent formation of the woman.

However, anticipating that humans, in their being the last and the newest species that God formed, might see a reason for entertaining hubris vis-à-vis other beings, the rabbis of yore prepared a rejoinder to rebuff such likely arrogance. Man would, therefore, need to be reminded that even the mosquito or the earthworm has been native to this earth longer than humans, for they preceded humanity in the order of creation. The psalmist further reminds us that humans have no special status among other creatures with whom we constitute one tapestry, for "in wisdom You have made them all; the earth is full of Your creatures" (Ps 104:24 NOAB).

And even further, all creatures depend on God's benevolence for their sustenance, as "the eyes of all look to You, and You give them their food in due season" (Ps 145:15 NOAB). Humans, then, were just another animal creature and are not portrayed as that one species that rules the world. The psalmist puts the kibosh on any human sense of superiority over other nonhuman beings, for they all "return to their dust" upon death (Ps 104:29 NOAB).

We sense the same when God says to Job, "Look! Here is a Behemoth [river horse or hippo] that I made just as I made you. . . . He is the first among God's works, and only his Maker can overpower him" (Job 40:15, 19

4. Rashar Gen 2:7.

KRAUS). God seeks here, comments Bible scholar Amos Hacham, to deeply drive into Job's heart the recognition of his human lowliness when compared with the river horse's supreme quality and its being the utmost choice in God's handiwork. "It was given the foremost prowess so no creature could lay its hand on it, except the Creator."[5]

Was Humanity's Making "Good" in God's Eyes?

Although finding his whole handiwork of creation to be "very good" (albeit not "perfect"), poignantly, God does not view the making of the human species as "good." Throughout the evolving processes of creation as a whole, and of the animal species specifically, the creator observed seven times that creation was "good," but did not do so after creating the two humans. Rather, in the second narrative of creation, God realizes that something was "not good" after all. Following the formation of a single man and relocating him to the garden of Eden, it dawned on God that it was "not good that man be alone."

This "unforeseen" glitch had to be fixed as the human earthling did not have an intimate companion. God, then, hastens to fill this void and make "for him a suitable [literally, 'a suitable helper as though against him'] partner," proceeding right away to form land and avian living beings (Gen 2:18–19).[6] It is apparent that God first thought that a compatible partner could be found for the man among those animals; their kinship and similarities being tangibly conducive. Or as Ecclesiastes sees it both animals and humans "have the same fate: as one dies so dies the other, and both have one and the same life breath; man has no superiority over animal; since both amount to nothing" (Eccl 3:19).[7] The ancient rabbis echo this sentiment: "[Man] eats and drinks like an animal, reproduces like an animal, excretes like an animal, and dies like an animal."[8]

Henceforth, God brought the animals "to the human to see what he would call them, and whatever the human called a living soul, that was its name." Naming is a most meaningful act of caring and love, requiring close attention to personal attributes and details of or hopes for the named individual. And it is with curiosity and awe that Adam enters into this intimate

5. Hacham, *Sefer Iyov*, 313, 315.

6. Author's translation.

7. Fox, *JPS Bible Commentary: Ecclesiasties.*

8. Midr. Ber. Rab. 14:3.

phase of learning about his fellow creatures, perhaps even through actual communication; a facility that trees and mushrooms also have.

According to the talmudic Rabbi Elazar, "Adam mated with each animal in his search for a suitable partner, but his mind was not at ease with or amenable to either one of them."[9] Nonetheless, since no animal matched the human's need for an intimate and compatible companion, a self-discovery by which Adam set himself apart from the other animals, God had fashioned a woman to meet it and brought her to him. Indeed, the man felt a true closeness and affinity with the woman; like with the animals, the man named her too: "She shall be called 'Woman'" (Gen 2:23 SB).

Remarkably, even after the individual making of the woman, God would still not note that either the making of the man or the woman, nor even of the two of them as a pair, was "good" as is; God did not do so in any of the two creation narratives. And while God deems the creation and existence of animals as "good"—none of them is viewed as either "bad" or "vicious"—humans, by contrast, were not appraised as good or bad because due to their unique free will, a conscientious decision that separates them from all other creatures, they can choose either option. God, who "make[s] peace and create[s] evil" (Isa 45:7 JPS) allows humans to choose between the two. Or as Viktor E. Frankl prefers in his *Man's Search for Meaning*: "There are two 'races' of men in this world, but only these two—the 'race' of the decent man and the 'race' of the indecent man. Both are found everywhere; they penetrate all groups of society. No group consists entirely of decent or indecent people."[10]

The Hebrew Mothers in Egypt Were "Animals"

Another attestation to the great similarity between humans and animals is found in the opening chapter of Exodus when the two midwives, Shifra and Puah, who delivered Hebrew babies in Egypt, favorably resembled their "clients" to "animals." The Pharaoh demanded of them an explanation as to why the male Hebrew babies escaped immediate death at the birthstool, given that he had ordered the two midwives to have the newborn boys killed upon their delivery. In response, Shifra and Puah argued that the Hebrew women were "*khayot*"(animals); before the midwife came to them, the hardy and lively Hebrew women already gave birth like animals do,

9. b. Yebam. 63a.

10. Frankel, *Man's Search for Meaning*, 86.

without any assistance in delivery (Exod 1:19). The eminent Bible scholar Amos Hacham agrees that understanding the verse as such is plausible. Clearly, the pharaoh himself did not challenge the midwives' explanation; his thundering silence indicated his acceptance of their equating humans to animals, at least when they delivered babies.

Nineveh's Livestock: Equal to Their Masters

The biblical view of an essential parity between humans and animals is revealed anew when the people of Nineveh learn from the prophet Jonah about God's doomsday design for their large city. They seek to avert that decree by enacting a series of gestures to appease God. Not only do they proclaim a fast, but they also impose the fast (food and drink) on their farmstead animals. And just like the people who covered themselves in sackcloth to express their remorse in their pursuit of a heavenly pardon, they also do the same to their animals, expecting them to join their mighty supplicatory cry "to God" on equal terms (Jonah 3:7–8).

The Talmud adds that the Ninevites used their animals as a bargaining tool to force God to pardon them, saying to Him: "If You will not have mercy on us, we will not show compassion"[11] to the animals. According to Rashi, a preeminent medieval Torah commentator, the Ninevites went on to separate animal mothers from their children, knowing how vicious it was (per 3:8).[12] The book's last verse confirms the efficacy of that action and hence the indispensable role of Nineveh's animals in sparing the city from God's wrath when the Lord admonishes Jonah: "Shall I not take pity upon Nineveh, that great city, in which there are . . . many animals as well?" (4:11 DAV).

Breaking a myth: man is neither the crown creature nor inherently good.

11. b. Ta'an. 16a.

12. DAV 232.

CHAPTER 3

Animal Lives Matter

The animals of the world exist for their own reasons. They were not made for humans any more than black people were made for white, or women created for men.—ALICE WALKER

What Is "Dominion"?

The creation of humans altered the *status quo ante* in that God charged the two humans with reigning and ruling over all other animals; it was at variance with the plain fact that the animals were first created for their own sake, as God had not designated them for servitude under a future human mastery. The (Hebrew) word to "rule over" (Gen 1:28) that God uses in calling upon humans to exercise over the animal kingdom reappears in multiple, yet diverse, contexts throughout the Hebrew Bible. It usually describes what a despotic regime does to its conquered foes, or how corrupt leaders or masters may rule over their subjects or slaves respectfully. The Israelite slave owner was forbidden to exercise ruthless dominion over a fellow countryman in bondage, which Rashi interprets as "exhaustingly so the body pulverizes" (per Exod 1:14). In contrast, gratuitous cruelty in servitude was the way the Egyptians imposed various harsh labors on their Hebrew slaves that "made life bitter for them" (v. 14 PLAUT).

Nonetheless, when God charged the two humans to dominate all animals it could very well be understood—by other biblical examples using the same word—as the way that a project manager controls his employees, like King Solomon who exercised authority or "had dominion over" the people who were "conscripted for forced labor" (1 Kgs 4:24; 5:13 NOAB), summoned for his buildup enterprise throughout the kingdom of Israel. Hence, humanity whom God charged to hold sway over the animal kingdom might opt to be gratuitously malevolent toward them, or rather benevolent and compassionate. The Bible will henceforth attempt seriously and consistently to tame humans to choose the latter.

Compassion, Not Repression

Indeed, God's first command addressing the treatment of animals did not demand humans to interact coldly or harshly with the fauna by holding sway over it like despotic tyrants do by tormenting their subjects, or slaves, to deprive them of their will and heart's desires. Doubling down on this convention is the Book of Proverbs' urging: "Know well the condition [i.e., appearance] of your flocks, and give attention to your herds" (Prov 27:23).[1] The word "know" is used profusely in the Torah's iconic demand of the Israelites to "know the alien's heart, for you were aliens in the land of Egypt" (Exod 23:9 NOAB), connoting compassion and congeniality. Rabbi Kook ruled out any divine acceptance of a man who hurts his fellow co-creatures by having dominion over them: "Far be it from such an ugly rule of slavery to be impressed by a permanent seal in God's world."[2]

The idea that animal lives matter to their creator reverberates in David's recognition that God "save[s] humans and animals alike" (Ps. 36:6 NOAB). Thus, he praises God's dominion for "giving drink to every beast [literally 'animal'] of the field [so] wild asses quench their thirst" or for provisioning prey "for the young lions . . . seeking their food from God" (Ps 104: 11, 21).[3] For it is God who avails sustenance for the animals, even "to the young ravens, when they cry" (Ps 147:9)[4]—all of them wait for God "to give them their food in due time" (Ps 145:15).[5] In a nutshell, a livestock farmer should seek the welfare of his animals and consider each individual's necessities, thus imitating God.

While shepherds see the lion and other ravening animals as their fiercest foes, it is clear that animals of the field were not created to serve man's

1. Author's translation.
2. Kook, "Vision," 2.
3. Author's translation.
4. Author's translation.
5. Author's translation.

wants, or even stay off the shepherd's flock. Why, God minds the needs of animals even if they conflict with those of humans. In the second version of creation, God does not tell the (male) earthling, following the subsequent formation of the animal kingdom, to lord over it, but only to give names to its species. Still, the very fact that God relates right from the first chapter of the Bible to what humans may do to animals—"have dominion over" them—or not do (i.e., eating them—an imminent prohibition) means that animals are not an afterthought, a negligible footnote; they are reckoned with like fellow creatures of their human counterparts.

Humans Cannot Dominate all Animals

Despite God's charge of humans to hold sway over the animal kingdom, even today humans have not penetrated every corner of the world of nature, and as such their "dominion" has not been exercised over many a species throughout the planet, like in "the uninhabited land, the empty wilderness" and "the barren waste" (Job 38:26–27 KRAUS). There, God tells Job that multiple animal species lived irrespective of their potential usefulness for humankind and off the sphere of man's influence. And that being the case, Amos Hacham comments, man "is not the purpose of creation . . . and man may not pride himself that he is the cause of the earth's harvest; why, also in places where man's presence is absent, there is an abundance."[6]

This idea is reflected in God's rhetorical questions to Job about how exactly man reigns over, let alone deriving direct benefits from animals such as the hippopotamus, the lion, the raven, the wild goat, the wild ass, or the wild ox. And since man cannot harness such land animals for his service, how much more so when it comes to birds, whether a stork, a hawk, or an eagle? (39:13, 26–27).

And as to the wild ox, would it—God asks Job—"agree to serve you? Will he remain by night at your trough? Can you keep him in the furrow with a harness? Will he follow the valleys after you with the harrow? Do you count on his great strength? Do you leave the heavy work to him? Can you trust him to come back, bringing the grain to your threshing floor?" (Job 39:9–12 KRAUS). Unlike its domesticated kin, the wild ox remained untamable until it was hunted out and rendered extinct in the land of the

6. Hacham, *Sefer Iyov*, 296.

Bible millennia ago, with the last individual of the species on earth meeting the same fate in Poland in 1627.[7]

Animals and Humans in Forced Servitude

God's instruction to humanity to domesticate all (beneficial) animals is not essentially different from the later biblical directive to Israelite owners of Israelite slaves: "You shall not hold crushing sway over him, and you shall fear your God" (Lev 25:43 ALT). Or in other words, such enslavement must be self-regulated, if not "enlightened," devoid of rigorous sway over the slave, with God monitoring compliance.

As it is, the Torah acquiesces in human slavery, and in that sense, there is no actual difference between enslaved non-humans and humans. Abraham and Isaac held slaves, as did Jacob, who mentions in a message to his brother Esau, even in one breath, that he has various livestock "and male and female slaves" too (Gen 32:6 ALT). Ecclesiastes's author (presumably, King Solomon) also owned slaves. A non-Hebrew (circumcised) slave may partake of the Passover sacrifice. Likewise, the Torah commands those with slaves and farm animals alike to provide them with a meaningful weekly Sabbath day rest.

Similarly, having dominion over non-human living beings is not too different from God's saying to the woman that her man "shall rule over you" in the wake of her defiant eating of the forbidden fruit in the garden of Eden. There are men, like Josephus, the Jewish historian (FIRST century CE), or even in our days twenty centuries later, who have understood these words to mean that "the woman is inferior to the man in every sense" for "God has given man the authority of a ruler" over her; she, in turn, must obey him and submit to his rule.[8]

Or there are the more contemporary words of Charles Darwin, who admonished as "barbarian" husbands whose "wives are commonly treated like slaves."[9] It is certainly absurd to justify a man ordering his wife around, beating her, and demanding her obedience and service at any given time because God said to the woman that her man "shall rule over you" (Gen 3:16 ALT). And since such a misogynistic idea that women are inferior to men should be unequivocally rejected, so is any purported divine permission

7. Wikipedia, "Aurochs."

8. Josephus, *Ag. Ap.* 2:25.

9. Gleiser, "How Darwin Felt."

for humans to fiercely subdue animals in their care. These living beings were created and ensouled by God, like humans; inflicting on them blood-curdling and spirit-breaking cruelties runs against the gamut of these truths. Speciesism, a misguided belief that one species is more important (to whom?) than another, is as toxic a concept and as ingrained today as racism and sexism have been ingrained in many societies, resulting in untold degradation and suffering.

Breaking a myth: animals were not created for human needs.

CHAPTER 4

Same Food for Humans and Animals

Man's normal sustenance is from plants just as it is with primates and large monkeys, even when their fangs are more developed than humans.
—Charles Darwin

In the Beginning, No Carnivores

When it comes to food, God exclusively weighs in with the two humans on the sustenance of all creatures; all were positively assigned the seeded plant, fruit produce, and the green plants on earth (Gen 1:29). God will soon repeat this staple of human sustenance by telling the earthling, "You may surely eat of every tree of the garden" (2:16)[1]—save from the tree of knowledge—and "you shall eat the plants of the field" (3:18 NOAB). God thus promulgates an all-plant food regimen in both accounts of creation as in Gen 1 and 2.

Notwithstanding the food choices of dinosaurs like the Tyrannosaurus Rex, the Velociraptor, the Allosaurus, the Spinosaurus, the Giganotosaurus, and the Deinonychus, who roamed on land for millions of years during the Jurassic and Cretaceous periods, Malbim, a renowned modern Torah commentator, posits in his germane interpretation that God did not permit the yet-to-become carnivore species, who in the first account of creation were created before the humans, to prey on other animals for food.[2] Likewise, God disallowed Adam to sustain himself by meat, even as the shape

1. Author's translation.

2. Malbim, "Malbim on Tanakh," Gen 1:29.

of human teeth and jaws indicates that it is not ideal for its consumption. Indeed, both creation accounts prescribe the plant-based diet for the human race and all other species with no exceptions.

God's silence on meat, both for humans and animals, is as expressive as God's positive assignment of solely herbivorous food to all species; from what was prescribed, they inferred what was proscribed. To wit, in contrast to herbivorous food, God said to Adam that "the animal of the land" [is] "not given to you," or more succinctly in the name of the talmudic Rav Yehudah: "Adam was not permitted to eat meat."[3]

Joseph Albo, a fifteenth-century Torah commentator, further explains in the *Book of Principles* that eating flesh would require "the gratuitous shedding of blood" (i.e., murder; see Lev 17:4; and commentary in chapter 1) through an act of "intense cruelty" spawning off "the teaching of a bad trait." This in turn would lead to serious damage to the soul—a price that is too high to be paid for eating meat, even when it is food that is "good and suitable for the human."[4]

Are You Eating Yourself?

In the Buddhist cycle of life known as *samsara*, a person's consciousness is taught that all humans might have once been born in an animal form. So forgoing meat is not practiced simply for compassion but rather in self-interest, for the animal you are about to eat is you or your loved one from a previous cycle of life.[5]

Science: The First Humans Ate No Meat

For most of the last thirty million years, writes American biologist Rob Dunn in "Human Ancestors Were Nearly All Vegetarians," most food consumed by primates was "vegetable, not animal. Plants are what our apey [*sic*] and even earlier ancestors ate." Occasionally, such plant-based food was negligibly supplemented by "meat of insect, frog, bird or mouse . . . albeit not of other species." Indeed, chimpanzees and other primates who

3. b. Sanh. 59b.

4. Albo, *HaIkkarim*, 15:3.

5. Rinpoche, *Words*, 225.

share the bulk of human genes rarely or never eat meat, preferring fruit, leaves, and insects.

Unlike unprocessed meat, plants are naturally glucose-rich, the sugar that is the brain's principal fuel source. So, "the job of a generalist primate gut is primarily to eat pieces of plants," fruit, and leaves. Hence, "if you want to return to your ancestral diet, the one our ancestors ate when most of the features of our guts were evolving, you might reasonably eat what our ancestors spent the most time eating during the largest periods of the evolution of our guts, fruits, nuts, and vegetables."[6] According to groundbreaking research led by University of Wyoming archaeologist Randy Haas in burial sites dating back between nine thousand and sixty-five hundred years ago in the Andes Mountains, plant-based foods made up the majority (80 percent) of individual diets for those prehistoric hunter-gatherers, with meat playing a secondary role at 20 percent. Thus, "the oft-used description of early humans as 'hunter-gatherers' should be changed to 'gatherer-hunters,' at least in the Andes of South America."[7]

"Far from being essential, for most people worldwide, meat has been only occasional, even incidental . . . but not counted on for daily nourishment," writes New York Times contributor Ligaya Mishan. Two million years ago, however, early hominids in the African savanna were already regular animal flesh eaters. Yet, "since we lack the great yawning jaws and bladelike teeth that enable true predators to kill with a bite and then tear raw flesh straight off the bone," meat-eating was an adaptation.[8] Similarly, the ancient Egyptian diet between 3500 BC and 600 CE was largely vegetarian too; it was primarily wheat and barley-based, plus cereals (millet and sorghum), with only a meager inclusion of fish.

In ancient cultures, vegetarianism was the general rule except in nomadic populations, and eating meat came later. Scientists, then, confirm what the Torah has been telling us all along, that the human species starts its dietary history as herbivorous. The human gut, however, was not created to be specialized, but accommodative to future changes, with Abel as a shepherd introducing dairy to the human plant-based dietary regimen. Nine generations later, God will permit the post-deluge Noah and all humanity to include meat in their food.

6. Dunn, "Human Ancestors."

7. University of WY, "UW Professor's Research."

8. Mishan, "End of Beef."

Veggie Pets Enjoy It More

A major study in the United Kingdom in 2021 found that while being the most palate-pleasing fare, plant-based pet food brands were also the healthiest and least hazardous options for dogs and cats.[9] That scientific finding effectively confirms that God's primal designation of "every green herb" to all species with "a living soul" was veritably sustainable, if not preferable. Isaiah prophesies that "on that day" (Isa 10:20), when the future peaceful earthly kingdom shall be established, all carnivorous animals will revamp their food and be fully sustained again by "straw," the way it used to be (see chapter 31).

Breaking a myth: creation commences with no carnivores on Earth.

9. Petfood Industry, "UK Pet Food Association."

CHAPTER 5

What Wrong Did the Snake Do?

Snakes hide in the grass, people behind their lies—UNKNOWN

Was "the snake" in Gen 3—this is how this iconic narrative introduces it to us, (like a well-familiarized figure from time immemorial)—a real living creature in the scheme of creation, or only a symbolic being manufactured for serving religious ideas? If it is only a literary device, what is its purpose then? To be sure, all other species (including snakes of their kind) were created in pairs to multiply and survive as a genus that God created for a reason. But this unique and singular serpent had no compatible partner. It did not need to reproduce like other animals because God destined it to live in perpetual enmity with humanity; its continuous role as such was assured for as long as humans were around.

By embodying the foremost antagonist of humans, the snake's task was to provoke them, as the story may suggest, to submit to their impulses and choose wrong over right. By constantly teasing humanity in this manner, such a metaphoric snake would effectively nudge humans to suspend their moral inhibitions and take actions far more destructive to their fellows—human and nonhuman alike—than what actual encounters between humans and venomous snakes might entail. The latter do their utmost to avoid humans anyway, preferring to bite and envenomate only their natural dinner. But the allegorical snake has been able to lure humans—despite their having preliminary hesitations (like the woman had)—into defiance of God's rules. Hence, Robert Frost's conviction that "the snake stood up for evil in the Garden."[1]

1. AZ Quotes, "Robert Frost."

The snake's ostensible luring of the woman to violate God's ban on eating the forbidden fruit was not what drove the woman to cross the Rubicon. Indeed, following her short dialogue with the snake, she did not rush to bite that fruit. The woman first observed that the fruit was good for eating, only to become obsessed with the tree's delightful look, then she realized its potential to make one wise. The process of first admiring, craving, and finally grasping what eating could do for her possibly lasted quite some time; even then she sufficed with merely picking a single fruit and just holding it in her hand—four distinct actions before finally succumbing to the fruit allure; so, she "ate, and she also gave to her man, and he ate" (he was standing beside her—Gen 3:6 ALT).

But is this the sole purpose of the story? This multi-themed tale cannot be read just as an allegory for didactic dividends. Rather, this text sheds light on the human–animal relations within creation. True, it all begins when the snake initiates a dialogue with the woman, baiting her to engage in it by posing a question: "Did God say: 'You shall not eat of any tree of the Garden?" (v. 1 STONE). The woman, perhaps, while accepting nonchalantly the serpent's ability to speak her language—one day, Balaam will react with the same equanimity when his jenny inquires why he struck her thrice—mistook the snake's question, delivered with a crafty literary hook, for a statement that distorted God's original, alert warning to Adam. (It is no wonder that some modern translators of the Torah, such as E. Fox and R. Alter, understood the snake's words just like the woman did; as an assertion rather than a question, admittedly provocative.[2])

Hence, the woman rushed to cut into the snake's question and counter back with what Adam told her after she was formed; that God only forbade them to eat of "the tree that is in the midst of the Garden" (v. 3 SB), or "the tree of the knowledge of good and evil" (2:17 SON), as God originally called it when commanding Adam to keep his distance from it. The woman was misled, then, not by the snake but by her man. Adam must have conveyed to her God's prohibition, adding on his own accord—effectively lying by "stretching" the truth—that God forbade both touching and eating of that tree.

Adam must have reasoned that if his helpmate did not lay her hand on the tree, it would be technically impossible for her to eat the fruit. This ruse of placing a hedge between the woman and the tree backfired; Avi Dentelsky even posits that the serpent is effectively the woman herself, and her

2. See the translations in Alter, *Five Books of Moses*; and Fox, *Five Books of Moses*.

verbal exchange with it mirrored her internal conflict as she was arguing with herself.[3] Thus, it was not a real but an imagined serpent with whom the woman discoursed; namely, with her adversarial inner voice. Hence, she practically invited it to assure her that good things would result from her biting into the forbidden fruit.

The Serpent Told the Truth

Still, a closer look at the text would reveal that God had anticipated *a priori* that Adam would positively eat from the tree of knowledge of good and evil. To be sure, God had forewarned him: "For on the day that you eat from it, you must die, yes, die" (v. 17 SB). Significantly, God did not stipulate that if Adam ate from the fruit, he would die on that very day. Rather, God was certain that Adam would opt to sample that fruit, even before the serpent would ever appear at the scene. The serpent's role in this saga was largely inconsequential and limited to triggering a short exchange with the woman; yet, it led in lockstep to the inevitable eating of what was forbidden to her and the man.

As it was, the serpent did not denounce God's fiat that banned the eating of the fruit, nor did it suggest to the woman to violate it. Indeed, the snake assured the woman that she and her man would not perish when they ate from the fruit. The snake reiterated essentially the same words God had originally said to Adam—"On the day you eat" rather than "If you eat"—for the dice had already been cast; eating the forbidden fruit was a foregone and imminent action just waiting to happen.

The serpent was right; the humans did not die immediately, not even soon after they sampled the proscribed fruit. As the serpent averred, their eating would result in peeling their eyes wide open as they became mindful of their nakedness and moved quickly to cover it. Again, the serpent essentially spoke the truth by echoing God's foreknowledge that Adam was bound to eat from the fruit, and would consequently acquire discernment as the talkative reptile predicted.

3. Dentelsky, "Adam uvehemah," 151–52.

Damned Be the Innocent Snake

At the brief triple trial in the garden, God did not even find it necessary to ask the woman to spell out her direct accusation against the snake: "The serpent deceived me, and I ate" (3:13 STONE). To excuse her illicit and deliberate action, the woman chose to vilify the animal who serves in the role of a punching bag, a pattern that humans continue and follow to this day. Without offering the snake the opportunity to speak up in its defense, although allowing it to the two other human defendants, God hastens to damn the serpent, finding it guilty as charged and condensing the verdict to "because you have done this" (v. 14 STONE), yet without specifying what "this" (*zoht*) exactly meant.

The serpent did not even try to persuade, let alone force the humans' hand to do what God had all along anticipated that they would surely do. It was not God's prescience that compelled the humans to sample from that fruit; rather, it was their own autonomous free will to act on it. Despite all of that, God called out the punishment that doomed the snake to become the perpetual archenemy of humans, who will henceforth try to "pound your head, and you will bite . . . [their] heel" (v. 15 STONE).

Laying the bulk of the blame for the two humans' "a-bite-too-far" on the serpent is not warranted if it is not an injustice, given its minor role in the forbidden eating. Even if the snake indirectly spurred the woman to do what she and Adam were bound to do anyway, they did not have to become such an easy prey to the snake's mild enticement. Herein we find the foundational portals of the biblical phenomenon where humans mess up and receive their comeuppance, but animals unwittingly get embroiled collaterally; despite their innocence, they are swept into the whirlpool of divine retribution.

While refraining from calling it "evil," God went on to damn this one creature; the only individual animal that God would ever curse: "cursed are you among all animals and all wild creatures " (v. 14 NOAB).

Nonetheless, God curses numerous humans as well, such as Cain for shedding the blood of his brother Abel: "You are cursed . . . [damning him to] become a vagrant and a wanderer on earth" (4:11–12).[4] God tells Abram, "I will curse" "those who damn you" (12:3 ALT). People who "do not hearken" to God's word are forewarned: "Damned be you, in your coming-in, damned be you, in your going-out" (Deut 28:19 SB). Similarly,

4. Author's translation.

God "will send the curse" to any charlatan acting in a dishonorable way by sacrificing "a blemished [animal] to the Lord" (Mal 1:14, 2:2 DAV).

Thus, since God cursed an animal—the serpent—God will also curse humans for acting wrongly in his view. To be sure, even God gets to be vilified: once by "the son of an Israelite woman" and "an Egyptian man" (Lev 24:11 SB), or when the corpse of an executed man is left hanging on the gallows after sundown—"for a hanging person is a curse of God" (Deut 21:23 STONE).

And still, this whole narrative where the snake is thrown under the bus as an outcome of the two humans' forbidden eating, will become a harbinger of the biblical phenomenon where God who dooms and designates humans to die for their wrongdoings would carry out their punishment, albeit ensued by collateral harm and ruination that inexorably befall blameless animals as well. This episode, where the woman scapegoats the serpent for having tricked her, despite the lack of textual support for such an accusation, will continue and fuel the instinctive human response to human-perpetrated atrocities by resembling these with the ways of animals.

In this way, we seek comfort in the self-delusional perception that committing violent and bloody barbarities runs against human nature and constitutes, therefore, a mere aberration from human norms; indeed, acts that only blood-thirsty animals ("beasts") characteristically perpetrate, even when no animal can reach the ferocity level of such deeds.

The Price of a Bite: An Endless Enmity

God could not have cursed snakes as such, because he created them as beneficial animals of their respective ecosystem, including aerating, tilling, and hoeing the soil from the inside out, and as a natural prophylactic to prevent rodent infestation. On the sixth day, when the earth brought forth various living beings, including "all crawling things on the ground of each kind, God saw that it was good" (Gen 1:25b ALT). Snakes, too, were included in that observation.

Among the roughly four thousand known species of snakes found worldwide, only about 7 percent are considered dangerous to humans or "medically important."[5] While most humans still see snakes with primal horror, mirroring subliminally God's enmity setting between them, snakes in general are completely uninterested in people, let alone seeing them as

5. Pinfield, "Addressing the Snakebite Challenge."

prey; indeed, snakes see humans as huge and dangerous predators that they would rather never be around. As a rule of thumb, snakes aren't naturally aggressive and are unlikely to strike unprovoked, only as a matter of last resort if they perceive threats "such as being stepped on, cornered, or handled. Snakes prefer avoiding human contact altogether, often choosing to flee rather than fight."[6]

To be sure, the snake, one of nature's underdogs, is more threatened by humans than vice versa. Nevertheless, despite the inherently shy nature of snakes and their usual tendency to hide, retreat, or escape from any contact with humans if given the opportunity, unlike the serpent in the garden, ophidiophobia, the innate and immense human fear of snakes, is the second most common phobia in the world. It terrorizes 51 percent of Americans and is more common than the fear of public speaking, heights, or flying.[7]

Human dread of snakes has thus become a curse unto all snakes, for humans would seek to dispatch the creeping creature, as God tells the serpent, by booting and striking its head. The "enmity" that God has set between both species simply because the first two humans chose to disobey God—while the serpent did not explicitly urge the woman to bite into the forbidden fruit, nor did it address Adam at all, who also ate of the fruit that the woman handed to him—has disadvantaged snakes far worse than humans. This is so even though snake bites kill myriads of humans annually, mostly in Asia, Africa, and South America, thus bringing many to believe that the only good snake is a dead one.

"Never wound a snake; kill it,"[8] said Harriet Tubman, a distinguished American abolitionist and humanitarian. Tubman was likely thinking philosophically about addressing, *mano a mano*, the root causes of the challenges people confront. Her bias, however, towards all snakes would be mirrored many decades later by Ross Perot, a 1992 US independent presidential candidate. Perot's rendition—"If you see a snake, just kill it—don't appoint a committee on snakes"[9]—reflected similarly the truism that humans and snakes share an eternal enmity towards each other.

Tubman's and Perot's deportment mirrors the human propensity to provoke snakes by handling or even attacking them when they are spotted

6. Enviroliteracy Team, "Are Snakes Aggressive?"

7. Reed, "Animal Phobia."

8. Quotation, "Quote by Harriet Tubman."

9. Brainy Quote, "Ross Perot."

lying in the road. In the rural southwest of the United States, snakes are rounded up by the thousands for commercialized rodeo entertainment, a popular and venerable "family-friendly" tradition that draws huge crowds. These snakes are hunted down in their dens and their catchers sell them by weight to the organizers. Snake "handlers" then take center stage in these roundup entertainment shows, where they are "prodded, kicked, or thrown around." Many of these snakes are put in freezers to chill, and have their fangs extracted or their mouths sewn "shut."

It is no wonder why many of these snakes appear at such shows "swollen and bloody, and too stressed or weak to defend themselves," before they are abusively tortured and then decapitated by machetes (or in past decades by bladed farming tools). "Officials invite children to skin snakes that aren't always completely dead, then rub their hands in blood and make prints on paper."[10] Snake meat is a part of local cuisine in Texas, Alabama, Oklahoma, Arizona, and Louisiana; it has been so for centuries in various countries in Asia, such as China (especially in Cantonese cuisine), Vietnam, Thailand, Malaysia, Indonesia, Cambodia, the Philippines, and Laos, even if not as a daily staple. Those who cook snake meat proudly point out that skinning a snake is as easy as peeling a banana, and that when cooked correctly, it is culinarily a palatable white meat; besides, the skin can be used for many applications. Humans, no doubt, are big killers of snakes.

10. Williams, "Rattlesnake Roundups."

CHAPTER 6

"Garments of Skin": Not Made *of* Skin but *for* the Skin

There is a charm about the forbidden that makes it unspeakably desirable.
—Mark Twain

The first humans, initially unashamed of their nakedness, realized after eating from the Tree of Knowledge of good and evil that they should cover their reproductive organs. To overcome their eventual death—a new concept gained from eating the forbidden fruit—they had to rely on their procreation, an ability that God blessed them with, like all fauna around them. Indeed, seeing that all new births in nature must have been linked, however mysteriously to the invisible God, their organs of procreation, they must have reasoned, ought also to be hidden to demonstrate reverence to the ultimate creator. Thus, they covered their genitals with fig leaves from the garden, sewing them into loincloths, which would also distinguish them from the animals.

Curiously, the Homo sapiens in Africa, who might have emerged as a distinct species some 300,000 years ago, needed 180,000 years of evolution before beginning to wear any clothing.[1] But before sending off the humans from the garden eastwardly after they sampled from the banned fruit, God "clothed them" with "skin coats" (*kotnot orr* in Hebrew), which he "made" for them (Gen 3:21 ALT). The Hebrew word *kotnot* ("tunics" or "coats") derives from a cognate Semitic word—*kitna* in Aramaic—that means flax or linen; this word will ultimately evolve etymologically into the European

1. Dunham, "Moroccan Cave."

word "cotton" (or a nuance thereof) that closely resembles the sounding of *kotnot*.

Does it mean, then, that, although forbidding them to kill animals for their flesh, God wanted the human pair to wear hides obtained either by the deliberate killing of animals or at the least from animals that had perished? After all, animals were already living on earth long before the humans arrived at the scene; naturally, they were dying, and their skins could be used for such garments. The narrative alludes, however, to none of these possibilities as to the provenance of such animal skin. Hebrew does not have a distinctive word for either leather or skin, as it uses one word for both—*orr*.

Hence, given God's effective prohibition against killing animals for sustenance, and even more so for making anything else from their skin, the "skin coats" that God tailored for the two humans should be understood as coats for the covering of their skin, rather than coats made of skin (leather). While essentially all translations from the Hebrew of this verse prefer "garments (or 'coats') of skin," commentator Avraham Ibn Ezra (eleventh to twelfth centuries) notes that the phrase could be understood simply as garments to cover their skin[2] (as much as "wood nails" are not necessarily nails made of wood but nails to drive in wood).

By contrast, Bible scholar Ken Stone endorses the idea—which reflects a widespread hermeneutical and folkloric premise—that God committed "the first murder in the biblical text"[3] by sacrificing and providing an animal for clothing the two earthlings with its skin. Nonetheless, such a claim is baseless with no textual evidence supporting it.

Guidance from Biblical Linguistics

When Noah's two elder sons, Shem and Japheth, covered his nakedness while he lay drunk in his tent, they "took a cloak and put it" (9:23 PLAUT) on him. The Hebrew word for that garment is *simlah*, and this item is not found in leather anywhere in the Bible. Therefore, it is unlikely that Noah's sons used leather-made apparel to cover their father's "birthday suit," even though leather was available since animals were permitted to be slain after the flood. The Torah also refers to Joseph's striped garment as a "coat" or "tunic" (*k'tonet*, in the singular). That it was not made of leather is evident because Joseph's brothers soaked the garment in goat's blood before

2. Ibn Ezra, "Ibn Ezra on Genesis," Gen 3:21.

3. Stone, *Reading the Hebrew Bible*, 39.

sending it to their father Jacob (see Rashi on Gen 37:3); leather would not have absorbed the blood effectively, jeopardizing their deception about Joseph's fate. Similarly, King David's daughter Tamar wore a "striped coat" (*k'tonet*)—so each piece of the fabric was made of a different color—a dress typical for "the king's daughters who were virgins" (2 Sam 13:18 JPS).

Aaron the high priest and his sons also wore "coats" (or *kootanot* in Hebrew) and "linen breeches" during their ministerial duties, specifically to "cover the flesh of nakedness" (Exod 28:42 STONE), and none of these garments were made from animal skin. The distinctions between such cloaks and Esau's garments are quite pronounced. When Rebecca dresses Jacob to impersonate Esau before their father Isaac, she adorns him with "the skins of the kids of the goats on his hands and on the smooth part of his neck" (Gen 27:16);[4] the Torah identifies here the animal source of Esau's attire.

This clarity is mirrored in the account of the prophet Elijah who wore "a leather belt around his waist" (2 Kgs 1:8 NOAB). The ancient sage Rabbi Haninah ben Dosa even attributes this leather to the ram that Abraham offered on Mt. Moriah.[5] Regardless of the actual origin of Elijah's leather belt, the commenting rabbi assumed it was crafted from animal hide. Unlike Esau's leather-made garments, the Torah does not even allude to the source of fabric God used for making the earthlings' first "skin coats."

And that permits us to infer that God had made them a cover for their skin, albeit not made of animal skin. A rabbinic gloss suggests that God made these coats from the skin that the garden's serpent sloughed off.[6] Even if the notion were deemed plausible, it would imply that God did not need either the snake or any other animal to perish for the making of the garments that he made to cover the skin of Adam and Eve.

Breaking a myth: God used no animal skin in making garments for Adam and Eve to cover their skin.

4. Author's translation.
5. Midr. Yal. 2 Kgs, 224.
6. Midr. Pirqe R. El. 20.

CHAPTER 7

Did Abel Slay Livestock for His Sacrifice?

Just as God's mercy is upon humans, so is His mercy upon animals.
—Midrash Tanhuma, Noah, 6

Approximately twelve thousand years ago, initially in Africa and subsequently elsewhere, humans started to domesticate and herd livestock, cultivate plants, tend crops, and establish permanent villages, or they were displaced by others who did.[1] In the Bible, Cain and Abel, the first two sons of Adam and Eve, symbolize this pivotal transition to agriculture and pastoralism in actual human history. Cain willingly offered his gift to God "from the fruits of the soil"; and Abel, a herder of dairy animals, followed suit. He chose "the choice firstlings of his flock"—the healthiest among them—to willingly offer to God, following his brother's example (Gen 4:3–4 ALT).

The Flock's Firstlings

Abel thus becomes the first biblical figure to assign a special status to the male firstborn of livestock; this practice will be codified in the Torah, requiring that such livestock be consecrated to God even before birth (Deut 15:19–20). These animals could not be put to work, shorn for their fleece, or used in any way that derived benefit before being sacrificed as an offering within their first two months, and only at the central sanctuary in Israel. This rule was aimed to reinforce the belief that all belongs to God, regardless of the farmer's efforts to increase his livestock, as the psalmist

1. National Geographic, "Development of Agriculture."

points out: "For Mine [are] . . . the cattle on the hills of oxen" (Ps 50:10).[2] Importantly, the law stipulates that the one who offers the firstborn (along with the priests who perform the ritual) partakes in eating the meat of these animals.

Abel Did Not Have a Slaughter Site

The text, however, does not suggest that Abel slaughtered his firstborn animals or ate of their flesh, as the sacrificial practices in the Torah would later prescribe. The narrative alludes to neither a demand nor a request that God made to him for such an offering, nor is there any mention of a covenant that God was planning to enact with him that might feature a sacrifice. Even when he "looked with favor on Abel and his offering" (Gen 4:4),[3] there is still the question of how Abel knew that God displayed such attention to it without any "fire from the Lord" that consumed his offering.

Fire was present when, nine generations after Abel, Noah, right after the flood, became the first biblical figure who voluntarily sacrificed animals to God. He constructed an altar for his burnt offerings, and their singed flesh emitted a distinct aroma, *nihoach*. Abram witnessed "a smoking fire-pot with a blazing torch" passing between the sacrificial pieces of his animal offering. Such a fire was visible both in the inaugural events of the Sinai sanctuary and King Solomon's temple in Jerusalem.

Likewise, when Gideon honored the angel of the Lord with his *mincha* offering, "fire sprang up from the rock and consumed the [kid] meat." Samson's (yet to be) parents, Manoach and his wife, also witnessed "the flame [that] went up toward heaven from off the[ir] altar" upon the rock, as did Elijah endeavoring to prove on Mt. Carmel that "the Lord indeed is God," when "the fire of the Lord fell and consumed the burnt offering" on the repaired "altar of the Lord" (Gen 8:20–21, 15:17; Lev 9:24; 2 Chr 7:1; Judg 6:21, 13:20; 1 Kgs 18:38 respectively).

But Abel's narrative alludes to neither altar nor sanctuary and certainly not to fire, smoke, or scent. When Abram offered animals at God's command, he meticulously divided the slaughtered animals down the middle, placing each half opposite the other. However, such details of the sacrificial protocol are absent from the Abel narrative; that could only be explained by the fact that there are no slain animals therein.

2. Author's translation.

3. Author's translation.

God Favors Green Offerings

Like Cain, Abel brought forth a *mincha* offering. The term *mincha* is repeatedly mentioned in the Bible in the context of a harvest offering. It is specifically detailed in Lev 2, where the *mincha* offering consists solely of plant-based elements such as grain, first fruits, corn, and olive oil, constituting a non-meat sacrifice. The Levitical Scripture presents this offering as a complete, if not a superior, substitute for an animal sacrifice. *Mincha* is also commonly interpreted as material gifts, including live farm animals, given to someone of a higher rank or social status. For instance, Jacob sent a *mincha* of numerous live animals to his estranged brother Esau before their reunion in Canaan, following Jacob's two-decade stay in Haran.

This compelling linguistic evidence suggests that Abel's offering of the best firstborn of his flock was made in a manner that did not necessitate their slaughter. Nonetheless, Bible scholar Gerhard von Rad presumes that Abel's "sacrifice of blood was more pleasing to the Lord"[4] than Cain's crops. Likewise, W. Sibley Towner believes that "the Lord apparently has always liked the smell of animal flesh."[5] Ken Stone agrees that God found "Abel's dead animals"[6] to be "pleasing."[7] Such assertions, reflecting the commonly believed notion that Abel slew his animals, have no smoking altar in the relevant text to make them credible, given that neither brother had built or used a preexistent one.

However, being the first person in the Bible to present God with an offering, Cain offered randomly from his agrarian yield, most likely not even the first produce to ripen, by depositing it in some unspecified location that the Torah neither describes nor identifies. Since Abel followed in his footsteps—"And Abel too had brought" (Gen 4:4 ALT)—it is reasonable to presume that, like Cain, he delivered his own *mincha* gift to the same place, without slaying any of his fine animals. Indeed, there is nothing in the text that alludes to the slaughtering of his livestock, let alone to what was done with their blood, fat, skin, or other internal organs. The Torah will provide such information in its future sacrificial protocol.

4. Stone, *Reading the Hebrew Bible*, 66.
5. Stone, *Reading the Hebrew Bible*, 67.
6. Stone, *Reading the Hebrew Bible*, 67.
7. Stone, *Reading the Hebrew Bible*, 37.

What Did Abel Do with His Finest Animals?

How then did Abel present his flocks' "choice firstlings"? The text does not explicitly state that he brought them to God, although this can only be deduced from the context. The Torah employs the term "bring" similarly when referring to the offerings of other choice firstlings, such as "the first of every fruit of the ground" (Deut 26:2 STONE). As the Israelites transitioned from desert nomads to farmers in Canaan, the "promised land," they were instructed to bring an unspecified quantity of their abundant earth produce to a sacred site that God would choose. There they would lay their elite produce before the Lord and prostrate themselves.

This offering was unique as it was not paired with animal sacrifices. Through this act, the offering person demonstrated his commitment to God by dedicating the finest of his harvest, relinquishing any personal gain from it, and thus returning it to God, the original benefactor. In doing so, the presenter eschewed pride in his prosperity, endowing instead a portion of his material success as a gesture of gratitude for God's grace.

Abel likely did something similar; he presented to God the fattest "firstlings" of his flock—those from which he would not gain materially—and plausibly set them free, or at the very least ceased to benefit from their provisions. Abel's offering might also have foreshadowed the scapegoat ritual (outlined in Lev 16 and referred to in chapter 1), where a goat is sent into the wilderness after the community symbolically transfers their sins onto it. This act would later evolve into a significant priestly ceremony during the Day of Atonement. Similarly, Abel may have released his sanctified animals to wander freely, laden with his thanksgiving for God's blessings.

Changing the Narrative on Abel's "Sacrifice"

It would, therefore, be highly logical to conclude that while Abel dedicated some of his best livestock to God by separating them from the rest of his flock, he did not slaughter them for a sacrifice. For Abel to slay animals—even as an act of homage to God—would have been a forbidden act due to God's total ban on killing animals for meat, which was currently in force. Thus, we may reasonably surmise that God's "regard for Abel and his offering" was earned because he did not slay the dedicated livestock. Although

God "had no regard" for the first offering that Cain offered from "the fruit of the ground" (Gen 4:3–5),[8] the Torah does not disclose the reason.

However, the Torah does not criticize Cain's produce offering per se, nor does it express any preference for animal offerings; how could it be when Lev 2 effectively elevates the voluntary land harvest offering above an animal sacrifice? Consequently, we are left with a metaphorical hung jury, unable to reach a unanimous decision about why God disregarded Cain's "green" offering.

God Is Blasé About Bloody Offerings

Did God "need" sacrificial animals from Abel or anyone else? The God who stated, "I will take no bullock out of thy house, nor he-goats out of thy folds. For every beast of the forest is mine, and the cattle on a thousand hills . . . for the world is mine, and all that is in it"? Would God, who prohibited humanity from eating animals, "desire" such "gifts"? Consider how absurd this is in light of these words: "If I were hungry, I would not tell you. . . . Do I eat the flesh of bulls, or drink the blood of goats?" (Ps 50:9–13 NOAB).

Tragically, the very first instance of offerings to God led to jealousy and violence, culminating in the first act of bloodshed recorded in the Bible when the land farmer slew the shepherd. Furthermore, when Cain was visibly crestfallen over his inability to please God with his apparent lackluster gift, God intimated that his action would be irrelevant to him whether "you offer well" or not.

In essence, God conveyed to Cain his indifference to any offerings as he did not advise Cain to improve the quality of his original offering and repeat it like a makeup offering. Nor did God suggest converting it to an animal sacrifice. What truly matters to God is whether Cain resists the sin of yielding to temptation, which is ever-present to entrap him, and that he must master it irrespective of any offerings made to God. This concept introduced in Gen 4:7 resonates throughout the Bible, often with many prophets minimizing the importance of animal sacrifices, despite their prevalent role in religious practices, with ethics having the upper hand.

8. Author's translation.

Bloodless Altars: Quite the Norm

Abel's offering that avoided the slaying of his dedicated-to-God livestock was only the harbinger, heralding for other biblical heroes how to pay homage to God without slaying animals. Although God commanded Abram to sacrifice a heifer, a goat, a ram, a turtledove, and a young pigeon to establish their covenant, it was a unique case; God did not require any other animal sacrifices from Abraham. Indeed, Abraham constructed altars in three different places to honor God, but did not present animal offerings on them, sufficing instead by merely invoking God's name.

Furthermore, Abraham does not perform an animal sacrifice when he and Abimelech, the Philistine king of Gerar, enact a covenant in Beersheba acknowledging Abraham's rights to a well, even though Abraham presents living animals from his herds to Abimelech without slaughtering them. Abraham also does not offer an animal sacrifice to God during the grand feast he made to celebrate the weaning of his son Isaac. Isaac, too, erects an altar and refrains from animal sacrifices, as does his son Jacob twice upon his return to Canaan (34:20; 35:7).

Similarly, Moses constructed an altar to honor God without animal offerings after the Israelites defeated the Amalekites shortly after the exodus from Egypt. The rich-in-livestock, two-and-a-half tribes of Israel (Reuben, Gad, and half of Manasseh) who settled east of the Jordan River, unlike the other tribes, also raised a "meatless" altar. Due to their distance from the central altar at Shiloh, they built a replica altar, not for sacrifices but as a symbol of unity and a testament that "the Lord is God" (Josh 22:10, 22–23 JPS). Gideon, the chieftain, erected another non-sacrificial altar named "Adonai Shalom" (Judg 7:24), and King Saul did the same to commemorate his military victory over the Philistines. What connects Cain, Abel, Abraham, Isaac, Jacob, Moses, the two-and-a-half tribes, Gideon, and Saul is their desire to honor God at a special site or altar, without the need for animal sacrifices. David, the psalmist, encapsulates this practice in writing, "The sacrifices of God are a broken spirit; a broken and contrite heart, O God, you will not despise" (Ps 51:17).[9]

Breaking a myth: Abel did not slaughter any of his animals when paying homage to God.

9. Author's translation.

CHAPTER 8

The Flood Is Coming

Just beyond the ticket booth, Father had painted the question on a wall in bright red letters: "DO YOU KNOW WHICH IS THE MOST DANGEROUS ANIMAL IN THE ZOO?" An arrow pointed to a small curtain. There were so many eager, curious hands that pulled at the curtain that we had to replace it regularly. Behind it was a mirror.—LIFE OF PI

It has taken God ten generations from the start of creation to realize "the evil of the human creature was great on the earth and that every scheme of his heart's devising was only perpetually evil. And the Lord regretted having made the human on earth and was grieved to the heart" (Gen 6:5–6 ALT). Similar to God's realization that it was not good for man to be alone, God presently admits in hindsight his error in creating the human species, seeing its constant moral devolution. Notably, God never regrets the creation of any animal species, nor does he deem any of them as "bad," let alone "evil," or having gone rogue, for it is humanity that failed God. Nevertheless, it is perplexing that God plans to "blot out from the earth the human beings," yet "together with animals and creeping things and birds of the air, [and God repeats] for I am sorry that I have made them" (6:7).[1]

1. Author's translation.

But Why the Animals?

That the word "them" must have meant humankind alone and not the other living beings should be evident from the mere fact that aquatic life was not going to perish in the forthcoming killer deluge; hence, being part and parcel of the animal kingdom at large must have meant that God had enough with humans but not with nonhuman beings. Surely, no animal could have played any role in the openly and rampantly violent robbery or the petty crime, for both of these societal woes doomed the human race to annihilation.

Some rabbis, however, felt it also necessary to link the animals to the overall state of human decadence; "certainly," they, too, must have acted immorally when mating unnaturally with different species. Rabbi Azariah (quoting Rabbi Yehudah Bar Simon) knows to say that "the dog mated with the wolf and the rooster did the same with the peacock"; thus, they too "corrupted their ways."[2]

To be sure, the Torah banned the livestock farmer from allowing two species to mate, though riding a mule—born to a donkey that mated with a mare—was common (and biblically licit) even among King David's children; Absalom and Solomon are noted individually for riding one, Solomon for his coronation as king of Israel on David's "own mule" (2 Sam 18:9; 1 Kgs 1:33). But that being the case, such forbidden couplings, even in the royal stables, were not prevented from happening. Indeed, while some rabbis opine that God prohibited all humanity from breeding different species to create a new kind (that God himself did not generate), other rabbis think that the Torah only prohibited the Israelites from actively facilitating such matings. Ergo, animals that did cross-mate but with no human intervention did nothing wrong.

Further, the talmudic Rabbi Yochanan comments that humans not only forced their animals to mate with a different kind but also forced themselves on animals perversely.[3] Thus, humans, guilty of evil acts, destined the animal kingdom alongside the whole of creation to a calamitous submergence.

In the Levitical legislation that prohibits either a man or a woman from mating with a livestock animal that the Bible exclusively condemns as "perversion" (Lev 18:23), *both* the human and the animal must be stoned

2. Midr. Ber. Rab. 28:8.

3. b. Sanh. 108a.

to death, even though it is clear that the animal was forced against her will into such a coupling. Hence Rashi's rhetorical question (per Lev 20:15): "If the person committed a wrong, what wrong has the animal done?" He thus explains that killing the animal is required because by enticing the human it became "the cause of the sin," and Chizkuni (another classical Torah commentator) adds, "lest it would cause another man to sin."[4]

The Talmud rubs salt into the animal's fatal stoning wounds as it excuses the animal's execution, viewing it as a means to avert the likelihood that, when it walks down the road, people would be upset to see it because it "caused a man to be stoned."[5] Such an "explanation" does not divulge how people would recognize that particular individual livestock, especially as it is embedded within its flock or herd and has no identifiable features distinguishing it from the rest of its fellows.

Yet, even in this flimsy talmudic reasoning, one could detect a tacit admission that the animal did not deserve its punishment; that it was to be carried out only to avoid a situation where people "recognized" the coerced-into-coupling animal and blamed it—the victimized party—for the execution of the man who violated her.

In his comment on Lev 20:16, Chizkuni seems to agree that in the case of a man forcing himself on an animal, the latter "did not commit a crime." Yet, the traditional commentator notes that only in the case of a woman forcing herself on an animal does the Torah note that both "retain the bloodguilt" because "the woman did not force it, and it is not hard to know" that the male animal was a fully willing accomplice in the proscribed mating. Indubitably, no animal deliberately seduces a human to engage in sexual intercourse, yet the animal must pay with its life for the depravity of the domineering human.

What the rabbis' commentaries amounted to was nothing but imputing humanity's culpabilities to the animals with no biblical allusions to animals' degeneration to back up such a narrative. The animals were, thus, predestined to perish in the forthcoming mega tsunami as collateral victims for man's moral collapse.

The talmudic Rabbi Yehoshua ben Karcha offers a different perspective, though still supportive of the logic behind the decimation of animals, by taking the anthropocentric view. To wit, animals were destined to perish because their subservient role in creation was to benefit humans. Therefore,

4. Chizkuni, *Perushei HaTorah*, 393.

5. b. Sanh. 54a.

the latter's forthcoming demise would render the animals dispensable and redundant with the extinction of humanity by water; hence, their collective death jointly with the humans they served would make sense.[6] Such a human-centered perspective is not unlike the ancient pagan Egyptian practice of killing food animals like ducks and geese, and then mummifying them for burial next to deceased humans to provide them with food in the afterlife; animals thus had to die because humans did.

Man Messes Up and Animals Pay the Price: Sodom

Such a knock-on effect on animals is evidenced in numerous subsequent biblical episodes, beginning with the death of animals in the "firebombed," morally degenerate twin cities of Sodom and Gomorrah. Believing that God, too, was bound by the moral laws he decreed for humanity, Abraham audaciously challenged God over the destiny of the innocent lives in the doomed-for-a-fiery-devastation twin cities of Sodom and Gomorrah: "Far be it from You to do such a thing, killing innocents and wicked alike, so that the innocents and the wicked suffer the same fate. Far be it from you! Must not the Judge of all the earth do justly?" (Gen 18:25 PLAUT).

As it was, God answered Abraham's successive laconic questions (18:23–33), which centered on collective punishment, by embracing the principle that the non-guilty should be spared at all costs, even if it meant that sinners would walk away from divine retribution. Yet, the lives of innocent animals were neither on God's nor Abraham's mind. Lot, his wife, and their two single daughters were taken out of the ill-fated Sodom by the two angels who did not even allude to the livestock therein.

Next was the "bloodying up" of the river Nile with the commencement of Egypt's plagues, God's comeuppance for the pharaoh's demurral to let the Israelite slaves go on a short religious furlough; it resulted in the extinction of the fish therein, and soon thereafter of multitudes of frogs forced out of the polluted river water only to perish on land.

Such was the lot of Egypt's livestock pestered by lice and swarms of insects before succumbing to the plague of "heavy pestilence." Boils and blains soon broke forth "upon man and animal," likely bilharzia that had spread from humans to the animals who had survived the previous plague.

When the fiery hail struck, it also exacted a severe toll on Egypt's farm animals, which endured the preceding woes only to be followed by

6. b. Sanh. 108a.

the horrific final plague that struck dead all the firstborn, both human and livestock, "in the land of Egypt."

The classical commentaries on this latest form of death by collective punishment address only the guilt, if any, of those felled Egyptians who were innocent (or not), even as they were uninvolved in enslaving the Hebrews, or not in a position to free them. However, the perished animals of the ultimate plague—who had somehow outlasted all previous animal-killing afflictions—are transparent to the commentators and ignored, even when theirs was an outright penalization of the innocent.

Moreover, on that eventful night of the exodus, the Israelites ate the flesh of a lamb or a buckling, whose blood they were to dab on the doorposts and lintel of their dwellings to escape the imminent deadly strike of the ultimate plague that would hit every Egyptian firstborn, human and livestock alike. Sheep and goats were religiously venerated animals in Egypt; their slaying was an offensive thing, a taboo in the eyes of the vegetarian Egyptians (Exod 8:22). Thus, to symbolize God's absolute supreme and ubiquitous reign, the Israelites, on the brink of their emancipation, slaughtered young sheep or goats in high numbers on the altar of a theological showdown between monotheism and its pagan "competition."

A week later, the drowning of Egypt's six hundred finest horses in the Sea of Reed (or Red)—which miraculously escaped the prior lethal strikes—also resulted from God's casting their human riders into the raging waters for heinously chasing the just-freed slaves, or at the least for their prior lackadaisical stance toward the suffering of the Hebrew slaves.

The most unfathomable ceremony of the Torah, known as the red heifer statute for neutralizing ritual defilement, is another prime example of ritualizing the cleansing of human contamination by killing a blameless animal, akin to the scapegoat of Yom Kippur (discussed in chapter 1). Such a rare red cow—in Hebrew *adhumah* ("red")—sounding like "*daam*" (blood)—was slain just to have its blood sprinkled "toward the front of the Tent of Meeting" (the mobile sanctuary at Sinai during the Israelites' long years of sojourning in the desert) before its carcass was burnt (Num 19:2–5).

The cow's ashes were then used in an obscure fashion to spiritually rid the polluting impurities incurred by a person who touched either a human corpse or even a human bone or a grave, (or was present in immediate proximity to it).

An innocent young cow was slain so that persons in a state of procedural contamination would be fit to enter their sacred shrine (to bring in another livestock animal for a sacrifice), with severe divine retribution designated for violators (Num 19:13). Maimonides argued that nine such cows were slain from Moses' time until the fall of the Second Temple.

Similarly, a biblical law known as "beheaded heifer" prescribes the neck-breaking of a she-calf in a ravine as a required ritual for the nearest community in whose vicinity a corpse was discovered, but without any clues as to the identity of the slayer. The dispatch of the innocent animal was to gesture the townsfolk's moral washing of their hands; indeed, a public admission that it was none of them who "shed this blood," or even saw the killing as it happened (Deut 21:1–9 ALT).

Yet, a heifer was to forfeit its life because a homicide was committed. Her slaying is reminiscent of the hairy goat that Joseph's brothers slew just to (ab)use its human-resembling blood by dipping their brother's striped (and now stripped off him) coat before they would have it delivered to their father Jacob, thus misleading him to think that his beloved son was slain by "an evil animal" (Gen 37:20, 33).[7]

And when an Israelite warrior, one Achan son of Zerah, kept to himself from the forbidden spoils of Jericho, the first city in the promised land to fall into the hands of the Israelites, he, "his sons and daughters, his ox, donkey, and sheep . . . and all that he had" (Josh 7:24)[8] were stoned and burnt by God's decree, even in the valley of Achor. Traditional exegesis explains that Achan's children were his accomplices in either hiding the loot or at least keeping hush about it, thus deserving their execution.[9] Nevertheless, no such commentary refers to the animals that were also killed due to their master's culpability; though innocent, they, too, became collateral victims.

Like in Jericho conquered by Joshua, where the entire population "and ox, and sheep, and ass" were "utterly destroyed . . . with the edge of the sword" (Josh 6:21),[10] King Saul is ordered by the seer Samuel to exterminate the whole nation of Amalek; a fate that had befallen their animals too. Much earlier, when King Saul began to reign as the first king of Israel, he sought to recruit a national people's army to defend the outlying town of Jabesh-Gilead from the bellicose threat of the Ammonite King Nahash. To do

7. Author's translation.

8. Author's translation.

9. Midr. Pirque R. El. 38.

10. Cohen, *Joshua and Judges*.

so, he resorted to the gruesome act of dismembering two yoked oxen into pieces. He then sent those cuts with messengers to towns throughout the land with the message that draft dodgers would see their oxen butchered likewise (1 Sam 11:7). Fearsomely, men came out at once to join King Saul's army. Surely, there would have been alternative punitive measures that the newly crowned king could have taken against anyone who shirked this call-up drive, but the sight of a piece of cut-up oxen was luridly effective.

Down the road when Doeg, a chief officer in King Saul's administration, ferociously murdered in cold blood the priests of Nob at the king's command for innocently feeding and aiding the fugitive David, whom the phobic Israelite monarch sought out, he also massacred by the sword the town's women, every child or infant "and ox, and donkey and sheep" (1 Sam 22:19).[11] Again and again, it is the innocent animal that is to be sacrificed and dispatched when humans botch up and corrupt their conduct.

Prophecies That Confirm the Pattern

Hosea is fully aware of the biblically ubiquitous phenomenon whereby animals pay the ultimate price for people's moral failures. He spells out Israel's acts of corruption: "swearing, lying, murdering, robbing, and adultery." These offenses will entail the "desolation" of the land—the Assyrian catastrophic devastation in 722 BCE—that will wipe out the people and collaterally the livestock together with all other wildlife, "the animal of the field, and the bird of the sky, and even the fish of the sea" (Hos 4:2–3).[12]

Jeremiah's prophecy about Judah's various failings depicts their resultant woes, including serial and extreme droughts, "for God had robbed the livestock of their pasture," affecting also the does who haplessly would have to abandon their newborn for lack of grass. Wild asses, and jackals too, would starve likewise with no herbage to be found (Jer 14:5–6).

These words are akin to Ezekiel's prophecy of the same harrowing days when he foretold the famine in Jerusalem due to its people's idolatry; it would yield the cutting off of its "human beings and animals" (Ezek 14:13). Zephaniah echoes these words almost verbatim in his prophecy on an eventual and universal calamitous Armageddon that will destroy animals, the birds in the air, and the fish of the sea (Zeph 1:3), while Zechariah prophesies on the nations that will wage war on Jerusalem and inflict

11. Author's translation.

12. Author's translation.

dreadful agony on her people. In retribution, God will strike the invaders with "the plague," whose ghastly effects would also "fall on the horses, the mules, the camels, the donkeys, and whatever animals may be in those camps" (Zech 14:15 NOAB).

The case of Nineveh stands alone as a sole exception to this consistent biblical pattern; in this instance, God spares this "great metropolis" (Jonah 1:2) whom Jonah warned, even if only pithily, albeit not pitiably, about its impending comeuppance due to the sinfulness of its populace. Its king, trying to avert the calamity, orders that people and livestock fast from food and drink, be covered with sackcloth, and "cry mightily to God" (3:8) as one for divine grace. The king understood that the same fate awaits all living beings—human and nonhuman—whose lives are interwoven, and consequently all must join efforts to save the city.

Thanks, however, to Nineveh's innocent children (as Rashi and Radak comment) "who do not yet know their right hand from their left" and its "many animals as well" (4:11 NOAB), God pardoned the whole city from its designated ruination; neither the children nor the stock animals therein deserved their would-be collateral demise.

Yet, beginning with the garden snake, which was hung out to dry due to the two humans' forbidden eating, we must now recognize that it was the forerunner of numerous episodes to follow throughout the Bible where collateral harm and demise befall blameless animals. Henceforth, God, who designates humans to die in compliance with the fiat "only for their very crimes may persons be put to death" (Deut 24:16; Jer 31:30; Ezek 18:20 NOAB), will soon carry out their capital punishment by a mightily unique deluge, yet allow the same fate to meet the untainted land, avian, and amphibian species just for being present in a global neighborhood infested with human maleficence. They perished collaterally because of God's fury unleashed on humanity with the enormous force of a colossal flood for discarding its moral compass.

Let us proceed now en route to the Noah saga and its monumental and sweeping permanent impact on the relationship between humans and fauna.

Breaking a myth: despite the biblical designation of capital punishment to the offender alone, animals, too, perish collaterally when God strikes down humanity.

CHAPTER 9

Who Eats First on Noah's Ark?

When I see how people behave, I understand why Noah brought only animals to the Ark—UNKNOWN

The Animals: Real Co-Players

The ark God charged Noah to build would allow every species to ride out and survive the forthcoming uber-deluge (not counting the numerous aquatic lives that would survive the earth's inundation). Indeed, he assigns no discretion to Noah in opting which animals to welcome on board; God's sole purpose is the preservation of all species—primates, badgers, and adders included—that God had created, all of whom were integral to a creation that God had viewed as "exceedingly good." In a nutshell, then, God charges Noah with taking the responsibility of the human race for preserving every species of the animal kingdom.

Hence, "all wildlife" from "all herd-animals" to "all crawling things," and "all fowl kinds" to "all chirping things" and "all winged-things came to Noah into the Ark, two by two" (Gen 7:14–15 SB), like Noah and his family did. Independently, they arrived as equal partners in this enterprise, rather than as a passively assembled lot; each genus being spelled out individually, like distinct nations, instead of being glibly lumped together as one indistinguishable lot like "the animals."

God informs Noah that "male and female . . . two of each shall come to you to keep alive" (Gen 6:19–20 STONE)—echoing the Torah's earliest references to the creation of the human pair (1:27; 5:2). Indeed, even "a man and his wife," the same diction (as in 2:25 and 4:1) that is used for the first human pair; translators, however, commonly—and conveniently—render it non-literally as "a male and his female" (7:2).[1] And when the flood commenced, "in pairs they came to Noah into the Ark, male and female" (7:9 STONE), seemingly aware of their gender and relationships.

Moreover, God instructed Noah to bring into the ark seven pairs, rather than one pair, from the "pure" species. He must have told Noah what animals qualified as "pure," a term that also describes certain accessories in the Israelite sancta (i.e., the lampstand and the table), or people who cleansed themselves from ritual impurities. But even more importantly, God refrains from calling all species that were not "pure" by their immediate antonym like "defiled" (or "foul" or "unclean"—*tameh* in Hebrew); a term that is used about people, or their polluted food, and even what could happen to the land of Israel. By using the longer phrase "that are not pure" (7:2 SB), God avoided relating to animals by a degrading or derogatory adjective, thus displaying distinct sensitivity to them.

All of these fine details are significant, for they attest to the respectful regard that the Torah has for all fauna that came upright to Noah, and God's close bond with them. The designated sustainers of their respective species did not come to Noah to appeal for his mercy; according to God's design, they came as equal co-players designated to become the indispensable building blocks in a regenerated world in the aftermath of the flood.

Noah's task, then, as God's steward, was to see to their preservation—"alive with you" and once again "to keep seed alive" (6:19–20; 7:3 SB)—of all species together, even with his resources and efforts dedicated to fulfilling this immense role. One rabbinic view posits that Noah also took with him on board saplings of figs, olives, and grapevines for replanting, presaging the need for them in a reconstituted life on earth.[2]

Stocking the Ark with Herbivorous Food

As far as food stocking on board, God tells Noah to "take every food that is eaten . . . to serve for you and them as food" (6:21 ALT). This food is the same plant-based or herbivorous food God had already prescribed to humans and animals on the sixth day of creation. Significantly, Noah is mentioned before the animals in eligibility to access this food. As it was,

1. Author's translation.
2. Midr. Ber. Rab. 36:3.

Noah (and his familial detail) was on a par with the animals, with Noah having no superior status on board, for they were all surviving refugees hunkering down in the ark and depending on God's benevolence.

Nonetheless, for the human passengers on the ark to edge out the animals for personal status, albeit subtly, God decreed that Noah and his family would be eligible to eat before the animals. And indeed, God mentions Noah before the animals when it comes to being the first in line for the herbivorous meal plan on the ark that will fully sustain all passengers, on four or two legs, winged or crawlers. It was a special gesture given to the humans on board that would symbolically distinguish them from the fauna on the ark.

God's permission for Noah and humanity after the flood to kill animals for food will entail a reversal in the order of who eats first, with God instructing farmers to feed their livestock before they eat. The idea is that with God's sanctioning humans to slay animals, humankind already has gained a higher ranking over them; it must concede, therefore, its privilege to eat before animals, which had symbolized its higher standing on the ark.

A Sense of Doom: Animals' Instinct for Natural Disaster

The animals' insight and ability to look for and discover the ark for a protective shelter from an incoming catastrophe is a literary reminder of their ingrained ability to sense one in real time. Although there is no definitive scientific evidence to vouch for animals' capacity to sense imminent natural disasters, and hence to flee from the scene, considerable anecdotal evidence may validate such phenomena.

The Roman historian Aelian wrote that in the winter of 373 BCE, before the Greek polis Helike was hit by an earthquake that triggered a catastrophic tsunami that submerged it, many residents wondered about the reason behind a large-scale exodus from the area of rats, mongooses, snakes, dogs, and other animals who had left the region several days before.[3] Similarly, minutes before the Naples quake of 1805, oxen, sheep, dogs, and geese were reported to have made alarm calls in unison. And just before the 1906 San Francisco earthquake, horses were said to have "run off in panic."[4]

In 2004, a catastrophic tsunami that followed a 9.1 magnitude undersea quake off Indonesia took the lives of about 225,000 people in South

3. Aelian, *Characteristics of Animals*, 2:82.

4. Tributsch, *When the Snakes Awake*.

East Asia. Many hours before it began, elephants and buffalo hastened for "higher ground, flamingos abandoned low-lying nestling areas, and dogs refused to go outdoors."[5] Given that the core of this natural disaster was the ocean shore, most wildlife escaped death by fleeing to safe altitudes.

No Second-Class Passengers on the Ark

Since all species mattered in God's world when the calamitous deluge was unleashed, the Torah, rather than offhandedly, asserts again that "all flesh that stirs on the earth perished, [as did] the fowl and the herd-animals, wildlife, and all swarming things that swarm upon the earth, and [lastly] all humans"; all who perished, the text tells us, possessed a soul or "the spirit of life" (Gen 7:21–22).[6]

Indeed, rather than summarize the catastrophic effects of the flood by saying that all life was lost to the killer flood, the narrator insists on being specific about the diverse species of animals that were wiped out. This is the case while referring to humans as a mere fellow species, even at the end of the casualty list adhering to the general order of creation (as in Gen 1). Similarly, when the deluge ran its course and it was time to open up the earth for its renewal, the narrator again informs us that "God remembered Noah and all the animals and all the livestock that were with him in the ark" (8:1).[7] These other species were high in God's "thoughts," all reckoned with, and far from being transparent in God's eyes.

The Dove and the Rainbow

Before disembarkation, Noah tenderly handles the dove that was with him, and she in turn becomes a symbol of restoration and revival, and most importantly, an iconic symbol of world peace. It isn't Noah who would symbolize peace, even as God is the very "Maker of peace" (Isa 45:7)[8], but "the dove."

Finally, God commands Noah to exit the ark with his family, and the various species of fauna "that is with you," for they should all return to the

5. Miller, "Animals That Detect Disasters."

6. Author's translation.

7. Author's translation.

8. Author's translation.

drying earth and renew the life cycle on the flood-stricken earth. Moreover, God expected the animals to start multiplying and increase their numbers, for their own sake, not for the benefit of man. Indeed, just like the Noah family, so all the diverse faunas from the creepers, the fowl, and the rest of their clans among them "came out of the Ark by their families" (Gen 8:19[9]), both human and animal pairs.

God also proceeds to proclaim the eternal rainbow covenant, which, judging from the rainbow's posture in the sky, like an upended archer's bow, could not be directed to shoot from heaven to earth. With such a symbol, both humans and animals standing on one equal footing, as God seeks to demonstrate here, would be assured that no future killer flood, like the one that God had unleashed on the whole earth, would ever again inundate it.

The ensouled animals are far from being a mere afterthought, with God repeatedly asserting in his rainbow covenant proclamation that humans and animals are on his mind: "I will remember My covenant which is between Me and you and every living creature" (9:15 SON).

Breaking a myth: animals aren't dumb, clueless, or unable to communicate. Rather, unlike humans, they may possess a sixth sense with which they anticipate impending natural catastrophes.

9. Author's translation.

CHAPTER 10

Noah's Altar: An Eternal Tragedy

Often it does seem such a pity that Noah and his party did not miss the boat.
—MARK TWAIN

Despite the Bible's references to the important status of animals in the post-flood world, alighting from Noah's ark heralds a radical change in the erstwhile peaceful relationship between humans and animals, especially as it had prevailed on board. It happened as Noah abrogated volitionally the legacy from the very beginning of human life that barred man from killing animals.

Noah surmised, however, as Rashi intimates, that God had ordered him to take along those seven pairs of "pure" creatures, to enable him to offer sacrifices after the flood. But if this were to be the case it would upend what God specifically told Noah upon disembarkation: "Bring out with you every living thing of all flesh that is with you: birds, animals, and everything that creeps on earth; and let them swarm on the earth and be fertile and increase on earth" (Gen 8:17).[1] This command had no strings attached.

Nonetheless, Noah proceeds on to do homage to God for his incredible personal survival amid a total waste by building an altar for the actual slaughtering of animals; no one before him had ever built one, neither Cain nor Abel. Noah, thus, becomes the first person in the Bible to erect a slaughter site on which he slays "from all pure animals and all pure fowl [as burnt] offerings" (8:20 SB); we are not told though what made him choose one sacrificial animal over the others, or even how many individuals from

1. Author's translation.

each "pure" species he butchered. The blood of these animals thus becomes the first blood to be shed following the flood.

What Is *Nihoach*?

Did Noah gratify God with his sacrifices? Or did God rather see them as a mere gratuitous flattering, if not an uncalled-for expression of thanksgiving? The biblical text says nothing about God being pleased or deriving any contentment from these offerings upon smelling "the *nihoach*" scent (v. 21).[2] Bible commentator Robert Alter suggests that this smell would henceforth be associated uniquely with the name "Noah," a name that his father Lamech derived from either the word for "consolation" (comfort) or "rest" (relief). The apparent offshoot word *nihoach*, which is quite similar to how the name Noah sounds, renders the scent that God "smelled" as comforting or a whiff that puts one in a state of restfulness. Subsequently, the word *nihoach* would be commonly accepted to mean a "pleasing scent."

Nonetheless, it is hard to see how the odor of the charred, butchered flesh (innards, skin, and feathers) of God's handiwork that gracefully survived the deluge would be soothing or comforting to the incorporeal God; it must have been so, however, in pagans' belief, the sacrifice ritual of which Noah likely imitated. After all, the pagans believed that their gods depended on their sacrificial food, and they would swoop down on it for nourishment.

To attribute to Noah's God a pagan-like contentment from the nauseating smell of charred skin or feathers is a very tall order, for it would mean that God, as a spirit, "enjoyed" smelling the "soothing savor" of Noah's scorched animals. That should present a serious challenge to the original meaning of *nihoach*.

Spices to Dispel the Stench

Indeed, when God instructs Moses to add to the sacrificial system "an altar on which to burn incense" (Exod 30:1)[3]—an admixture of spices, to be offered twice a day at the time of the communal sacrifices—its goal was to

2. Author's translation.

3. Author's translation.

offset the foul smell of singed flesh emanating from the main altar. In *The Guide for the Perplexed*, Maimonides comments,

> Since many beasts were daily slaughtered in the holy place, the flesh cut in pieces and the entrails and the legs burnt and washed, the smell of the place would undoubtedly have been like the smell of slaughter-houses, if nothing had been done to counteract it. They were therefore commanded to burn incense there twice every day, in the morning and the evening [see Exod 30:7, 8], to give the place and the garments of those who officiated there a pleasant odor . . . [the burning of aromatic incense was thus intended] to support the dignity of the Temple.
>
> If there had not been a good smell, let alone if there had been a stench, it would have produced in the minds of the people the reverse of respect; for our heart generally feels elevated in the presence of good odor, and is attracted by it, but it loathes and avoids bad smell.[4]

Other Biblical Meanings of *Nihoach*

Hence, it is no wonder why the Bible expresses divine displeasure with the smell of animal offerings as in its loaded assertion when God informs the Israelites that "I will . . . make your sanctuaries desolate and I will not smell the scent of your pleasing odors [*nihoach*]" (Lev 26:31 NOAB). God is in no need for holy shrines and their respective altars, where people who spurn his laws bring sacrifices believing they would gratify or appease him. To begin with, God does not savor smells like people do. But even if God did, it is only the people who, while resisting his way, consider such a smell as *nihoach*, namely, being sweet and pleasant; you, but not I.

The prophet Amos echoes this very sentiment speaking for God: "I hate and loathe your festive offerings, and I will not be appeased [literally 'smell delightfully the offerings'] by your assemblies" (Amos 5:21 DAV). The prophet Ezekiel tells us that such aroma billowed up from Israel's idolatrous altars that "offered pleasing odor to all their idols" (Ezek 6:13 NOAB), or from such provoking-to-God sacrifices that "sent up their sweet aroma" (Ezek 20:28).[5]

4. Maimonides, *Guide to the Perplexed*, 3.45.

5. Author's translation.

Rabbi Yitzhak Hebenstreit posits in his *Sefer Kivrot HaTa'avah he torat hatsimchoni*: "Fresh animal flesh does not appeal in its scent, let alone make us crave for it; only the opposite is true as it creates repugnance and even disgust in us upon looking at it. Only after it absorbs the cooking scents of various vegetables and herbs that cancel out its original smell can one crave it, but only when its first smell and look have dissipated, so you cannot notice that it was a dead animal."[6]

When Meat Is "Home Alone"

In the summer of 2022, residents of an apartment building in the city of Eilat, Israel, were smelling for a few days a strong foul odor that made it almost impossible to breathe. Since the residents associated the odor with a rotting animal carcass or a human corpse, they called in their despair the local fire squad to break into an apartment that they suspected to be the source of that foul smell. When the first responders did so they discovered on the kitchen table a plate topped with steaks and meats left over by the resident who went on vacation for a few days.[7]

Noah's Slaughter: Uncalled-For and Malicious

When Abel found his way to dedicate animals to God—without slaughtering them—the Torah indicates that God "regarded" (or took note of) this gesture; at least that is how Abel felt about it. Rabbi Chaim ibn Attar (eighteenth century), commonly called the *Ohr Hachaim*, posits that it was due to Noah's sacrifices whereby God committed himself through the rainbow covenant that "never again shall all flesh be cut off by the waters of a flood, and never again shall there be a flood to destroy the earth" (Gen 9:11 ALT). Nevertheless, the Torah text does not even allude to Noah's sacrifices, let alone linking them to God's assurance.

Glaringly missing, however, from the Noah narrative is God's approval of his iconoclastic action, being the first person to build a slaughter site and sacrifice animals on it. God's response to this outrageous action is inconsolable and devoid of any scintilla of acquiescence. It thus looks odd, if not unsettling, that amid an unending graveyard of all that had lived, Noah

6. Hebenstreit, *Sefer*, 67–68.

7. Ifergan, "Dayarim."

slaughters fellow flood survivors to thank God for his survival. Their blood was the first fluid to spill over the drying and meant-to-be "purified" earth.

Noah hadn't done a single thing yet after building his altar to offer thanksgiving sacrifices on it before God "smelled" them, only to say promptly "in His heart [that] . . . the inclination of the human heart is evil from its youth" (Gen 8:21 NOAB). The scent emitted from Noah's slaughtered and now burnt animals was not aromatic but nauseating to God; it was an admission that humanity has remained as vile as it was before the flood with no change for the better. In making those sacrifices, Noah failed in becoming the progenitor of a new humankind and was indistinguishable from his generation that perished in the flood; from being "righteous" he descended into being "the man of the soil, [who] debased himself" (Rashi's unique rendition of Gen 9:20).

God's subsequent requirement that Noah follow seven laws, which the rabbis infer and delineate, including the prohibition of murder, sexual debauchery, stealing, and cruelty to animals, attests to the essential idea that humans are not inherently good. Ergo, humans need an ethical code of behavior; only if heeded, humans might become good. After all, even these demands do not ensure compliance by man, albeit only the possibility for it.

To be sure, God is not presently lamenting the people's wrongdoing that drove him to unleash the killer deluge, which in turn wrecked countless human and animal lives alike; God had already done that. Nor does God decry the continuation of wicked human conduct after the deluge, for that is yet to unfold. Rather, smelling the very first singed flesh of animals and birds sacrificed by a human to do homage to him, even on Noah's altar, brings God to grieve over this evil action of gratuitously wasting the lives of living beings "that He has made" and spared from the flood.

When reading survivors' memories from the Holocaust (or other accounts of mega atrocities that humans committed), one never comes across a ceremony, or even a prayer, that thanks God for one's survival from the genocidal inferno. Rather, there is an unfathomable bemoaning of the destruction of a whole world, with its unanswerable questions. For example, Jeremiah, who survived the Judean calamity (of 586 BCE), rather than ceremoniously thanking God who spared his life, instead laments, "Remember O Lord, what has befallen us; Look, and see our disgrace. . . . Why have you forgotten us completely? Why have you forsaken us these many days?" (Lam 5:1, 20 NOAB).

Like Noah, Job was a uniquely righteous hero of the Bible. But God had visited egregious woes on him when his ten children perished at once and his possessions were wiped out. When Job had new posterity and renewed prosperity, he did not bring sacrifices to God who had blessed him with his new fortunes; how could he when the fresh memories of his dead children were still vivid with him? God's early hope that Noah would be the catalyst of a dramatic change in people's conduct, or that the flood would at least purify the earth from "humankind's evildoing," went sour following Noah's watershed animal sacrifice.

The highly dense, if not tense, journey on the ark with limited resources that lasted about a year recorded no hostility among the species. Noah's slaying of animals, who like him were fortunate to have endured the same catastrophe that befell the planet, was unprecedented and hard to understand for its cruelty. God neither solicited nor appreciated his smoky expression of gratitude at any time. Nonetheless, once Noah slaughtered animals to thank God for staying alive, God would soon permit—albeit not command—such action to permanently stay on, even as a means for procuring food; a mysterious shift, indeed, in God's stance on killing animals.

Breaking a myth: God did not find the smell of Noah's charred sacrifices as either aromatic or pleasant, let alone meaningful.

CHAPTER 11

What Is Wrong with Animal Sacrifices?

Until we stop harming all other living beings, we are still savages
—THOMAS A. EDISON

Abram's Sole Animal Sacrifice

Although God conceded the flawed component in human nature immediately after Noah's animal offerings, the sacrificial institution would become a fixed biblical fixture. Ten generations after Noah, it is Abram's "Between-the-Pieces-Covenant" with God that promised him a numerous posterity and a vast land, while affirming the sacrificial system as a way to serve God. Indeed, God instructed Abram to ritualize their mutual covenant by slaughtering animals "to Me." But that, too, was a unique command because God would never ask Abram for another animal sacrifice.

Still, many years afterward, God asked Abraham to offer up his son, Isaac, "as a burnt offering upon one of the mountains," only to nix that illegitimate command in the nick of time (albeit through his messenger). After all, it was a trial (not a genuine demand). Instead, Abraham offered to God on the same altar that he had built for the sacrifice of Isaac a stray ("a delayed") ram that was entangled in a bush. And in so doing, Abraham expressed his belief that the sacrifice of an animal carried for God the same weight that the offering of Isaac would, as though there was no difference in the gravitas of a human or animal sacrifice. No wonder why the famed Israeli poet Yehudah Amichai called the ram "the real hero [with 'his human eyes'] . . . who seemingly volunteered to die instead of Isaac."[1]

1. Amichai, *Selected Poetry*, 219.

But even more importantly, God never asked Abraham to slay the animal. After all, Abraham would slaughter a ram that did not belong to him, with Mt. Moriah being a three-day walking distance from Abraham's domicile in Beersheba, the ram most likely belonged to another shepherd. But after its entanglement in a thicket, it could not catch up with the rest of the flock.

As such, this effectively pilfered substitute sacrifice was blemished and uncalled for given that Abraham violated the requirement to do one's utmost and return a lost livestock animal to its owner (Exod 23:4, Deut 22:1–2). Above all, God neither requested Abraham to slaughter the ram nor accepted it subsequently as a sacrifice; God would never allude to it at all.

That one divine request of Abraham for butchering animals to enact their mutual covenant is the sole exception to the otherwise total absence of any such requests from God of Abraham himself, or his son Isaac, or Isaac's successor son Jacob. Isaac would never offer animals to God, not even voluntarily, though he does erect an altar like the three slaughter sites that his father did; altars that featured no animal offerings.

Jacob, throughout his lifetime, would opt twice to offer animals as a sacrifice to God—with many years wedging between these offerings—but God would never allude in any way or fashion to these displays of tribute. To be sure, Jacob erected six pillars or monuments (pouring oil on two of them) in comparison to his two actual slaughter sites. Altogether, animal offerings to God by the Hebrew patriarchs were a negligible ritual; requested only once and offered otherwise voluntarily (four times), even as God would be oblivious to them all in their aftermath.

No Sacrifices in the Early Exodus

The next biblical reference to animal sacrifices after the patriarchs is invoked when Moses and Aaron first faced the pharaoh on behalf of the Israelite slaves. They deliver God's iconic message to the pharaoh: "Let my people go so that they may celebrate a feast to Me in the wilderness" (Exod 5:1).[2] "Let us go, pray, three days' journey into the wilderness that we may sacrifice to the Lord our God" (Exod 5:3 ALT). In a subsequent encounter with the pharaoh, Moses even demanded sacrificial animals for this purpose, but the pharaoh did not sanction this furlough.

2. Author's translation.

When the Israelites leave Egypt with their numerous livestock they do not, however, make any sacrifices, as Moses told the pharaoh that they would do, and not even after their miraculous crossing of the Red Sea that was quite reminiscent of the alighting from Noah's ark. And similarly, no animals were slain on the altar that Moses built in the aftermath of the Israelites' military victory over the (henceforth notorious) Amalekites a few weeks into the exodus.

It was rather Jethro, the Midianite pagan priest, who brought his daughter Zipporah, Moses' wife, and their two sons to Mt. Sinai some seven weeks after the exodus for family reunification, who voluntarily sacrificed burnt and feast offerings—likely Israelite livestock animals that he must have obtained after his arrival—in gratitude to God for extricating Israel from Egypt. Nonetheless, Moses does not avail himself of any charcoaled meat that Jethro provided—nor do Aaron, his brother, and the Israelite elders who joined together to welcome Jethro; the Hebrews were satisfied with merely breaking bread with Jethro.

From the First Sacrifices to the Golden Calf Fiasco

Only after Moses began to ascend Mt. Sinai en route to receiving the two tablets of God's laws—seven weeks into the exodus—did he proceed to offer animal sacrifices "to the Lord." Forty days later, when Moses descends from the mountain with the tablets to deliver them to the people, a colossal disaster breaks loose when the people renege on the Decalogue covenant by worshiping a golden calf.

Moses' altar and sacrifices yielded no positive outcome, given that Moses shattered to smithereens God's carved and inscribed tablets to prevent the covenant from becoming effective and render his people guilty of idolatry. When God summons Moses anew to the top of Mount Sinai to receive a replacement set in place of the smashed one, he builds no altar as before. That might imply that Moses realized that celebrating the covenant with animal offerings as he did before did not lead to a happy end, but rather to a dreadful outcome (See Exod 32:5–6, 19–20, 28).

Indeed, according to many commentators, including Rashi, God's call for the making of a portable sanctuary—*mikdash*—and its accessories that included an altar, came only in response to Aaron's crafting of the pagan golden calf and building a slaughter site for it on which animal offerings were brought up. To wit, animal offerings as a fixed feature in Israel's ritual system came only as a consequence of that disgraceful and flagrant violation of the Decalogue's unequivocal prohibition on idolatry.

And that being the case, the itinerant sanctuary and its altar emerged only as a substitute for the golden calf, if not its antidote—a "kosher calf"—to nudge the Israelites back to the service of one God alone, sans an intervening accessory. Without that traumatic debacle, there would likely be no divine call for erecting a slaughter site for Israel's livestock to be slain there in the service of God.

The Decalogue's two versions in the Torah—the essential bedrock of biblical laws—do not even allude to sacrifices. Hence, the prophet Jeremiah (like Amos before him) will remind his reluctant hearers centuries later that when their ancestors left Egypt, God did not command them to offer animal sacrifices (Jer 7:22; 14:12); rather, only to imitate him in performing "kindness, justice, and righteousness; for in these things, I delight" (Jer 9:24).[3]

The Plant-Based Offering: God's Favorite

When the Book of Leviticus—the Torah's grunt book on matters of animal offerings—begins to flesh out the Bible's foremost protocols on sacrifices, it becomes evident that the individual animal offerings were essentially voluntary rather than obligatory. Hence, "Should any person from you brings forward an offering to the Lord" (Lev 1:2 ALT) implies an option in the sense of "if it is the case" rather than a solid demand.

This rendition is later confirmed with "when you slaughter a well-being for an offering to the Eternal" (Lev 19:5),[4] which does not mean that "you must" (or "should") but "in case that," like in numerous other places elsewhere in the Torah (e.g., Exod 21–22). Namely, for an individual to bring an animal offering is, thus, a choice rather than imperative—he might or might not do so. When it is obligatory and for one time only, the Torah knows well how to command, "Go . . . and slaughter" (the Passover lambs; Exod 12:21 PLAUT), or as when God said to Abram, "Bring me a heifer" (Gen 15:9 NOAB).

Furthermore, when one brings to God a livestock offering, God calls it merely "your offering" (as in Lev 1:2; 2:13 NOAB) to underline its optional character, an offering that God did not demand; if it was positively

3. Author's translation.

4. Author's translation.

required, God might likely say instead, "My offering" (Num 28:2 NOAB). And how meaningful it is that even the procedure for voluntary animal offerings has an alternative that constitutes the Torah's favorite sacrifice—the "near-offering of grain-gift for the Lord" (Lev 2:1),[5] which was the first grain to ripen of either wheat or barley.

Why was the grain offering far superior to the animal offering? The latter could only be made by folks of means, for in biblical days, the cost of a sheep was valued as the wages of four work days. The price of a ram was the equivalent of eight work days, and for an offering of a calf, one had to work twenty days. For a grown ox, one had to labor for four months to afford its market value.

But bringing choice flour enabled the poor to participate in this major ceremonial ritual while being able to afford its bearable cost. Hence, the Torah describes the person bringing such a grain offering as "a person [literally, 'a soul']" to drive home the message that he offers not less than his very personhood (Lev 2:1 PLAUT). Or, as Rashi describes God's view of such an offering, "I will regard it as if he had offered his very soul," and not just "your offering" (1:2 PLAUT) as when describing the animal sacrifice.

It was not only that the produce offering democratized the sacrificial system by enabling the have-nots to partake in it. And that was especially so since any slight blemish in the animal's skin or anatomy would be a cause to either disqualify it as a bona fide offering before the slaying or, even worse, after the slaughter. If that were the case, the offering person would have to bring another animal; however, in the gifting of choice grain, such a disqualification did not exist.

Even more so, the plant offering allowed people who opted for it a better sense of nearness to God than those who brought animal sacrifices. For while the animal-sacrificing person may only bring and slaughter it independently outside the Tent of Meeting before conceding the slain animal to the Kohen (priest) to continue for him the sacrificial protocol, the person bringing a near-offering from the produce of the soil may himself pour the requisite oil and frankincense on the flour before conceding his gift to the Kohen (Lev 2:1). Consequently, his involvement with the offering was more elaborate than for the one who sacrificed an animal. This is a significant factor because it rendered the bringer of flour more proactively involved in the service of God, and with less reliance on the Kohen as a facilitator between the gifting person and God.

5. Author's translation.

Blood and Purity Don't Mix

Last but not least, the Torah makes three references to two major accoutrements in the sanctuary (or the tabernacle)—the table and the seven-branched menorah (lampstand)—that are the only vessels there that God portrayed as "pure" (Exod 31:8, 39:37; Lev 24:6 STONE). Even the ark, ensconcing the two tablets of the covenant, let alone the sanctuary as a whole, is never referred to as "pure." Yeshayahu Leibowitz (after a comment by Chizkuni) explains that both "pure" accessories never came in contact with any blood of animal sacrifices. "This comes to teach us that even the blood of the offerings called 'holy ones' (*kodashim*) has a blemish . . . as it is impossible that bloodshed would also be pure."[6]

And it is for this reason that God would not have King David—"the Messiah of Jacob's God"—build a temple, his great desire to do so notwithstanding, for he shed "much blood" of people on the battlefield, even in waging "great wars" (see also in 1 Chr 22:8). The sword that kills a human, or the knife that slays an animal in God's temple could never be "pure."

W. Sibley Towner's assumption that "the Lord apparently has always liked the smell of barbeque,"[7] is thus found hollow. And it must similarly be rejected on account of the rabbis' assertion that God receives more willingly the affordable grain gift that the poor present than the animals from the sacrifices of the rich; the offering, then, of the former's "soul" is superior to the offering paid from the wallet of the prosperous.[8]

God Wants Ethics, Not Dead Animals

When King David bought a piece of real estate in Jerusalem—the threshing floor (and the future site of the Jerusalem temple) from the Jebusite Araunah—his people were agonized by a deadly plague epidemic. "And David built there an altar to the Eternal and sacrificed burnt offerings and peace offerings, and the Eternal heeded his prayer for the country and the plague that afflicted Israel stopped" (2 Sam 24:25).[9] Notably, God was moved by David's supplicatory prayer for compassion, as the blood of the animal offerings alone could not have induced God to end the disastrous disease.

6. Leibowitz, *Seven Years of Discourses*, 395.
7. Stone, *Reading the Hebrew Bible*, 67.
8. Midr. Tanḥ. Vayikra:He.
9. Author's translation.

Isaiah, Hosea, Micah, and Jeremiah called upon their people to end idolatry and repair their flawed morality while emphasizing that God did not find their sacrifices "pleasing," or even acceptable (Jer 6:20). Hosea lambasts the Judeans for bringing their sacrifices to the temple solely for eating from their meat while believing that such sacrifices would be reckoned as meritorious and protect them from due punishment for their wrongdoing, even as "the Lord does not want" these sacrifices at all (Hos 8:13).[10] Jeremiah invokes also the ghost of the Shiloh Temple—a predecessor of Solomon's Jerusalem Temple some twenty-five miles and a few decades apart—where God first caused his name to dwell, only to enable its ruination later (after a catastrophic war with the Philistines). And what God "did to it" could not have been passed over, given the people's moral "wickedness," notwithstanding the numerous animal sacrifices that were presented there (Jer 7:12 NOAB).

It was for these vices that the First Temple would be destroyed (by the Babylonians in 586 BCE); the people's animal offerings did not bring them any closer to God's word. Likewise, the Second Temple—its sacrificial system notwithstanding—would ultimately be set ablaze (by the Romans in 70 CE), for similar ethical vices (e.g., internal, causeless hatred among the people, failure to rebuke those who needed to be admonished, the loss of shame).[11] In short, the whole sacrificial cult did not induce a more faithful people to God's way despite an uncountable number of animals slain at the altar with nothing auspicious to show for it. Like many other prophets, Isaiah insisted that heeding God's word regarding the ethical treatment of fellow humans was much more important than attempting falsely to honor God by participating in the sacrificial cult. Those animals were not what mattered to God, unlike offering "kindness" (Hosea), "obeying the voice of the Lord" (Samuel), or "justice and loving kindness, and walking humbly with God" (Micah) that did.

Curiously, why did the prophets choose to specifically demote the religious value of the sacrificial system, rather than other ritual demands, such as the dietary restrictions? After all, the Torah does not state which religious precept takes priority over the other. Some observers pointed to God's essential opposition to animal offerings because these sacrifices were the most likely among all other ritual requirements to mislead man into thinking that he did his part in God's service by partaking in the cult, and

10. Author's translation.

11. b. Šabb. 119b; and Yoma 9b.

it mattered not whether his ethics were skewed. No presenter of sacrifice had ever received a good word from God for a job well done, not even if his name was Noah or Job, the Bible's foremost persons of integrity and fealty to God.

Like Job, Isaiah and the other like-minded prophets attempted to send home the message that the gold standard in obeying God was one's code of ethics and not the gifting of animal sacrifices to God: "You have not brought Me your sheep for burnt-offering, or honored Me with your sacrifices. I have not burdened you with offerings" (Isa 43:23).[12] Malbim elucidates, "The burnt offering that you brought, not for Me you did. For I need no sacrifice . . . as I derive no benefit from the sacrifice."[13]

David the psalmist called out unabashedly, "Sacrifice and offerings You do not desire . . . burnt offering and sin offering You have not required" (Ps 40:6 NOAB). And then again: "I will praise God's name in song and exalt Him with thanksgiving. And this will please the Lord more than an ox, more than a bullock with horns and hooves" (Ps 69:30–31).[14] The irony of fate is that the king who eagerly desired to build a temple for God in Jerusalem, he and not another, nullified with such words the indispensable need for its sacrificial cult, a most important component of its tasks.

One needs neither temple nor a sacrificial animal to do "what is right and just," which ranks "as the Lord's elected choice over sacrifice" (Prov 21:3).[15] God prefers that peace and tranquility dwell among people over peace between people and God if they seek to keep or restore it by making animal sacrifices. Or phrased alternatively, "The sacrifice of the wicked is offensive to the Lord, but the prayer of the upright is His delight" (Prov 15:8), thus sealing the deal on God's favorite offerings. Rabbi David HaKohen (Rav Kook's primary disciple known as "the ascetic rabbi") commented that the delay in rebuilding the Third Temple is a heavenly sign that it is inappropriate to serve God by killing animals.[16]

12. Author's translation.

13. Malbim, "Malbim on Tanakh," Isa 43:23.

14. Author's translation.

15. Author's translation.

16. Stav, "Kasher parveh."

Job's Insights

Job maintains throughout his poignant and profound disputation with his friends that how folks treated others—e.g., "grieve for the poor" and providing "for the orphan," or clothing the naked (Job 30:25; 31:17, 19 KRAUS)—scored much higher with God than their adherence to the sacrificial cult. He most likely reached these insights from his own experience, for it was Job himself who would daily arise in the morning to offer animal sacrifices for each of his ten children lest they "sinned and cursed God in their heart" (1:5 KRAUS), while feasting and wining jointly in their soiree get-togethers.

Yet, these ongoing burnt offerings that the non-Israelite Job presided over—as his priest and at his slaughter site—did not nudge God to save his children from being killed as the house of the eldest son collapsed on them all—the work of Satan that God would not forestall. All these dead animals to appease God were for naught!

At the end of the Job saga, God angrily admonishes Job's three friends for misrepresenting him to Job. For the sake of flattery alone, they justified on God's behalf the calamity that befell Job, attributing it to their concocted sins that he must have committed, while Job spoke the truth in his heart vis-à-vis God. Hence, each one of the three was to take "seven bulls and seven rams [an unprecedentedly large sacrifice for a contrite single person attesting to the severity of their iniquities], go to my servant Job, and sacrifice for yourselves a burnt offering, and my servant Job will pray for you" (42:8 KRAUS).

As it was, these sacrifices were not meant to appease Job; he had to be reconciled by a personal and direct verbal apology. As animal sacrifices cannot atone for interpersonal offenses, Job's friends could only offer them to God, provided they first expressed their remorse to Job. Indeed, Job's prayer to God to forgive his friends made it amenable to him to accept their repentance, rather than their animal offering, which had always been ineffective in "swaying" God this way or another. After all, Job's animal offerings on behalf of his children could not save them from the tragic doom that Satan perpetrated, albeit with God's acquiescence.

We see the futility of such offerings of "oxen and sheep" and once again the offering-up of "a bull and a ram" (Num 22:40; 23:2, 4 NOAB) on each of the seven altars that Balak, king of Moab, built in his pathetically desperate attempts to solicit Balaam to curse the Israelites, an action that the latter would not take without God's consent. Again and again, animals are doomed to lose their life when humans beseech God for clemency or make another petition, even as such sacrifices cannot show results. Though God's graciousness and mercy are mysterious (Exod 33:19), animal offerings cannot start to manipulate such divine attributes.

Breaking a myth: animal sacrifices score low in the service of God and are empirically dispensable.

CHAPTER 12

Animals Become Food

I have, from an early age, abjured the use of meat, and the time will come when men such as I will look upon the murder of animals as they now look upon the murder of men.—LEONARDO DA VINCI

God's Mysterious Permission to Harvest Meat

Noah blazed a new direction for humanity, not only by being the first human to kill animals for a religious sacrifice. Even more significantly, he introduced meat into humanity's diet regimen after God nixed his prohibition against eating it. That meatless era had lasted ten generations from Adam's first day to God's sudden and mysterious permission to the post-flood Noah and sons to wield "fear and dread [on animals for] . . . they are given in your hands, every moving thing that lives shall be food for you; and just as I gave you the green plants, I give you everything" (Gen 9:2–3).[1] Indubitably, the animals were fully restored to the renewed life cycle of life and multiplying.

And yet, Noah was not allowed to have his meat as rare or medium: "Only, you shall not eat flesh with its life, that is, its blood" (9:4).[2] The prohibition of eating any of the animal's blood meant, simultaneously, as Rashi comments, that God forbade Noah and all humanity ever after to tear off a limb from a living animal and eat the sliced-off cut while keeping the animal alive, albeit bleeding, and suffering, yet still breathing. Such an evil

1. Author's translation.

2. Author's translation.

practice would prevent the animal's remaining flesh from quickly spoiling as it would be if the animal had been slain, but its flesh could not be preserved and remain edible without keeping it in a cold place.

Although God permitted the post-flood Noah and all generations henceforth to kill animals for food, God did not restrict Noah to "pure" animals alone. Still, God's concession was neither a command nor was it even made into a value that would endear meat eaters to God. Yet, that sanctioning that suddenly upended the exclusivity of the plant-based indigenous diet smacks of an apparent compromise (or conceding an emerging reality).

What's Behind God's Shift?

Why did God relent on killing animals for food—that which he forbade heretofore? Was it because Noah was the first to pivot and cross the Rubicon by offering sacrifices on his altar? Though God cited no reason whatsoever for this dramatic reversal, the traditional argument that the Ohr HaChaim advocates is that Noah merited the killing of animals for food since he saved their species from extinction by having them on the ark.

This view is morally untenable; you do not rescue a fellow creature from a dire menace to later kill it yourself. Ohr HaChaim reasons further that God rewarded Noah for his vigorous labor in caring for the animals aboard the ark. The reasonableness of this argument is also unsustainable; Noah's hard work of preserving the species was a divine command that, like most other commandments, did not entail a promise of a reward.

Also, animal flesh was not needed for his sustenance because, as we just saw, when meat was permitted to Noah, "green plants" were already available to him to feed on, just as it had been before the flood and on the ark itself. Even the dove's return to the ark with a fresh olive tree leaf signaled that fruit trees were already reemerging, ready to yield produce. It is inconceivable, therefore, that God would call on Noah to leave the ark if plant food security was not assured on land.

Did God Attempt to Trade Human Blood for Animal Blood?

Rabbi Joseph Albo points out that the original ban on eating meat led indirectly to the murder of humans. God permitted, therefore—albeit not demanded—the consumption of meat to highlight the difference between killing a human being—"for in God's image He Made the humankind"[3]—and allowing the dispatch of animals for food.[4]

Indeed, before the flood, man committed homicide directed at his fellows but not against animals; the Torah does not cite any killing of animals by humans, but it notes instances of men shedding the blood of other men. Cain, who slew his brother Abel, is the first. And then, Lemech—five generations later—brags vulgarly to his wives of his vengeful slayings of his fellows: "Aye—a man I kill[ed] for wounding me, a lad for only bruising me!" (4:23 SB). Neither one of these two first murderers suffered any actual adverse or punitive outcome in the aftermath of their actions, neither by God nor by man. Indeed, God had not yet prohibited murder per se, presumably expecting that humans would not slay each other of their own accord.

Nonetheless, human propensity for slaying their fellow men was immensely upsetting to God, even as he rebuked Cain after he slew Abel: "What have you done? Listen, your brother's blood is crying to me from the ground! And now, you are cursed from the ground." (4:10–11 NOAB). Hence, since humans killed other humans before the flood but did not turn their arms on animals, they might kill, perchance, fewer people, if not avoid manslaughter altogether, by turning now their unabated bloodthirstiness unto animals, trading homicide with zoocide.

Ergo, right after permitting the slaying of animals for food, God issues a warning to humans and animals alike whereby all will be held accountable for shedding human blood. God then decrees the unequivocal warning that was never pronounced before, that of capital punishment: "He who sheds human blood by humans, his blood shall be shed. For in the image of God, He made humankind" (9:6 ALT).

God's stance was clear; while humans may kill animals for food, an animal that killed a human being, even in self-defense, God would personally avenge the shedding of such human blood, if a court did not (for the lack of two eyewitnesses). The era of the cordial relationship that existed for ten generations, even when man was merely wielding dominion over animals, had come to an enigmatically mysterious end; hence, Stone's musing: "No wonder the animals dread us."[5]

However, the permission to kill animals for food did not prove to be a game-changer for overhauling human wickedness altogether and bringing

3. Author's translation.

4. Albo, *Sefer HaIkkarim*, 3:16.

5. Stone, *Reading the Hebrew Bible*, 178.

an end to homicide. If speculatively that was the reason for God's sanctioning of zoocide, then God's attempt to "flatten the curve" of homicide failed miserably. For certain, the human species has continued increasingly to massacre both its fellow members and animals, starting to do so with the latter when God authorized Noah to harvest them. This grim reality of life raises the question whether God's green-lighting of meat for Noah was given merely on an ad hoc basis and hence has long expired. Indeed, the contemporary Orthodox Rabbi Avraham Stav raises the question whether God's sanctioning of meat was eternal and unconditional and whether it should be reinterpreted in every generation.[6]

Breaking a myth: though permitting it, God had never commanded humans to eat meat.

6. Stav, "Kasher parveh."

CHAPTER 13

Dying for Meat

The beef industry has contributed to more American deaths than all the wars of this century, all-natural disasters, and all automobile accidents combined. If beef is your idea of "real food for real people," you'd better live real close to a real good hospital.—Neal Barnard, MD

From Noah to Abram: A Consistent Diminution of Lifespan

Even as it informs us about the Noachian genealogical roster of his descendants, the Torah spells out the longevity only of Shem's line (Noah's eldest son), which leads to Abraham nine generations hence. What could be the purpose of telling us the lifespan of each generation? Or what do these numerical details add to the narrative, even as we learn that Noah had lived 950 years, the first 600 of which were before the flood?

While we need not necessarily take these numbers by their face value, Shem lives to be "only" 600 years, but his son, Arpachshad, lives a "mere" 438 years and his son, Shelah, lives to be 433 years. Shelah's son, Ever, lives 464 years, while Peleg and Rehoo, representing the next two generations, plummet their longevity to 239 years each. Next, Serug lives to be 230, while his son, Nachor, lives to be 148. Terah, his son, lived to be 205, and his son, Abraham, will be 175 at the end of his life. Ultimately, Ps 90 will note that "the days of our years are three-score years and ten [is it an allusion to King David's lifespan that ended at seventy years?] or even because of strength four-score years" (v. 10 JPS). By contrast, with Adam's longevity of 930 years, an uptick for Methuselah's 969 years, and his grandson Noah's 950 years, we witness a stable human lifespan over ten generations with negligible vicissitudes.

Does Eating Meat Shorten the Human Lifespan?

What happened to human longevity between Noah and Abraham, a drop of 775 years, especially when we consider the immensely longer lifespans of the ten prediluvian generations that featured no real fluctuations in their longevity (Gen 5:5–32; 11:10–27, 32)? The Ohr HaChaim's scholarly long commentary on Gen 6:3 may imply that God's original plan was for people to live for a good number of centuries. Realizing, however, that humans were morally going astray profusely during most of their long days, God pivoted and shortened their longevity to lessen the extent of their wanton actions.

However, if that was God's real purpose behind the precipitous shrinking of humans' lifespan, then the whole idea flopped since humans continued to lead immoral lives even while living fewer years, and at the same time good and ethical people (e.g., Abraham) were also living much shorter years than the prediluvian generations whose nefarious deeds led to the colossal deluge.

So, as that proposition must be tabled, we may explore another avenue. Was it because meat was added to humans' meal plan, with Noah still belonging to the nine generations that preceded him, who had never eaten meat? Of course, this is only circumstantial evidence to explain the dramatic decline in man's longevity that cascades steeply in the post-flood era. Yet, it is a likely signpost pointing to humanity's falling lifespan that coincides with man's turning to meat for food. This consistent drop in humans' longevity is a factor that ought to be juxtaposed with what science knows to tell us about eating meat, namely, the following:

- Our human species is not ideally made to consume high amounts of animal protein.
- The heavily and traditionally meat-eating indigenous Inuit (formerly known as Eskimo) ethnicity of the (North American) Arctic, where plant-based food is scarce, has a shorter lifespan—"10 years lower than in Canada as a whole." The Intuit diet (among other factors) plays a role in determining longevity, as "protein, and especially animal protein, consumed in excess . . . places serious burdens on the body."[1]

1. Dr. McDougall's Health and Medical Center, "Extreme Nutrition"; Mariotti, "Animal and Plant Protein"; Richi et al., "Health Risks"; Physicians Committee for Responsible Medicine, "Cancer."

Rabbi Yitzhak Hebenstreit maintains that "eating meat runs against human nature; consequently, eating it damages and shortens man's years. If one acts against nature, it would be inconceivable that nature would favor him to complete his time [on earth], as nature cannot bear those who challenge her."[2] Admittedly, the Bible is not a medical manual for a healthy diet; with many authors over many centuries, its respective messages are diverse and inconsistent. Nonetheless, the case of Daniel doubles down on this thesis.

Daniel and Friends: Thriving Without Meat

In Daniel, the chronologically latest book of the Hebrew Bible, we see a reversal from meat eating to pure herbivorous food. Daniel and three other friends were exiled to Babylon with other Judean youth (in the sixth century BCE) for their good looks, splendid education, and impressive intelligence in order to serve King Nebuchadnezzar. Daniel and his three friends, however, were reluctant to eat the dainty but religiously proscribed food that was given to them from the king's table. He was able to convince the personal chamberlain tending to their food to substitute their dietary regimen with a plant-based meal plan for ten days, an adequate time to determine whether their new food (quite likely composed mainly of raw seeds, rice, legumes—such as peas and garbanzo—peanuts and nuts) compromised their health or abated their good looks.

When the experience ended, it became evident that Daniel and his three friends did not only look healthier and were more vibrant and joyous than before, but they even surpassed the other lads who had stayed with the king's food. The four friends' intellectual aptitudes and wisdom sharpened and stood out among the other youth. What is unique in this narrative of the Book of Daniel is that it informs the reader that Daniel would live a long life (approximately one hundred years), as though to imply that his ultimate longevity was linked to his meatless diet. This detail, appearing in the book's opening chapter (Dan 1:21) rather than in its last, which would be most appropriate to sum up Daniel's life, especially in the context of his food, seems editorially deliberate.

2. Hebenstreit, *Sefer*, 65–69.

CHAPTER 14

Taming Meat Eaters

And Ofer [not quite four years young] . . . then asked me if there are people who kill the cow to take from her the meat, and I—what could I say to him?—said "yes."

And then he started to run over the whole house, back and forth, maddeningly, and he also yelled . . . "Do you kill her? Do you kill a cow to take her meat away? Tell me! Yes? Yes? You do it to her deliberately." That very moment I grasped . . . perhaps for the first time, what it is; that we eat living creatures, that we kill them to eat them, and how we train ourselves to understand that on our plate we have a chopped-off leg of a chicken, and Ofer was unable to lie to himself like that.

—David Grossman, *A Woman Running from the News*

When "Is the Beef"?

After he invited the three "wayfarers" (who were God's messengers) to his desert tent, the Torah tells us that Abraham rushed to prepare a special beef meal in their honor. By the same token, when Isaac had sought to confer on his eldest son Esau the birthright blessing, he asked his hunter son to celebrate the special event with meat "delicacies such as I love . . . so that my soul may bless you before I die" (Gen 27:4 STONE). And when Jacob and Laban, his father-in-law, entered a mutual treaty vow of stretching a border-line between them at the Gilead Mountain, Jacob slaughtered animals for the ceremonial feast. The most likely reason the Torah notes these culinary details is that meat was not a usual fare or commonly anticipated as a daily meal, and that it took a special occasion to offer and eat meat. Otherwise, meat was mainly available in a sacrificial center when celebrating a festival (Deut 12:7; 1 Sam 9:12; Prov 7:14), or for marking the expiration of an oath.

In the same spirit, upon approaching the promised land, Moses envisions ordinary farmstead meat consumption in the land, apart from the elective sacrificial priestly protocol that availed meat to the participants. Yet, he associates such mundane eating with "an obsessive desire" or "craving," rather than viewing it as an essential or normative human need.

The medieval commentator Rabbi Jacob ben Asher (thirteenth–fourteenth century CE), known as Baal HaTurim, ignores the common rules of Torah punctuation and reads Moses' restrictive rules on consuming (secularly slaughtered) meat outside the sacrificial system as a call to stay away from eating meat altogether. Thus, Moses says, "When you say 'Let me eat meat,' for your soul craves to eat meat, whenever your appetite's craving may be, you shall eat meat, [yet, let it be] far away from you." While Moses' actual words refer to the great distance between the meat craver's domicile to "the place" where the meat of sacrifices would be available, the creative commentator coerced the text to express his frowning on meat in general by ascribing the distance not to the cultic altar, but rather to the eating of mundane meat per se (Deut 12: 20–21).[1]

Laws to Tame the Eating of Meat

All in all, once we get into the fine print of the Torah, beyond its sanctioning of eating meat and its attendant taming protocol (as in Lev 11 and Deut 14), it is quite possible to notice the overarching sense that slaughtering animals for food is flawed in principle, if not in practice. The Torah tries to curb and minimize the consumption of meat by allowing livestock meat to be consumed as rarely (or as often) as an average Israelite hunter would indulge in eating game meat: "And you may eat in your cities according to your full heart's desire, just as the gazelle and the deer are eaten, so too may you eat [farmstead meat]" (Deut 12:20–22).[2]

Hence, even as the Israelite was permitted to burn the midnight oil and hunt on occasion "deer, gazelle, and roebuck, wild-goat, ibex, antelope, and mountain sheep" (Deut 14:5), the Torah wants him to match the rate

1. Ben Asher, *Baal HaTurim Chumash*, 20.

2. Author's translation.

of his mundane livestock meat eating with his infrequent consumption of such game. For indeed, harvesting venison for Israelite hunters was not an everyday occurrence.

This might even be intimated in the story about Esau, a career hunter, who could come home empty-handed, if not famished. Similarly, when Jacob presents himself to his father as Esau to falsely receive the birthright blessing that Isaac had saved for Esau, the father asks him to explain his deftness in obtaining the game so quickly. Jacob must perforce ascribe "his" good hunting chops to God's grace, if not luck.

The Torn Flesh

To place more speed bumps between meat and people, the Torah also forbids the eating of a "torn animal" (if retrieved from a predator). Rather, it designates for dogs such flesh to show symbolic gratitude for the dogs that did not snarl at the Israelite slaves upon their exodus from Egypt. Nevertheless, the Torah does not caution or forewarn any harsh divine retributions against those who would eat such proscribed meat, nor does it reward those who would not. Violators who ate such meat were merely required to launder their garments and bathe in water (Exod 22:30; Lev 17:15; 22:8). After all, the eater did not dispatch the animal himself and only scavenged its flesh. Ezekiel, the prophet-priest, alludes to the eating of meat that "was torn by animals" among his people, though he absolves himself from doing so, at least since his "youth" (Ezek 4:14).[3]

The Torah's benign objection to eating from such meat—and, given that meat as such was not a frequent dish—consuming the retrieved meat of a stock animal that was fatally mauled or mangled by a predator allowed shepherds the opportunity to partake of it whenever that was available. Otherwise, slaughtering a farm animal for its meat was a luxury and self-defeating.

Bloodless Meat

A sterner means for the Torah to lessen the rate of meat consumption was to essentially prohibit right away all traces of blood in the meat, with blood being the foremost symbol of the creature's soul given to it by the creator.

3. Author's translation.

The fiat to rid it from the consumed flesh, as God told Noah, is reiterated at least eight more times in the Torah with God warning all Israelites and aliens sojourning among them who eat any blood that he "will cut him off from among his people!" (Lev 17:10).[4] Those eating any animal blood incur God's wrath ("concentrated attention"), so that "I will turn away from all My other pursuits to punish" them (Rashi's take). At the same time, refraining from eating bloody meat also yields a reward: "So that it will go well with you and with your children after you forever" (Deut 12:28).[5] The import of both the warning and the (rare!) promise of a reward for fulfilling this requirement attests to its gravitas among other religious obligations.

When eating blood, teaches "Sefer HaChinukh" (the anonymously written "Book of Education" from the late thirteenth century), "We acquire a bit of the trait of cruelty in our souls." Since the animal and the human body are similar in that "the blood keeps it alive, animals' life depends upon their blood to which their spirit is connected; it is well-known that animals have spirits, which the wise men call a living spirit." So, "If a man eats blood, as Nachmanides posits [when commenting on Lev 17:11], there will be density and coarseness in his spirit. [Ergo] it is inappropriate that the [human] soul will eat the [animal] soul."[6] Likewise, the contemporary modern Orthodox Rabbi Yitz Greenberg posits, "Blood is seen as the carrier of life. The prohibition is a reminder that the ideal remains not to take another life. . . . Not consuming blood is humanity's acknowledgment of violating the sanctity of life" when it does.[7]

Rabbinic Voices That Go Even Further

The Talmud agrees that what stood behind the permission for the Israelites to eat secularly slaughtered meat was the people's "evil impulse," and that a total taboo on meat was impractical due to humans' craving for it. Hence, it was a concession to wean them from eating the flesh of an animal carcass.[8]

Thus, the Talmud (in interpreting Deut 12:20) further teaches that meat eating should be limited to the moment of craving, when the amount consumed is minimal—merely to slake the urge; meat should not be eaten

4. Author's translation.
5. Author's translation.
6. "Sefer HaChinukh," 148.2.
7. Greenberg, "Covenant."
8. b. Qidd. 21b.

then at an hour of great hunger. Ideally, meat may be eaten, albeit occasionally, lest its cost drive the person to poverty. Meat may be an indulgence only for the wealthy, and those who are not should subsist on lighter foods such as vegetables and fish. Even then, meat should better come from one's farm animals (as Deut 12:21 implies)—though sparingly lest the farmer lose his entire livestock—and not be purchased in the market.[9]

One of the cases where the Torah calls for the stoning to death of a person to "remove the evil from your midst [so] all Israel shall hear and they shall fear" is when both parents of an irremediable "wayward and rebellious son" accuse their child before "the elders of his city" also of being "a glutton and a drunkard" (Deut 21:18–21 STONE). Though there had never been an actual execution of such a child, Rashi comments that the son overindulged himself with meat and wine despite the biblical warning—"Be not among winebibbers; among gluttonous eaters of flesh" (Pro 23:20 SON).

The talmudic sage Rabbi Yochanan thus posits that parents should teach their child proper behavior by training them to expect neither meat nor wine.[10] Rabbi Yehudah, the preeminent talmudic scholar, views Lev 11:46 as forbidding anyone except Torah scholars from eating either stock meat or poultry,[11] likely because they would know how to limit their meat intake to a bare minimum. When the Torah permits, however, lust-driven meat eating, it is evident that it is only retroactively acquiesced, and that it is seen as a luxurious activity that ideally should be avoided. Another traditional commentator, Kli Yakar, goes even further by positing that eating meat is "a little like defying the will of Heaven."[12]

Rabbi Avraham-Yitzhak Kook writes similarly that "taking animal life to fulfil needs and pleasures is a general moral concession [and hence] a deficiency in the human race" that fleshes out its "natural repugnance." For the destined fate of a kid is not to "slake one's despicable craving" in a "desirous stomach."[13] Rabbi Joseph Soloveichik in his (posthumously published) *The Emergence of Ethical Man* echoes such sentiments: "There is a distinct reluctance, almost an unwillingness, on the part of the Torah to grant man the privilege to consume meat. Man as an animal-eater is looked upon skeptically [if not mistrustingly] by the Torah." Humans have

9. b. Hul. 84a.

10. b. Hul. 84a.

11. b. Pesaḥ. 49b.

12. Kli Yakar, "Kli Yakar on Deuteronomy," Deut 12:20.1.

13. Kook, "Vision," 1, 7, 8, 14.

no right to meat—if only because the flesh of the eaten and the flesh of the eater are not much different from either one. And as a matter of principle, the dispatch of animals for eating their flesh is pure bloodshed. No wonder, then, that neither God in addressing Noah, nor the Torah afterward, sings praises for meat consumption by "bloodthirsty and flesh-hungry humans"; rather, their voice concedes a defeat to man's "evil drive."[14]

Breaking a myth: eating meat is not a biblical value.

14. Soloveitchik and Berger, *Emergence of Ethical Man*, 31.

CHAPTER 15

Traversing the Sinai Desert Without Meat

It always seems to me that man was not born to be a carnivore.
—ALBERT EINSTEIN

The Craving for Meat

A month into the exodus, traversing the Sinai desert with their numerous flocks and herds, the Israelites were exhausting their small flour provisions that they carried off from Egypt and became nostalgic about "the flesh pots" and "the fish" that they recalled eating in Egypt. While eating meat was considered to be "offensive" by the vegetarian Egyptians who worshiped animals—they looked down with disdain on every non-Egyptian shepherd as one who ate lamb (Gen 43:32; Exod 8:22)—the evidence shows that even in bondage the Hebrews could keep their husbandry of livestock (Exod 12:38).

Nonetheless, their present grumbling and craving for meat indicated that the Israelites at Sinai did not slaughter their livestock to satiate their culinary urge. Slaying individuals from their livestock for meat would be counterproductive or at least luxurious, for besides milk, the sheep was also a resource for fleece. God resents the quest for meat because it contradicts his idea for the meatless manna regimen—a whole vegetarian staple to sustain the people fully. It was sugar-like, frost-like, flaky stuff "like coriander seed" (Num 11:7 JPS).

The Abarbanel posits that God told Moses that meat was "not an essential food," even as it was "gluttony, intestines-filling, and excessive craving that plants in man malicious and cruel blood"; henceforth, that is the reason why Israel had to sustain themselves on mere manna.[1] Or as God calls it "bread from heaven" (Exod 16:4 NOAB), for which David the psalmist hails God, "who gives bread to all flesh" (Ps 136:25).[2] Just like the first ten generations of humanity, this first generation of liberated Hebrew slaves was to suffice with a plant-based (and dairy) meal plan as their only source of nourishment.

The Deadly Quail Revenge

Nonetheless, God responds to the first Israelites' nostalgic longing for meat by sending quail to cover the camp. There is no clear indication that the Israelites caught and ate them. Still, a year out since the exodus, the obsession with meat flares up again in the Israelite camp with a similar renewed grumble: "Who will give us meat to eat?" (Num 11:4 SB). Again, God responds by sending to the griping Israelites droves of quail, a bird whose capture to this day at Sinai is primitive, yet easy and effective; the small bird's exhaustion following its migratory flyway makes its capture very facile once they ram into stretched-out nets between trees by the seashore.

Although God himself sent the quail, what happened next was disastrous. "The meat was still between their teeth, not yet chewed, when the anger of the Lord flared up against the people" (11:33),[3] resulting in the death of numerous Israelites, even as they were eating quail meat right after capturing it. Their burial site was named "the graves of craving because there they buried the people who lusted" (11:34),[4] thus connecting these mass deaths with improper and gratuitous lusting for meat.

Modern medicine recognizes the quail poisoning phenomenon, coturnism (derived from the scientific name of the quail, *Coturnix*). Though such quail poisoning dissipates from the quail's body a few days after being captured, the Israelites, desirous to satiate their craving at once, would not wait. To make things worse, not sufficing with an adequate amount of that quail meat, the Israelites wolfed excess amounts of it voraciously, thus increasing the level of deadly toxicity in their body.

1. Abarbanel, "Abarbanel on Torah," Exod 16:4.
2. Author's translation.
3. Author's translation.
4. Author's translation.

The Israelites' obsession with meat and its traumatic results at Sinai continued to reverberate vividly in Ps 78, which admonishes the Israelites for "rebelling against the Most High God in the desert . . . by demanding the food they craved . . . meat for His people. . . . He rained flesh upon them like dust, winged birds like the sands of the seas; He let them fall within their camp, all around their dwellings. And they ate and were well filled, for He gave them what they craved. But before they had satisfied their craving, while the food was still in their mouths, the anger of God rose against them, so He slew of the lustiest among them, and smote down the young men of Israel" (vv. 17–31 NOAB).

CHAPTER 16

Slippery Slope: From Sacrifice to Hunting

Hunting and fishing involve killing animals with devices, such as guns, for which the animals have not evolved natural defenses.—Marc Bekoff

Nimrod: The First Hunter

Only three generations after Noah, it is Nimrod, his great-grandson from the lineage of Ham, who becomes the Bible's first hunter; he turned zoocide—beyond livestock—into a career, or at least pastime, as a form of "sports" or a hobby. By intently entering the natural habitat of animals—the largely unsettled areas—Nimrod expands the scope of animal killing from farm to non-domesticated animals. Hence, the Torah echoes twice Nimrod's self-praise of his prowess and exploits for his unprecedented hunting skills: "The first mighty man on earth. He was a mighty hunter before the Lord" (Gen 10:8–9 ALT).

Nevertheless, Torah blogger Ofer Burin notes that "it might have been expected that Nimrod's heroics would turn out to be a central biblical story. Yet, this is where it starts and ends, with a couple of verses for 'a mighty hunter,' even if he is the first powerful individual in the Bible. A mighty hunter does not interest the Bible whose heroes are different from Nimrod who might be an intriguing character, yet biblically-speaking unimportant."[1]

1.Burin, "Elohim."

The two other professional hunters whom the Torah names, Ishmael, "an archer-bowman," and Esau, his half-nephew (and a son-in-law to boot), are also peripheral players and outliers to the core interest of the Bible.

The Daunting Herod

Herod, the notoriously brutal, violent, and murderous Judean king under Roman tutelage was hated by his Judean subjects and "was ever a most excellent hunter, where he generally had success, by the means of his great skill in riding horses; for in one day he caught forty wild beasts."[2]

Esau: Nimrod's Successor

The Torah remembers Esau in the main for cavalierly conceding his firstborn prestigious status to his twin brother Jacob. He reasons that sooner rather than later he would have a deadly encounter with an animal. Esau, in other words, did not anticipate living long years given his vocation, which he considered as life-threatening.

Such professional mishaps that Esau must have feared presented themselves anew even in the summer of 2020 when an archery hunter in the state of Oregon, who had first injured an elk, was charged by the wounded bull and gored in the neck to his death.[3] And again, in January 2023 when a butcher died while trying to slaughter a pig in Hong Kong after he was knocked to the ground by the struggling animal and sustained a lethal wound from his fifteen-inch meat cleaver. The butcher had been about to kill the pig—which he had already shot with an electric stun gun—when it regained consciousness and knocked him over with his butcher's knife.[4]

Esau's fear for his life, however, would never materialize. Ishmael and Esau will live a long life and expire naturally; neither by an animal's claws, antlers, or fangs. According to a story in the Talmud, Esau was killed by his nephew (Khushim, Dan's son), on the same day of his twin brother Jacob's burial, both at age 147.[5] According to another rabbinic legend, Lamech, Cain's fifth generational descendant who was blind but a skilled hunter, accidentally killed his elder progenitor while he was hunting with his son

2. Josephus, *J.W.* 1:21.
3. Burkhead, "Oregon Bowhunter."
4. Magramo, "Struggling Pig."
5. b. Sotah 13a.

Tubal-Cain, who directed his bow and arrow. Hearing a noise in the bushes, they shoot what they think is a wild animal. But they soon discover that Lamech's arrow killed Tubal-Cain. In his overwhelming remorse, as Lamech struck his head with his powerful hands, he inadvertently killed his son too.[6] This legend thus implies that even as hunting might have preceded Nimrod, hunters recognized the possible serious risks their occupation or activity could entail.

Hunting: Not So Popular in Israel

The Torah, as we saw, permits the overall sparsely livestock-meat-eating Israelites to moonlight and hunt "deer, gazelle, and roebuck, wild goat, ibex, antelope, and mountain sheep" (Deut 14:5).[7] Yet, archeological evidence minimizes the prevalence of hunting among them. Notwithstanding the discovery of deer bones on Mt. Ebal, an early Israelite worship site in Samaria (dated to Joshua's settlement period, i.e., twelfth century BCE), the overwhelming percentage of the excavated bones—evidence of food consumed at this site by the ancient Israelites—was of livestock.[8] After all, goat meat was readily available, especially since its flavor when charcoaled and seasoned is not different from venison, albeit deer must be laboriously harvested away from man's habitation and subjected to restrictive laws to make it conform to the biblical protocol.

. . . And Trapping Even Less So

Israelites who burnt the night away and hunted periodically were hardly engaged in animal trapping. When Isaac sends off Esau to hunt game for him, he does not even allude to trapping gear. While the Torah forbids categorically capturing a mother bird (whether laying on eggs or with fledglings in the nest) that one encountered outdoors (see chapter 27), it seems that trapping was limited only to birds. The prophet Hosea refers only once to "the snare of a bird" (9:8),[9] as does Amos to a bird's "trap on the ground" (3:5 DAV) or as the psalmist does twice. The Book of Proverbs also invokes

6. Midr. Tan. Ber. 11.

7. Author's translation.

8. Berkowitz, "Mount Ebal."

9. Author's translation.

the "snare of the fowlers" (6:5),[10] as does Jeremiah in referring to his causeless enemies who "have hunted me like a bird" in the book of Lamentations (3:52 NOAB).

According to recent research conducted in northern Israel, miniature bird bone-made flutes were used some twelve thousand years ago to produce the sounds of raptor birds that facilitated the hunting of water birds and possibly also the hunting birds. Archaeologist Guy Bar-oz also detected evidence from five millennia ago in the Middle Eastern desert, which he dubs "desert kites"; it was a mass-hunting system comprised of a system strewn over hundreds of meters, and at times several kilometers, ending with a built-up round pit presumably designed for capturing animals.[11]

Taming the Hunters

The Bible's constricting rules of slaying an animal pose real challenges to normative hunting. An animal hit by a straight shot of an arrow most likely would not simply fall to the ground; it would, rather, try to escape being wounded. An injured animal is doomed to die sooner rather than later, while suffering gratuitously and immeasurably. Such prolonged and intense agony contradicts the purpose of the ritual slaughtering of livestock or birds (other than chickens that are never mentioned in the Bible) that God instructed Moses about (Deut 12:21).

The biblical protocol for hunters demanded, therefore, that once the animal (or bird) was downed it had to be slaughtered with a final cut to the throat, provided that it still possessed a glitter of life that remained in her, so that as much blood as possible might drain into the soil "like water" (Lev 17:13) and then covered by earth. An animal that was killed instantaneously was disqualified for food because it was not slain by a knife, and thus considered carrion.

This requirement weighed low on the rabbis' minds, judging by their insights derived from Isaac's sending off his son Esau to "take your gear, your quiver and your bow, and go out to the field and hunt game for me" (Gen 27:3).[12] In the rabbis' view, Isaac expected his son to comply with the spirit of that (future) Torah law. For the rabbis, "your gear" referred to Esau's knife for ritual slaughter.

10. Author's translation.

11. Archeology Newsroom, "Team Discovers"; Spitzer, "'Desert Kites.'"

12. Author's translation.

Stepping Up the Taming by Covering the Animal's Blood

Additionally, the hunter must cover with soil any blood that was spilled, even along the animal's "misery trail," for the soul that is one with the blood must return to the earth from which all life emerged. The Jewish practice to bury people whose violent death bloodied their clothes or personal items, not in the customary shrouds but in and with those clothes, shoes, and objects that were stained by their shed blood, is reminiscent of the biblical requirement of interring the blood of the slain animal. It is a way to express fury against the act that ended that life.

"Leaving the blood out, exposed to the elements and wild animals, shows disrespect" to the slain animal, writes Rabbi Zev Farber.[13] Burying the blood, then, is a gesture of respect in which the hunter expresses his shame and self-guilt upon gazing at the dispatched game's soul before its flesh is eaten. Both when it comes to the burial of bloodied humans and the blood of dispatched game, the burial of their spilled blood is expressive of respect to the blood, which is the soul.

At the same time, it is reminiscent of another Torah requirement to bury by nightfall even an executed criminal's body that was slung on a stake; for "a corpse left hanging after sundown is a curse or blight to the departed spirit that once inhabited it," if not a disrespect shown to God himself (Rashi).[14] Thus, the Torah shows sensitivity and reverence for the final respect due to both a human and a hunted animal.

Rabbi Avraham Yitzhak Kook, in his *Vision of Vegetarianism and Peace*, avers that covering the blood and making it disappear is a moral caulking that somewhat alleviates the hunter's shame and frail sense of morality. To cover the blood from the top and below requires more time at the very site where the animal painfully breathed its last; it is akin to a "protest against God for the permission" to "snuff out the life of any sentient animal soul," and to eat its meat out of "lust" in repudiation of "the sense of good and just."[15]

A keystone rabbinic perspective on pastime hunting was manifested in the response of Rabbi Ezekiel Landau (Noda BiYehuda or "known in Judah") to a question he was asked in eighteenth-century Prague about the permissibility of hunting. Unless hunting was for one's livelihood, such a

13. Farber, "Mitzvah."

14. Alter, *Five Books of Moses*, 984.

15. Kook, "Vision of Vegetarianism," 11.

cruel pastime for pleasure conflicted with "the way of the children of Abraham, Isaac, and Jacob."[16] This view seems to mirror the biblical condemnation of hunting (Prov 12:12) where the wicked covets the catch and desires to go and hunt the innocent, whether fauna or humans, rather than till the field to make a living.

Breaking a myth: hunting is not a biblical value.

16. "Noda BiYehudah II," Yoreh Deah 10:15.

CHAPTER 17

The Fear of Animals

Fear an ignorant man more than a lion—A TURKISH MAXIM

The Canaanites Are Feared Less

Once humans had begun to target wild animals, their anxiety and concern, if not a perceived sense of danger to their safety, must have become an enduring reality. The Torah, however, does not report any instances of animals targeting humans; it uses the fear of them to explain to the Israelites that the disdained Canaanite neighbors were better than roaming animals as neighbors.

The extent of either humans' fear of animals or wild animals' dread of the sight of people becomes evident when God informs the Israelites en route to the promised land that their current numbers are inadequate to effectively replace and inhabit every defeated and abandoned Canaanite town or settlement. Therefore, some of these would not be conquered "in one year lest the land become desolate." If the land were purged all at once, the Canaanite population would be replaced, not by Israelites but by numerous "wildlife of the field," perceived as more frightening neighbors than the morally odious and militarily feared Canaanites (Exod 23:29 STONE). Or in Moses' words, "Your God will dislodge these nations before you, little by little; you may not finish them off quickly lest the wildlife of the field become too many for you" (Deut 7:22 SB).

How much better it would be, then, for the new owners of the land, the Israelites, if Canaanite cities that the Israelites had not yet tried to capture were to be tolerated, if only temporarily, even though the presence of pagan Canaanites in the land was, in principle, proscribed. That would be a better alternative to animals of the land roaming in would-be prematurely vacant Canaanite towns.

Similarly, when Jeremiah prophesies (Jer 50:39 NOAB) about Babylon's demise with her population dispersed and gone, it will be "wild animals [who] shall live with hyenas . . . and ostriches shall inhabit her," replacing her people. Indeed, after Jerusalem was devastated (586 BCE) and the temple site became "desolate, foxes walked upon it" (Lam 5:18 JPS). Human presence deters animals from inhabited areas, for it is the animal that fears humans, even as people are scared of animals too, albeit for an arcane prejudice.

The Prophets Spread Fear of Animals

Hosea mirrors the ubiquitous dread of predators when describing God's response to his people's haughty hearts that led them astray to forsake him and forget his kindness. Hence, he depicts the enemy nations (Assyria and Babylon) that God will unleash on his people or the plague that will devour them "like a lion" or "a [lurking] leopard . . . [even] like a bereaved bear [that would] rip open the enclosure of their heart" or like "the animal of the field [that] will split them open" (Hos 13:7–8 DAV).

The prophet Amos—relating most likely to personal experiences as a shepherd—reflects humans' innate fear of lions as he uses this hyperbole: "like when a man flees from the lion." Yet, the question begs the answer: Could a man outpace a lion and flee? To be sure, the maximum running speed at which a lion can chase prey is about sixty kilometers per hour, which is faster than the speed of the fastest man on the planet, Usain Bolt (who in 2009 clocked 9.58 seconds to break a world record in the one hundred meter dash, which still stands as of 2025)—or running the length of a football field in six seconds. However, due to their large size, lions cannot maintain such a fast pace for a distance of more than one to two hundred meters; a human cannot and, therefore, should not try to outrun a lion, for that is what the lion's prey does.

Admittedly, Amos expresses an inherent and typical human dread of encountering a lion, even as he projects his fear of the crown predator onto Israel's super-powerful external enemies. He thereby seeks to impress and prod his hearers to tremble before God's word, even more than they are scared of a lion. Indeed, rather than fear God, who, as Jeremiah says, "does roar from on high," even "mightily" so (Jer 25:30)[1]—an idea that both Amos and Joel uniformly phrased "And the Lord roars from Zion" (1:2 and 3:16 respectively NOAB)—yet, to these prophets' chagrin—Ezekiel joins them too—the Israelites do not tremble from God's roar but from the lion's triumphant roar (after a hunt) that can be heard up to five miles away. It is louder than a rock concert and almost as piercing as a jet plane at takeoff.

When Isaiah prophesies about the forthcoming Assyrian military assault (probably the Sennacherib's devastating campaign in 701 BCE) on Judean territory, he describes the Assyrian warriors' roar "like that of the lion, they roar like young lions; they growl as they seize their prey and carry it off with no one to rescue" (Isa 5:29).[2] The indirect message that inheres this resemblance of the Assyrians to lions is that, unlike other instances where lions prey on livestock, and a successful rescue effort should be expected from the shepherds (Isa 31:4), such attempts to salvage the vanquished Israelites would not be made in this instance. (Isaiah's contemporary fellow prophet, Micah, echoes the same sentiment in 5:7.) Isaiah betrays again his innate trepidation of lions in particular and also of other wild animals even in his depiction of the idyllic messianic times when "no lion shall be there [i.e., the land of Israel], nor shall any ravenous animals come up on it" (Isa 35:9).[3]

Jeremiah (2:15) attests to the same idea when he likens the Assyrian and Babylonian monarchs, who had devastated the kingdoms of Israel in 722 BCE and would later do so to the Judean kingdom in 586 BCE, to roaring and growling lions. He thus warns Zedekiah, the (last) Judean king, not to rebel against Babylon for God entrusted to their king wild animals—per chance elephants, if not lions—whether real ones (or as aliases to symbolize might and fright)—to employ militarily against the Judean king if he risked a losing war of mutiny against Nebuchadnezzar.

Fear in the Poetical and Wisdom Books

David in Ps 22 echoes the human atavistic fear of animals, which turned his "heart like wax" that melted "within my inmost parts." He resembles his human "company of evildoers" who had besieged him, a likely allusion to King Saul and his troops who chased and surrounded him, or more

1. Author's translation.
2. Author's translation.
3. Author's translation.

generally his struggles with other enemies, with dogs, even with many and strong bulls, "the horns of wild oxen," and "a ravening and roaring lion." Such animals, even in such metaphors, did not physically harm him, but they did scare him.

These literary stereotypes of fearsome animals were inherent in people's minds, albeit contradicting young David's empirical experiences when, even as a lad, he boldly pursued and extricated prey from the jaws of powerful predators (see chapter 21). Similarly, when Elifaz assures his friend Job that when his painfully shattered life is restored to its former state of success and wellness, Job "will not fear the animal of the earth," and that such wild animals "will be at peace with you" (Job 5:22). Though the Book of Job does not allude to Job's fear of animals during his prosperous days, Elifaz seems to harbor such a ubiquitous trepidation.

The Book of Proverbs humorously uses that innate dread to jibe at the lazy person, who cites such a fright as the reason for not going about his business: "There is a lion outdoors; I shall be slain in the streets" (Prov 22:13).[4] To be sure, lions do not naturally stroll in open streets unless the "lion" referenced here is a mere metaphor for a human gangster.

Rabbis and Academics Fuel human Fear

Rabbis, too, have their share in sustaining that essential dread of animals. In commenting on the biblical demand "not to stand by the blood of your neighbor," the Talmud provides examples for a likely application of that life-saving obligation: when a person drowns in a river, when "an animal drags him away," and when robbers attack him.[5] The likelihood of such lethal human–animal encounters is by far the least realistic one among these three perilous situations. After all, the rabbis could not have cited even one bona fide, biblical lion-related incident to back up their didactic example. Rather than provide more likely scenarios for saving a life, such as when a devastating fire threatens lives, or when a house collapses on its dwellers, the rabbis chose to point out that animals were likely to slay people.

That choice is also manifested in the liturgy that the rabbis wrote. We thus read in the prayer that one invokes before traveling to a new destination (that takes longer than an hour to reach) a petition to God to "save us from . . . any enemy . . . and robbers and evil animals on the road." The

4. Author's translation.

5. b. Sanh. 73a.

iconic High Holy Days prayer Untaneh Tokef—"Now, we declare"—notes the various ways of dying: "by fire" and "by water," "by the sword" and "by the beast."[6] The inclusion of predatory animals among such likely threats to one's life merely reflects a conventionally canned standard conception that sees animals as a notable cause of death.

Yuval Noah Harari echoes the prophets' and the rabbis' primal fright of predator animals as he writes for his young readers, "You feel safe" because animals like tigers, lions, crocodiles, and snakes "cannot come at you out of the TV or escape from their cages. But what if the tigers were out, prowling around your neighborhood? Would you feel safe leaving the house to walk to school or meet a friend?" Harari seems here to overlook the fact (like the Book of Proverbs does, albeit with a chuckle) that human presence deters animals from inhabited areas (an aspect discussed in detail toward the end of chapter 20).

Yet, Harari describes what he thinks children were certain to feel and do in ancient times: "Whenever a lion or a bear appeared, humans had to run away and fast!" Hence, "If you heard a noise in the dark, it could have been a lion coming to eat you. If you quickly climbed to the top of a tree, you survived. But if you went back to sleep, the lion ate you."[7] Truth be told, neither running away from a lion nor a tree would shelter a human from a lion, even if nimble and strong enough to climb up a tree, as lions are big cats who can climb up trees well. The tilted trunks and thick branches of most trees in lions' natural habitat are easy to climb and perfect for jumping onto and moving around. Chapter 21 addresses the likelihood of lions eating humans.

6. Kol Haneshamah, *Prayerbook*, 349.

7. Harari, *Unstoppable Us*, 3.

CHAPTER 18

Rebecca and Who Gets to Eat or Drink First

Who feeds a hungry animal feeds his soul.—Charlie Chaplin

When Abraham's servant—commonly identified as Eliezer—arrives with a caravan of ten thirsty camels at Aram Naharaim, the residence town of his master's extended family, he eyes Rebecca as a desirable bride for Isaac, Abraham's son. The decisive reason for choosing her as a potential bride from among all the other maidens, who walked at the same time to the spring to draw water to bring home, was not solely her kindness and promptness in offering him—the slave that he was at a foreign town with no privileges at the town's well—water to drink from her jug.

Rebecca also hastened to shoulder the arduous and time-consuming task of filling the troughs with water she had drawn for the ten camels in Eliezer's convoy; she hauled up water, jug after jug, until the camels stopped drinking altogether. In this episode, Rebecca introduces a new standard of conduct whereby humans should precede livestock in access to water when drinking from the same source. Yet, the fact that drawing water receives this special attention in the story is both a testimonial to Rebecca's generous heart and the significant importance of animals in creation, far from being an afterthought or a negligible component of the narrative at hand.

This precedent is upheld anew when Joseph, the pharaoh's chief steward, invites his brothers to his house where Joseph sees to their getting water before their donkeys are fed with fodder; again, the donkeys' eating mentioned in the narrative is noteworthy, for their presence in the story is reckoned with a broad brush. Similarly, when the Israelites quarreled with Moses and Aaron about the dire lack of water in Kadesh, their grave fear was the imminent death by thirst of "we and our animals," as both are mentioned with no daylight between, like two integral components of one whole. In response to the people's distress, God charges Moses with bringing water out from "the rock" to "give drink to the assembly and to their animals" (Num 20:8 STONE). Time and again, God consistently refers to animals in one breath with man, solidifying further his respect for the nonhuman sentient entities, even if priority in accessing water is given to humans.

When Animals Eat First or Last

When Abraham's servant inquired with Rebecca whether there was any extra space in her father's house for his crew of underlings to stay the night, Rebecca first informed him—though that was not what Eliezer asked her about—that there was plenty of food for the camels, as feeding the camels was foremost on her mind. It is only now that Rebecca extends a hearty invitation to Eliezer and his men to enjoy home hospitality at her father's house. Hence, when they reached Rebecca's family's house, Eliezer unharnessed his camels first and fed them from the house's bran provided to him; only afterward was food brought for him too.

We come across the same pattern in Joseph's house in Egypt when his brothers were invited to lunch with him, but only after the steward of Joseph's house provided provender to their donkeys. And again, in the town of Giv'ah, a traveling man and his concubine, his servant boy, and their two donkeys were invited for a night stay at the house of an old resident. The first thing the host did was to prepare food for the donkeys before the three guests ate and drank as well (Judg 19:21).

This order, whereby the animals eat before humans, contrasts with God's directive to Noah about the food that he should store in the ark: "every kind of food that is eaten . . . [is to] be for you and for them to eat" (Gen 6:21);[1] the humans on the ark were, thus, given the right of way to this food before the animals. This contrasted order (from the hosting protocols in either Rebecca or Joseph's home) was most likely a symbolic gesture for the humans on the ark so they would subtly maintain a higher standing over the animals; after all, both could be viewed as equal to each other given the fact that both ate the same plant-based food, the only kind of sustenance that Noah stocked on the ark.

1. Author's translation.

The same concept applies to accessing the available-for-all produce that grows in fields left untended and unharvested during a Sabbatical Year. Though livestock and wildlife must be permitted to enter and eat such ownerless fruits, precedence in the pecking order is given to the farmer (who owns the property during the ordinary six years of cultivation), his servants, employees, and other fellow residents, even before the animals. And still, humans and animals alike are permitted to eat (just like they were on Noah's Ark) the same food that a fallow field yields on its own, so their essential equality is thus manifested (Exod 23:11; Lev 25:7).

Nonetheless, in the post-flood age, after God permitted humans to kill animals for food (while not allowing animals to reciprocate and kill humans, not even in self-defense), the elevated status of humanity was, thus, displayed. Humans were not, however, to flaunt their prominence above what it already was; their elevated station as a species was to be evinced, but up to a point. Domesticated animals, the Torah says, should, therefore, be fed before their owners themselves eat for God's assertion—"And I will give grass in your fields for your livestock, and you will eat" (Deut 11:15)[2]—mentions the animal before the human.

With that, God reversed the pecking order on the ark (or in an untilled field on the Sabbatical Year), so that the stock animals that could become themselves at any day the farmer's food would precede him in line for food. Indeed, that already was the case at both Rebecca's family home and Joseph's house.

But by granting humans the right of way to water as Rebecca does at the well, which will become a societal value to remain a constant and fixed order, the Torah might be intimating that animals can sustain dehydration longer than humans. Being thirsty is much more difficult than being hungry, and humans have a lesser ability than animals to withstand it. The requirement to first feed the animals is a likely intimation that God lacks trust in man; if allowed to eat first, like in accessing water, humans might forget, after all, to feed their farm animals. What happened at the well of Aram Naharaim and later at Rebecca's (or Joseph's) house thus firms up the Bible's hospitality protocol addressing humans and animals alike.

2. Author's translation.

CHAPTER 19

The Primacy of Plant-Based Food

I am a vegetarian for health reasons—the health of the animal.
—ISAAC BASHEVIS SINGER

When God permits Noah to eat meat, we cannot fail to note the prominent role of the plant-based diet in human sustenance; animals' meat may be added to one's meal plan "like the green herbage" (Gen 9:3 STONE). "I think," commented the first-century Philo of Alexandria, the Hellenistic Jewish philosopher, "that God's mentioning of the green plants attests to the human need and imperativeness of eating them."[1]

By the time Isaac decides to proffer on Jacob, who through mummery and guile presented himself to his father for the "death-bed blessing," which he had designated for his elder twin brother Esau, Isaac had already sensed that he—whose voice was "the voice of Jacob," but his hands were "Esau's hands"—was none other than Jacob himself. Even though Jacob fooled his father, Isaac was not deceived when blessing Jacob: "May God grant you from the dew of the heavens and the fat of the earth, an abundance of grain and drink" (Gen 27:28 ALT).

Still, others might argue that Jacob did manage to mislead his father who earnestly believed that he was blessing Esau. Did Isaac not "tremble with very great trembling" (v. 33 SB) when Esau showed up to receive his blessing, even as Isaac came to realize that he had just conferred this blessing on Jacob, the blessing that he intended for Esau?

Now, if Isaac did know that he conferred his first blessing unto Jacob, though his younger twin son sought it perfidiously, then its agricultural

1. Philo, "Midrash of Philo," Gen 9.3.8.

substance makes perfect sense. Assuming, however, that Isaac thought that Jacob was Esau, for that is whom Jacob said he was—"I am"—this agrarian blessing, then, is quite stupendous for Isaac conferred it on his son, the hunter.

Even when Esau showed up for his blessing, and Isaac knew without a doubt that he was conferring it unto Esau, Isaac remained consistent with his former blessing, thus wishing upon Esau "the fat of the earth" and "the dew of the heavens" (v. 39 ALT), while not alluding even to an ample harvest of prey. Isaac, who loved the taste of meat, whether of livestock or venison, dispensed his blessings to his two sons by not alluding to thriving flocks or herds for Jacob, let alone copious game for Esau. He wanted his sons to derive their sustenance from farming the soil, from plant protein rather than animal protein.

Jacob Stays off Meat

Two decades later, as a salaried shepherd employed by his father-in-law (due to his marriage with Leah and Rachel), Jacob reminds Laban of his noteworthy ethical integrity during all these years. He tells him that even "the rams of your flock I have not eaten" (Gen 31:38 ALT), which would have been his right to do. It appears that Isaac's blessing, void of any reference to meat, became a well-nigh reality, even in Jacob's food sustenance, while shepherding Laban's flocks for two decades. That should not come as a surprise, given that the only food cooked by Jacob that the Torah cares to tell us about was a hearty red lentil stew, that even Esau voraciously gulped down after bartering his first-born status for it.

The Torah mentions only two occasions in Jacob's life when he offered animal sacrifices: when he first entered into a kind of non-belligerence pact with Laban (as mentioned before), and once again in Beersheba, many years apart, just before going down to Egypt as an old man to see his beloved Joseph. Nevertheless, Jacob does not partake in any of those sacrifices, as there is no explicit reference to his doing so. Indeed, the Torah never tells us distinctly that Jacob ate meat, leaving us to wonder with good reasons whether Jacob sufficed just with plant-based food.

The biblical text is overt about when one eats meat; thus, when Abraham prepares a full meal for the three angels who visited him, "he took cream and milk, and the calf which he had prepared, and placed these before them . . . and they ate" (Gen 18:8 STONE). Or, when Moses tells the complaining Israelites that God will provide them meat (quail) in the evening and bread (manna) in the morning. Similarly, the prophet Elijah has ravens who bring him twice a day "bread and meat" (1 Kgs 17:6 NOAB). These mentions of meat in the Bible could only be significant because meat eating was not a regular fare.

The End of Meat Does Not Worry the Pharaoh

That most Egyptians also did not eat meat might be inferred from the two dreams that Joseph interpreted for the pharaoh's butler and baker, his fellow inmates in the royal prison. Both dreams, one about grapes and the other about white bread, were plant-based edibles. The elevation of such plant-based food over the flesh of animals was embedded even in the pharaoh's dual dream, which he later asked Joseph to interpret for him after his magicians would not provide him with a solution.

The first dream involved seven foul-looking, meager-fleshed cows that ate up seven plump cows yet remained as emaciated as before. This dream that prefigured the likelihood that Egypt would run out of meat did not perturb the monarch. It was not a serious concern for the pharaoh, whose people viewed "all shepherds" as "abhorrent," as Joseph tells his brothers (Gen 46:34 NOAB). Sforno, a classical commentator (echoing Ibn Ezra who noted before him that the Egyptians were not meat-eaters), explains: "They despised shepherds because they despised sheep, both as food and for sacrifices."[2] Hence, we can surmise why the worry-free and undisturbed pharaoh went back to sleep despite the demise of the fair-looking and well-nourished cows.

But another different dream woke him up "a second time": that of seven wilted and scrawny ears of grain that swallowed up seven other full and goodly ears. At this time, the pharaoh could not go back to sleep, for he realized that his other dream might portend the cessation of grain. Indeed, with his spirit agitated, the pharaoh, unable to return to sleep, looked for a strategic plan to prepare for such a calamity; after all, Egypt relied on its land produce as its primary staple food, reminiscent of Isaac's double blessing to Jacob and Esau.

Breaking a myth: meat is not a staple human food.

2. Cohen, *Soncino Chumash* (SON), 288.

CHAPTER 20

Predatory Animals Fear Humans

It is harder to crack a prejudice than an atom.—ALBERT EINSTEIN

Framing "a Vicious Animal" to Hide Human Cruelty

Thirteen generations after Noah, the Torah will first use the term "a vicious animal." Though it was the human, not an animal, who acted maliciously, a concocted "vicious" wild animal was falsely indicted for what was an appalling human action. Indeed, upon seeing Joseph approaching them in Dothan, his rankled brothers begin to conspire: "Come now therefore, and let's slay him, and cast him into one of the pits, and we will say, 'an evil animal has devoured him'" (Gen 37:20 SON).

Joseph's brothers nefariously abused that innate rife dread of predatory animals that contrasted with the facts on the ground as they schemed to deceive their father into thinking that Joseph fell prey to an "evil animal." Curiously, this human attempt to ascribe to a wild animal what the brothers were plotting to do to Joseph was that which moved Judah, the influencer brother, to sell him to the approaching Ishmaelite merchants, rather than targeting him for elimination.

Judah had assumed that the brothers had a bona fide legal case against Joseph that warranted his execution; in that case, there would have been no need to hide behind a vicious lie by attributing Joseph's demise to a predatory animal. Yet, once he heard his brothers planning to resort to that deceptive subterfuge—"an evil animal"—to explain away Joseph's plotted assassination, Judah realized that there was no rightful justification at all for slaying Joseph, and he, therefore, swapped that idea with a "mere" selling off Joseph as a slave.

The story is shrouded in fog as to what exactly happens next. Joseph's brothers might have sold him off into slavery to Ishmaelite merchants heading to Egypt. More likely and unbeknown to the brothers, Midianite traders overheard Joseph's desperate cries and pulled him out of the pit that his brothers had cast him into, and subsequently sold him off to the Ishmaelites who passed nearby. Now, with Joseph being gone, his brothers smeared in the blood of a goat—that they slew merely for this purpose because its blood resembles human blood (Rashi)—the striped tunic that they had stripped off him before casting him into "the pit." They then sent it to their father Jacob, only to mislead him about Joseph's horrific demise.

Here again, we witness the human autopilot attribution of human acts of evil to predatory animals because odious and ferocious deeds were perceived as suited to carnivore animals but not to the human race—an impulse that began with the woman in the garden by blaming the serpent for her illicit action. Jacob's spontaneous reaction upon receiving the bloodied tunic of his beloved Joseph from his other sons dovetailed with their perfidious act, for he cried out, "A vicious animal devoured him" (v. 33).[1] Jacob presumably believed that Joseph was "torn to shreds" (by a predatory animal, even as that did not happen at all; the real "predators" here were his brothers who used an act of skullduggery to make their father infer that a ravenous animal slew his son). But the fact of the matter is that Jacob did not hesitate to send young Joseph alone on his way from home in Hebron to look for his brothers in Shechem, some sixty miles away, because he did not anticipate, let alone fear, a dangerous encounter between his son and a wild animal.

Joseph's Bloodied Tunic Was Unscathed

It is against this background that Jacob looked at Joseph's bloodied tunic sent to him by his sons at Dothan; he could have seen immediately that it had no evidence of any fragments of skin or flesh, especially since it was intact. A predatory animal would have at the least scratched or punctured it. How to explain, then, Jacob's attribution of Joseph's demise to "an evil animal," particularly when the Torah does not record any lethal confrontation

1. Author's translation.

between a human (including himself) and a predatory animal in prior generations?

Indeed, wouldn't Jacob wish to go to the site where his son's tunic was discovered and look for any remains of Joseph's corpse to be buried? Did he refer, if only subliminally, by these words to his own two hot-tempered sons—Shimon and Levi, who had already exhibited their ruthless lawlessness in the atrocious massacre of Shechem (Gen 34)—who might have murdered Joseph in a new frenzy? And since he opted not to search for any remains of Joseph's devoured corpse so they could be interred, one might suspect that he did not necessarily buy the literal "vicious animal" narrative.

Yet, even by expressing these words, "an evil animal"—whether he meant a real animal or any of his sons—both Jacob and his sons betrayed an inherent dread of predators. Jacob's trepidation might have been augmented by his brother Esau's reasoning as to why he, being a hunter, did not need to be his father's successor son. Esau, anticipating his looming death, appears as conceding an entrenched consternation of predators; although going after the same prey, he was never assaulted by any of his animal competitors.

Rebecca Sees No Danger to Jacob from Wildlife

To be sure, Jacob's earlier life experience of walking alone in open fields—he had left his home in Beersheba for Haran, a veritably long distance—confronted him with no danger from wild animals. Rebecca sent him off on such a major journey, for she feared for his life, not from wildlife, but from the hands of his twin brother, Esau, whose birthright he stole.

Rebecca, a meticulously detail-oriented individual, didn't find it necessary to equip her beloved Jacob even with a personal weapon, let alone guiding her son about the behavioral patterns of predatory animals, maybe because she knew that big carnivores generally try to avoid confronting humans. Rebecca did not even bother to assign a hireling companion for Jacob, as the presence of two is likely to ward off a rogue predator who might uncharacteristically act aggressively, even deep in the animal's natural habitats. (One day Kish would send his son Saul with a servant to look jointly for his strayed jennies; see chapter 22.)

Presumably, Jacob might already have known that most wild animals are disinclined to hunt humans whose considerable height walking on two legs and with two eyes up high on the front of the head, besides two high arms, would likely signal to such animals that they are looking at a probable big and strange-enough predator. So, swerving and dodging it, rather than attacking it, might be a better option. Jacob must have also known that a human who keeps calm when sighting a four-legged predator in order to appear non-threatening, while maintaining a respectful distance, is less likely to provoke an aggressive response. Similarly, he must have known to avoid animals' turf when predators are poised to hunt at dawn and dusk, and that wearing bright and contrasting clothing would distinguish him from prey. Besides, he must have known not to camp for the night near animal trails or overhangs, scratch marks, scat, small piles of dirt, pine needles, tall grasses, or leaves.

Indeed, Jacob, who had expressed to his mother reservations about his consternation of tricking his blind father lest he called his bluff for pretending to be Esau, voiced no reservations about encountering predatory animals on the road to the far-off Haran to which both of his parents sent him, albeit for a different reason.

On the Road Alone

On his first night away from home, Jacob parked in "a certain place" (Luz, to be known later as Beth-el). He then "took from the stones of the place," putting them "at his head, and he lay down in that place." Rashi explains that Jacob feared "vicious animals," so he gathered some stones for protection; hence, Jacob trusted that a mere small stone barrier, "a gutter" (per Gen 28:11) would thwart any animal from threatening him. But Jacob did not need those stones as his journey to Haran was quick and carefree.

During the twenty eventful years Jacob spent in Haran while working as a shepherd for Laban, he experienced the effects of predators on his flocks. But when he laments to his employer that "these twenty years I have been with you . . . what was torn up [by mauling animals] I brought not to you, I bore the loss" (Gen 31:38–39 ALT), he says nothing about any personal fear for his life from those predators that snatched and carried off some individuals of his flocks.

More Biblical Evidence: Animals Avoid Humans

Animals of the field ate carcasses but not live humans. The Torah warns the Israelites against defying God's way, lest "your carcasses will be food to all birds of the sky and the animals of the earth, and there will be no one to frighten them away" (Deut 28:26).[2] Evidently, the animals would not be the ones to slay the Israelites for the abandonment of their divine commandments. Their death would be the result of the plague or other deadly diseases, or even the sword; the animals would only forage on their exposed corpses. And while the Bible tacitly, yet perceptibly, admits that ordinarily such carrion eaters may effortlessly be driven off from human carcasses, God would reverse the normative pattern when his wrath was kindled.

This reality, whereby the animals of the field come to mind as foragers, rather than as animals that prey on humans, is reflected clearly in the verbal exchange between Goliath and David before their duel. Goliath: "Come to me, and I will give your flesh to the birds of the sky and the animals of the field."

David retorted, "This day the Lord will deliver you into my hands, and I will strike you down and remove your head from you. And I will give the dead bodies of the army of the Philistines this day to the birds of the sky and the wild animals of the earth, that all the earth may know that there is a God in Israel" (1 Sam 17:44, 46).[3]

The heroic saga of the seven-month-long lone vigil by King Saul's concubine, Rizpah, daughter of 'Aiah, over the seven impaled young bodies of her two sons and five other grandsons of Saul, is another attestation of animals' fear of humans (2 Sam 21:8–10). King David (ruthlessly and contrary to two laws of the Torah) surrendered these seven youngsters to the Gibeonites to be the target of diabolical blood revenge for King Saul's breach of the non-belligerence pact that Joshua had entered with the Canaanite nation centuries before. At least that was the official version of David's historians in the second book of Samuel. Of course, David's motive might have been the practical eradication of the last male heirs of King Saul's bloodline.

The Bible notes that during these dry season months (spring to fall) Rizpah single-handedly warded off any scavenger, either fowls or animals of the field, from approaching those seven condemned languishing corpses; they were not to be buried until the first rain arrived to signal the end of the dry spell and the curse of the famine. During these seven months, the animals feared the intrepid Rizpah, who single-handedly kept them at bay.

2. Author's translation.

3. Author's translation.

Finally, the Torah demands that every Israelite man fulfill the commandment of making three annual pilgrimages from their villages or towns to the current religious center ("the house of the Lord your God"; Exod 23:19; 34:26 NOAB) for a sacrificial duty; only in the days of King Solomon was it established permanently in Jerusalem. In such journeys, most pilgrims must have used rural routes that required several, if not more, days to complete in either direction. The Torah was unconcerned with risks from dangerous encounters between pilgrims walking on such roads or trails and wild animals.

Explaining the Biblical Record

Despite the prophets' numerous references to scary lions, wild animals do not attack people in the Bible unless they are God's envoys (see chapter 30). How can we explain this phenomenon whereby humans, albeit much slower and weaker than these wildlife animals, indeed possessing no natural defensive means for protection, nor fangs, talons, or antlers, are not considered by big carnivores as primary prey? These would ordinarily leave humans alone, perhaps being more afraid of them than to attempt to snack on them. In general, a lion (or a mountain lion) would try to avoid confronting a human, even veering from a path where a human walks, especially if more than one human is present.

The Talmud goes even further by positing that if a human fell into a lions' den, that alone would not mean that the person would be slain by these predatory animals, especially if the lions were already satiated and spread about, rather than constricted in a narrow space. There would thus be plenty of time for such an individual to either extricate himself or be helped out by others.[4] Humans are not the normative typical quarry that lions tend to hunt simply because humans often don't live among animals in the wild or frequently wander alone into the lions' territory, especially when lions typically hunt at dawn, dusk, and night.

"Humans are one of the few creatures that lions fear" contends Nathan Myhrvold, an accomplished observer of lions in their natural habitat.[5] Biblical commentator Yosef Braslavi, basing himself on "lion researchers," agrees: "Only when startled at its crouch or interfacing with a human who leaves it no space for maneuverability,' let alone with one who seems like

4. b. Ber. 33a; Yebam. 121a.

5. Myhrvold, "Lions."

posing a threat to lion cubs, does the lion resort to an offensive mode. Possibly, the human upright posture and their scent, which differ from those of their usual quarry, deter lions from confronting them—save in cases when a lion has accidentally preyed on a human, mistaking them for a four-legged animal. Lion prides would attack human settlements only as rarely as a plague in case of acute hunger."[6]

Patrick Pester, writing for Live Science, suggests that since "humans are bipedal, walking upright on longer legs," it makes them visually "larger in appearance [and that] is threatening . . . [even as it communicates] the signal to predators that you are trouble." Hence, "Hearing a human voice would deter approaching humans." Warm-blooded animals harbor a deep innate fear of man, and generally don't hunt them; no large animal sees humans as its natural prey. When they do attack humans—several people will be enough to keep even most polar bears away—it is the result of feeling threatened (especially when they are scared for the safety of their young), but attacking to protect isn't the same as hunting a human for food.[7]

Blame the Animal First

The entrenched fear of animals also permeated the Shaba National Reserve in Kenya when the body of Joy Adamson, who wrote *Born Free* and was featured in the iconic movie about Elsa, the lioness she raised, was discovered by her assistant on January 3, 1980. He had first presumed that a lion slew her as the media reported. However, the police investigation found "that Adamson's wounds were too sharp and bloodless to have been caused by an animal," and concluded she "had been murdered with a sharp instrument." A disgruntled laborer formerly employed by Adamson was found guilty of murder and sentenced to indefinite imprisonment. George Adamson, Joy's husband, was also murdered nine years later in 1989 near his camp in Kora National Park while rushing to aid a tourist being attacked by poachers.[8] In both cases, humans were the true evil beasts, but in Joy Adamson's case, the lion was instinctively the prime suspect until proven otherwise.

6. Braslavi, *Arayot*, 60.
7. Pester, "Humans are practically."
8. Adams, "Author Joy Adamson"; Associated Press, "George Adamson."

Other Contemporary Encounters

- In January 2020, a mother and her three children were found alive after getting lost in the Amazon jungle between Peru and Colombia, the natural habitat of more than four hundred mammals and four hundred species of snakes. They survived on wild berries, seeds, and fruits for thirty-four days. An almost identical story took place in the same Amazon jungle in 2023 when four children, ages thirteen years, nine years, four years, and eleven months, survived a small plane crash and were found alive forty days later.[9]
- That same year, a Bolivian man was separated from his three hunting buddies in the same Amazon rainforest; he endured thirty-one challenging days. As far as wild animals, he reported one punch-up encounter with a boar and a successful dodging of a jaguar who stalked him, yet he remained unscathed.[10]
- A year later, a hiker lost his way in the wilderness of the Santa Cruz Mountains in California for nine days. He had a mountain lion following him, but it kept its distance without threatening him.[11]
- The most publicized case of survival in the Amazon jungle is the one that famously became the subject of a book, a documentary, and a feature movie—*Miracles Still Happen* (1974)—telling the story of the seventeen-year-old Juliane Koepcke, who had endured, while being seriously injured with bleeding cuts on her arms and legs, ten days alone in the Amazon rainforest after the Lansa Flight 508 plane crash in late December 1971.[12]
- A rare cougar attack in 2023 on an eight-year-old boy in Olympic National Park in Washington State was quickly foiled when the child's mother scared off the animal by merely yelling at the mountain lion, forcing it to casually abandon the scene, leaving the young boy with only minor scrapes and punctures.[13]

9. Ng, "Mother and Three Children"; Smith, "How 4 Children Survived."
10. Davies, "Man Survives Month."
11. Neath, "California Man."
12. BBC, "Juliane Koepcke."
13. Propper, "Rare Cougar Attack."

Evidently, in neither physical nor merely visual encounters mentioned above did wild animals that teem the wilderness or the rainforest harm any human; as a rule of thumb, predatory animals neither regard humans as prey nor are likely even to try to attack a human accompanied by another person.

- Nonetheless, rare exceptions to this general rule do take place, like the one in 2018 when a lone hiker on Mount Hood, Oregon, was likely killed by a cougar, as deemed by the type of injuries inflicted on her. It was the first fatal attack on record by a cougar in the state.[14]
- In March 2024, two young adult brothers walking in the woods in Northern California were assailed by a mountain lion who mauled one of them to death, seriously injuring the other. Admittedly, it was a rare attack—California's first fatal cougar-on-person attack in two decades. Still, even as humans kill far more cougars than the other way around, some cougars who do not "play by the rules of disengagement" managed to kill twenty-eight humans during more than a century (or since 1890) throughout North America; a statistically negligible aggregate number.[15]

Other rare physical confrontations end with the humans triumphing over predatory animals even without a firearm or a knife, as in the following instances:

- In 2021, Rajagopal Naik, his wife, and their child were riding on a motorbike back home (India) when a leopard leaped at them from behind the bushes, getting a hold of the child. With everything happening so fast, Naik managed to hit the leopard on the head and then suffocated it to its demise.[16]
- In 2022, a leopard that escaped through a damaged fence surrounding the Kruger National Park in South Africa crossed paths with Ndumiso Mona (twenty-three), who was on his way to fetch his kids from school. Hearing a growl behind him, he turned around as the big spotted cat suddenly pounced on him, hitting him on his head with its paws and almost tore his nose apart. But Mona brawled with the wildcat, fighting back with his bare fists until the animal fell. Mona kept

14. Urness, "Oregon's First Fatal Cougar."
15. Casapani, "Mountain Lion Kills Man." Predator Defense, "Cougars at Risk."
16. Newsflare, "Man Kills Rogue Leopard."

on strangling it while calling for help. Another man who overheard his call hit the leopard on the head with stones, causing it a death blow. Because of the rarity of leopard attacks, its carcass was sent for veterinary analysis to explain its aggressive behavior; a traditional local healer believed that the animal was "frustrated."[17]

Breaking a myth: while humans are prone to fear wild animals, the latter's dread of humans is by far more empirically warranted.

17. Ginindza, "How I Fought Leopard."

CHAPTER 21

Is the Lion as Powerful as One Thinks It Is?

The lion's power lies in our fear of it.—A NIGERIAN MAXIM

The Lion's Popular Image

The Bible is rife with people's first names borrowed from the animal kingdom; this category is the largest one in the Bible except the theophoric category (where names incorporate the name of or refer to the divine). Men were named (in Hebrew): "wolf," "raven," "bird," "dove," "donkey" and "foal," "addax," "snake," "mouse," "rabbit," "dog," "lion," "deer," "camel," "wild ass," "fox," "horse," and even "worm," "flea," "grasshopper," and "fish." Women were named: "sheep," "she-bird," "falcon," "ibex," "bee," "calf," "rat," "sheep," and "wild cow." In naming someone after an animal, it was believed that the prowess and energy of such animals could mysteriously endow that person. It also attests to the proximity and closeness people felt for the animal, both physically and emotionally, or to the appreciation of its favorable attributes.

Jacob's blessings for his twelve sons gathered around his deathbed in Egypt employ several references to animals that he embedded within his farewell biddings for some of them. The animal's highlighted special characteristics were such that Jacob wished for his sons to adopt and emulate. Prominent among them is Judah, whom he likens to "a lion cub" broadcasting leadership and royalty. With that, the lion makes its debut in the Bible, where it will henceforth be mentioned more times than any other wild animal.

Generations later, when Jacob's descendants approached the promised land from the east seeking passage through the land of Moab, the lion would be associated with being the foremost predator. King Balak, distressed over the approaching Israelites to his land, sought to hire Balaam—a non-Hebrew prophet (others view him as a "sorcerer")—to curse his prospective trespassers. In his sublime, albeit enigmatic poetry, Balaam compares Israel to a bloodthirsty lion that drinks "the blood of the slain" (Num 23:24 NOAB). Indeed, the prophets Isaiah, Jeremiah, Hosea, and Amos relate to the lion as the scariest animal, even when the Bible does not earnestly describe the animal as dangerous to humans.

The Lion Was No Match for Samson

Balaam's image of the ravenous lion is reversed as the Bible tells the story of the super-strong man, Samson, the first known human who slew a lion with his bare hands. With his brawn, he effortlessly slew a young lion in the vineyards of the Philistine town of Timna(ta) after the animal roared at him. Rather than seek to de-escalate the encounter and disengage from the young lion's scene, Samson quickly charged the lion. Grasping it by its hind legs, he hastened to tear the lion "apart barehanded as one might tear apart a kid" after it is butchered (Judg 14:6).[1]

Traditional commentaries justify the act as self-defense by saying that the young lion approached Samson, an exceptionally powerful "ironman," to assault him. The young lion, however, only roared in Samson's direction, which meant that it did not intend to charge at him. "Lions don't roar when hunting"; rather, they "usually act stealthily and silently to avoid alerting their prey." In this case, the lion roared to avoid actual contact with Samson by showing off its "good condition and [its readiness] to defend its territory and pride. Roaring before attacking would be counterproductive" for achieving their goal.[2] The lion reserves its bloodcurdling roar to the moment after it ravened a quarry (Ps 22:14).

Given Samson's muscular size (plus his unshorn long hair that could resemble a lion's mane) and that humans are not lions' natural prey, we may infer that the lion's roar was meant to broadcast to Samson that he was trespassing into its territory and to intimidate him out of doing so. Had

1. Author's translation.

2. Sinclair, "Why Do Lions Roar?"

Samson disengaged and withdrawn from the lion's "sphere of influence," there would be no need for a violent clash.

The narrator of this story suggests, however, that Samson's killing of the young lion was enabled by "the spirit of the Lord [that] came mightily upon him" (Judg 14:6 JPS) before he dispatched it; this may suggest that God imbued Samson with the intrepidity of mind that emboldened him to take on the lion. But we do not find in other references to humans triumphing over a lion, like young David or Benaiah (a mighty member of the future King David's guard) that God infused either one with grit and a booster shot of prowess like with Samson, even when none of these two subsequent lion slayers came close to resembling Samson's hulking stature.

Samson's rapid dispatch of the lion would lead to a series of seemingly unrelated knock-on events, ultimately resulting in his very demise and his complete failure to relieve his tribal predicament vis-à-vis the Philistines. Though he killed many of them, the tribe of Dan still needed to seek an alternative land to the tribal territory it had before being unable to defend it from the Philistines; it would be just difficult to see God's presence in any shape or form associated with Samson's gratuitous routing of the lion. We thus may speculate why the narrator here wanted us to know that Samson did not tell his parents about his encounter with the lion, which looks like a negligible detail in the complex scheme of events that ensued. Might it be that he did not find the slaying of a young lion, who, other than a roar, made no offensive move against him as a feat to brag about to his parents?

Shepherds Pursuing Lions

The next biblical confrontation between a human and a lion is featured, rather retroactively, in young David's pitch to King Saul when he pleaded to be the one who would challenge and strike down Goliath in a duel. Though a mere shepherd youth, David makes his case to the king: "Whenever a lion or a bear came, and took a lamb from the flock, I [alone] went after it and struck it down, [even being successful at] rescuing the lamb from its mouth; and if it turned against me, I would catch it by its cheeks, strike it down, and kill it. Your servant has killed both lions and bears" (1 Sam 17:34–36 NOAB). From King Saul's prompt embrace of David and sending him off to take on Goliath (even as David could not fit into the war gear of the tall king), it can be inferred that Saul believed David's plain telling of his exploits with predators.

David's daring valor will resonate years later in Hushai's reminding Absalom during his war of rebellion against his father that the latter was endowed with "the heart of a lion"; a heart that is not likely to "melt" by fear (2 Sam 17:10 NOAB). To be sure, David credits God with delivering him "out of the paw of the lion, and out of the paw of the bear" (1 Sam 17:37 JPS); in Ps 22 he likely intimates his short petition to God before pursuing such predators: "Save me from the mouth of the lion" (v. 22 NOAB). But David was not merely delivered from the jaws of lions; rather, he rescued a lamb from the jaws and paws of lions and bears with his bare hands. And in any event, these predators only braved a baby sheep, not even a fully grown one.

Hired shepherds in the ancient Near East were not obliged to make good on or indemnify the employer for livestock lost to predators. In the absence of a witness to corroborate a hired shepherd's professional vigilance, the Torah required an oath to attest to it (Exod 22:9–12). Despite such a legal recourse, it was common for shepherds to pursue a lion that snatched an individual from the herd.

Isaiah's assertion that the lion "will not be terrified" or "daunted" at the shouting of "a band of shepherds" summoned to retrieve its catch (31:4),[3] buttresses the fact that shepherds (like young David) were wont to pursue the predator to save what they could. Amos agrees that exploits like David's were the norm among shepherds, albeit less successful than what David related to Saul. Though Amos admits that shepherds did chase lions who ravened on their flocks, they still ended up rescuing "from the mouth of the lion [merely] two legs, or a piece of an ear" (3:12 NOAB).

Likewise, the Talmud presumes that a skilled shepherd may be able to rescue any individual from the herd under his watch, even from the jaws of either a wolf or a lion, "by chasing away a predator of this kind." Such a shepherd would face "the lion with other shepherds and with sticks chase it away."[4] As we saw (in chapter 14), it made sense for a shepherd to try and extricate what he could from the predator, but not because he needed to prove to the owner that livestock was lost to a marauding animal. Rather, pursuing the predator and rescuing the dead carcass, or the mortally injured animal, would earn the hireling shepherd meat for his next meal that was usually austere or meager. The average diet of an Israelite, let alone that

3. Author's translation.

4. b. B. Met. 93b.

of a herder, included meat only on few-and-far-between solemn occasions (a festival, vow payment, and honoring guests).

The lion's relative weakness vis-à-vis man is well reflected in David's poetical tribute after learning about the heroic fall of King Saul and his crown prince Jonathan in battle against the Philistines on Mt. Gilboa: "They were stronger than lions" (2 Sam 1:23 JPS). That man could be stronger than a lion in a face-to-face encounter became evident again when one of King David's heroic men, B'nayahu ben Yehoyada (Benaiah's son of Jehoiada), had dispatched a lion by descending into a narrow desert pit on a snowy day to interface with the animal that slipped into that ditch (23:20). The lack of any wiggling room compounded by the cold temperature were factors that the Bible likely notes deliberately to aggrandize B'nayahu's exploit, for lions in contrast to humans are at their peak performance when it is cold and where they face no escape route. Lions are fiercer when deprived of prey, as livestock are corralled and do not go out to graze in the open.

Nonetheless, the pit might have been dug to entrap the lion in it, though one might question the purpose of hunting the lion since we are not told that it had posed any danger. But people being people, the culprit is always the animal. Hence, some commentators know to tell us—irrespective of what the Bible does not say—that the lion, "driven by the cold from the forests, had made its lair in a dry tank near some town, and thence preyed upon the inhabitants as they went in and out of the city. And Benaiah pitied them, and came to the rescue" of the terrorized inhabitants after it "did much harm". Alternatively, "Benaiah went into a cave . . . to shelter himself a while from the cold, when a lion, being in it for the same reason, attacked him, and he fought with it and slew it."[5]

Slaying a Lion by Hand

A similar confrontation was reenacted in April 2022 when a man in Eastern Uganda wrestled with a lion in a brutal battle. Although sustaining severe injuries after fighting off the lion near his home, the man was able to kill the animal with his bare hands.[6] Such contemporary stories (see the previous chapter) help reinforce and corroborate similar biblical human–lion encounters ending with the humans being triumphant.

5. Bible Hub, "2 Samuel 23:20 Commentaries."

6. Davis, "Man in Uganda."

The Prophets: Weak, Weak, Weak Is the Lion

That the lion is bound to lose its showdown with a human who interfaces with it is reflected likewise in Ezekiel's comparison of the kingdom of Judea in its final years to "a lioness" confronting strong humans. Despite the roaring of Judah's "young lions," namely, her evil and oppressive last kings (in the late seventh century and early sixth century BCE—Jehoahaz, Jehoiakim, Jehoiachin, Zedekiah), none of her rivals, Egypt and Babylon, the superpowers of the day, was fearful of them. Being wobbly and weak lion whelps, their powerful human rivals put one of them in "hooks," another in a "net," "in their pit," "in a cage," and "into strongholds" (Ezek 19:2–9 JPS)—metaphorical references to the humbling and disastrous downfall of Judah's last four monarchs. Yes, these Judean royal lion cubs roared, but they failed to impress the mighty and violent men who dethroned them, if only because they had ignored God's roar, as Ezekiel avers, while trusting solely in their own.

Ezekiel similarly identifies Egypt's Pharaoh, who considered himself "a lion among the nations" (32:2 NOAB), as an utterly failed and defeated monarch at the time of Judah's fall into the hands of the Babylonians. The prophet Nachum shares the same image in referring to the eventual collapse of the oppressive Assyrian Empire and its capital Nineveh that will be brought about by a sword that "shall devour your young lions" (2:13 NOAB).

Humans vs. Lions in Contemporary Times

The revered rabbinic guide for religious living, *Shulchan Aruch*, features the lion as a paragon for a bright-eyed and agile animal; it, therefore, urges each follower before everything else in the morning to "be like a lion and overcome his inclination . . . [to stay in bed and procrastinate, but rather] rise from sleep before dawn to serve his Creator."[7] In reality, however, the lion is the least active of all big cats as it goes on a hunt only when its hunger is beyond tolerable. It has been argued that a typical lion prefers to be a scavenger rather than to prey proactively on live quarry. Carcasses that the lion did not kill itself (their death was rather brought about by either a natural cause, like a disease, or by other predators such as leopards,

7. Karo, *Shulchan*, 1:1.

cheetahs, hyenas, or wild dogs from whom lions are likely to steal prey), provide more than one half of the lion's sustenance.[8]

So, as much as the lion pilfers flesh from other species, there is enough evidence that humans also rob such flesh from lions. The media knows to tell us about tribespeople in Africa who regularly steal food from groups of lions to provide their families with substantial meals. In so doing, they practice kleptoparasitism (the very common prey-stealing from another animal's kill, as observed among certain species of wild animals in Africa).

Taking meat from lions is thought to be a common practice among the nomadic Mbororo in North Cameroon. "One village in the Central African Republic is known to allow lions living in the surroundings, solely for easy access to meat." Another study in Uganda reported "nine cases of humans actively scavenging meat from lions and leopards."[9]

In 2012, the British *Daily Mail* reported about three tribesmen tracking a pride of lions, with vivid photos taken in real-time. Led by a sixty-five-year-old man, they soon stumbled on a band of fifteen bloodthirsty lions tucking "into a dead wildebeest. Their huge teeth could be seen dripping with the blood of their kill." The men "confidently walked towards" the pride.

As the men approached the ravenous pride and "got closer to the dead animal, all of the lions dispersed, and instead watched eagerly from the fringes" as the men stole the meat without being challenged. Anthony Bond, the reporter of this story, added that the whole incident seemed to him as evidence that humans take part in this behavior "regularly."[10] Still, other observers of lions argue that the animal is particularly aggressive and dangerous to humans when protecting its carcasses.

To be sure, man-eating lions are still around in contemporary Africa, especially in Tanzania, home to the highest population of lions on the continent, and in Zambia. These lions have been deprived of their natural prey sources, so they have resorted to going after human prey. In April 2025, a lioness mauled to death Peace Mwendwa, a fourteen-year-old girl, after snatching her from her home on a ranch in the village of Emakoko near the Nairobi National Park in Kenya; when her body was discovered, 80 percent of it was already consumed. A spokesperson for the local wildlife services pointed a finger at "human encroachment on wildlife habitats" as a likely

8. Schaller, *Serengeti Lion*, 260–70.

9. Zielinski, "Humans Steal Food."

10. Bond, "How to Steal."

explanation for the lion's attack. He maintained that "deadly lion attacks are relatively a rare occurrence that account for less than 2 percent of all reported incidents involving humans and wildlife."[11]

In 1898, a pair of male lions was responsible for the slaughter of 134 construction workers on a bridge in Tsavo, Kenya. These lions dragged many of them from their tents at night or picked some off in daylight if they wandered too far from their group. Between 1990 and 2004, Tanzania alone saw 593 deaths from African lion attacks; many of the victims, however, were poachers.[12]

Although the Bible also cites examples where lions kill humans, they do so only as God's envoys. These cases, alongside other animals who God recruited to do his bidding, are narrated in chapter 30 because their behavior was uncharacteristic and extraordinary due to the divine mission they were fulfilling. Nonetheless, the biblical reality is that a normative lion did not pursue human beings to attack them, and as it naturally feared them, it did not endanger them.

11. Nied, "Girl, 14, Dies."

12. Tsavo National Park, "Man-Eating Lions"; Thompson, "Yes, Lions Will Hunt."

CHAPTER 22

Whom Did You Call "an Ass"?

Concerning the difference between man and the jackass: some observers hold that there isn't any. But this wrongs the jackass.—Mark Twain

Disparaging the Lowly Donkey

Sobering up from an unwarranted sweeping adulation of its generals in the Great War (1914–1918), public opinion in Great Britain reversed course in the late 1930s, adopting the stereotype of "lions led by donkeys"; the donkeys being the uncaring, incompetent generals, responsible for thousands of their men's deaths through sheer callousness, and the lower-ranked men being the "lions."

Such low esteem for the donkey in contemporary times is evidenced in the common derisive word in modern times like "jackass," which stands for a stupid, annoying, or detestable person. Monikers like "dumbass," "badass," or "asinine" join other derisive idioms like "a donkey remains a donkey" or "a donkey jumps first." Such derogatory aliases or diminutive references to the donkey are hardly found in the Bible, an animal mentioned (with various derivatives, e.g., "jenny," "foal," "calf of she-donkeys,") 156 times, but none connotes negativity, just the opposite.

Ezekiel's griping against the sinners in the land of Israel "whose flesh is like the flesh of asses" (23:20 JPS) is a comparison of the sinners' whoredoms to the donkeys' lewdness; despite the negative context, the fact remains that the prophet puts donkeys and certain humans, albeit such with defective morality, on a par. He thus personifies the donkey even when the prophet focuses on the similar lasciviousness of humans and animals. Jeremiah, who refers to "the burial of an ass" (22:19 JPS)—a dishonorable burial—anticipates that the deposed-by-the-Babylonians Judean monarch, Jehoiakim, would receive such a "burial," namely, no burial at all, like an ass' carcass that is taken out of town and is then left abandoned and exposed to the elements and scavengers, with none attending to its grave, nor moaning or mourning for it.

The rebellious Judean vassal king was dragged in chains with other captives, who were being carried off to Babylon (2 Chr 36:6) and probably died on the journey. His corpse was presumably left behind unburied as the Chaldean army marched home. Since the Torah mandates the burial by nightfall even of an executed felon, the fact of Jehoiakim's dismal fate cannot be anything but a lament against the Babylonians, who would disgrace and abuse a dead body by not burying it.

Yet, it was not only an ass's carcass that might not be interred—Samson found a fresh jawbone of an ass in a field (only to use it as an uber-lethal weapon against Philistines)—but humans too. The bodies of the slain-in-war King Saul and his three sons were also left unburied—King Saul's body was beheaded—exposed for all to see on the walls of the town of Bet Shan.

We similarly read in chapter 20 about the king's two sons and five grandsons, whose corpses were not buried for seven months. The bodies of the vanquished Judeans—"The young and the old are lying on the ground in the streets . . . fallen by the sword" (Lam 2:21 NOAB) and discarded by their heathen Babylonian conquerors in 586 BCE "to the birds of the air for food" and "to the wild animals of the earth" (Ps 79:1–2 NOAB). Alas, humans find it easier to relate to "the burial of an ass" than to the "burial" (or rather to the non-burial) of King Saul's sons and grandsons, or to the scattered bodies in devastated Judea.

Honoring the Worthy Donkey

Indeed, we can't glibly assume, based on this sole reference by Jeremiah, that carcasses of donkeys were haphazardly discarded at the nearest ravine. Rather, an archeological dig in an excavated Canaanite site in southern Israel, dated to the Middle Canaanite era (1550–1700 BCE), discovered donkeys' burial sites. One of those skeletons was identified as belonging to a donkey who had received a ceremonial internment. Notably, this was a familiar phenomenon in the east of the Nile Delta, where donkeys were found to have been buried next to dignitaries, so honoring the animal took a central place in Egypt's culture.[1]

The donkey species in the Bible is not only spared from any pejoratives; on the contrary, it was a favorite and highly esteemed animal. Thus, we find that the animal is mentioned in narratives where one might wonder why the biblical narrator spends precious ink and parchment, if not laborious stone carving, on such seemingly dispensable references to the animal.

When Joseph summons his brothers—who are clueless about his true identity—to his vizier's house in Egypt for a joint dinner, they dread being arrested and taken into slavery together with "our asses." With dawn, however, the brothers were "sent off, they and their donkeys" (Gen 44:3),[2] to return to their home in Canaan with a fresh supply of grains.

The brothers' recorded consternation over the would-be confiscation of their donkeys, while they might be taken into slavery, or their noted-down departure from Egypt with their donkeys—how else were they supposed to make their way to Canaan?—seems gratuitous, while adding nothing to the storytelling. These citations about the donkeys speak volumes of the deep attachment beyond the monetary value that the brothers felt for this animal—an animal that stood as a paragon for precious livestock—ergo, it entered the list of animals gracing Jacob's blessings to his children.

Two Sons and a Donkey

Our search for the true biblical image of the ass takes us first to the encounter in the desert between an angel of God and Hagar who ran off from her mistress Sarai while pregnant with Abram's son. The angel informs Hagar that she will bear a son, Ishmael, who will be "a wild-ass [an untamed, and powerful animal that no stranger would rule over him] of a man" (16:12).[3] Indeed, Ishmael is destined for future success. The angel's likening Ishmael to a wild ass says a lot about the animal, whose agility and love of freedom make it a fitting symbol for Abram's beloved firstborn son.

With such a divinely proffered precedent, it is not surprising that Jacob's deathbed messages to his sons mention the donkey even thrice. Thus, even as he concludes his blessing to Judah, whom he first likened to a lion, Jacob refers twice to donkeys in his foremost blessing to Judah, who "binds

1. Dohm, "Dressed-Up Donkey"; Way, "Assessing Sacred Asses."
2. Author's translation.
3. Author's translation.

his foal to the grapevine, his jenny's colt to the grape-bough" (49:11).[4] It was essentially the affluent and bigwigs who could pay for pricey wine that Judah's offspring would produce and transport with donkeys from the hilly Judean plain to a nearby seashore port (likely in Gaza or Ashkelon) to export overseas via Egypt.

The dual mentioning of a donkey, even as a pack animal, yet in the lucrative grapevine business, symbolizes the future wealth of the Judahites, which the donkey would facilitate on their behalf. The donkey's even gait and sure-footedness, so well-suited to hilly paths, made it the most popular of all the animals for riding in those rough regions, and for which it deserved a citation.

It is the same animal that Jacob reinvokes in his subsequent blessing to his other son Issachar whom he compares to a strong donkey "lying down between the saddlebags in a goodly homestead" (49:14).[5] Further, rabbinic tradition views this blessing as more than symbolizing thriving agriculture, but rather a spiritual flourishing in Torah learning. Thus, the donkey becomes a paragon for true learners of the Torah by carrying considerable weight at a consistently slow pace, as it does not run.

For the rabbis, Jacob meant to describe Issachar as a wise student who carries on his back the heavy weight of Torah learning; such a wise scholar was not judged by fast and original brilliancy but by faithful daily learning, line by line, and page by page, after the pattern of a donkey's gait. Rashi, on his part, compares an ox—the biblical "twin" of the donkey—to a wise Torah scholar, without whom there is no proper instruction (per Prov 14:4 that praises the ox for plowing and cultivating the land, thus enabling it to yield produce). In plowing the land, the ox is an example to the learners to plow in the field of wisdom and knowledge; in so doing, they also will generate a generous harvest. Thus, the donkey and the ox teach people how to labor for and cultivate the service of God through Torah scholarship.

"The Donkey" in the Binding of Isaac

Significantly, Abraham takes his donkey to Mt. Moriah for a rendezvous with God and destiny—to be known henceforth as the Binding of Isaac. As Rashi has it, besides Isaac, the sacrifice-designate, Abraham takes two more companions, his eldest son Ishmael and his closest servant Eliezer.

4. Author's translation.

5. Author's translation.

The narrator of this episode could have easily done away with any of the two allusions to Abraham's donkey in this unique drama without impacting the suspenseful flow of this succinctly narrated story. Yet, "the donkey" is a player here to be reckoned with taking on the role of carrying the firewood for Isaac's sacrifice. On the third day, when only Abraham and Isaac leave for the designated place of the altar, Isaac does what the donkey had done heretofore—hauling the wood. In so doing, Isaac elevates the status of the donkey in this mega event of the Bible.

Moses' Family and "the Donkey": En Route to Egypt

Similarly, when Moses returns to Egypt upon God's command to oversee the exodus of the Israelites from Egypt, he "took his wife and sons, put them on the donkey, and returned to the land of Egypt" (Exod 4:20).[6] Yet, at some point on that journey Moses sends them back to Midian. Just like Abraham's donkey journey to Mt. Moriah, Moses' repairing to Egypt with "the donkey" appears to be permeated with crucial importance, for the donkey is mentioned in the same breath with "God's staff" that Moses also took along. Again, the reference here to "the donkey" is not gratuitous, but is respectful of the animal's role in a historic event that should be acknowledged.

"The Jenny" Helps to Save a Life

We again encounter the same concept in the important story of the prophet Elisha—"a holy man of God," who was treated most generously by "a great woman" each time he visited her village, Shunem. When her only son passed out from sunstroke and was deemed dead, she was determined to bring him to Elisha to heal him at Mt. Carmel, a considerable distance from her village.

Though having men in her employ, it was she who saddled the jenny that she used to ride on the new moon and on the Sabbath to learn the word of God from Elisha; like a helping partner, the jenny enabled the woman to seek that knowledge. Presently, it was the dangerously sick son of "the great woman" riding the jenny—most likely in a two-man saddle—with her servant. However, she did not ride on another donkey; she walked simply

6. Author's translation.

behind them. The reference to the jenny is ostensibly gratuitous in this story. However, like in the other stories, it was again important for the Bible to share some of the credit for the miraculous revival of the child by the "man of God" with the animal that carried him there (2 Kgs 4:8–37 JPS).

The Donkey's Unique Status

The favorable image of the donkey received another booster when the Hebrews were instructed to dedicate to God the firstborn stock animals they possessed, besides their firstborn sons, at the same time of the exodus. Such dedication was meant to recall the tenth plague that slew all firstborn males in Egypt, human and animal alike, but passed over and skipped the Hebrews' households. The Torah singles out the firstborn donkey among all the firstborn farm animals by making it eligible—even effectively required—to be exempted from being slain (like all other farm animals) when its human owner offers a lamb or kid in its place. Robert Alter (quoting H. C. Propp) observes that "a donkey was worth several times the value of a sheep, so the sheep substitution would almost certainly be embraced rather than the alternative of destroying the donkey"[7] (by breaking its neck or decapitation).

This unique dispensation given to the donkey stems, as Rashi renders Exod 13:13, from the Bible's resemblance of the Egyptian firstborn to asses (per Ezek 23:20), and as an expression of gratitude to the many donkeys that the Israelites, hastily departing from Egypt, loaded their hefty and precious possessions on. Most significantly, the status of the ass is also comparable to the status of the firstborn sons in Israel who must also be "redeemed" by their father (for they were spared from the devastating tenth plague) when he presents a priest (from the tribe of Levi as God decreed) with five pieces of silver, an object of equal value, or nowadays an equivalent gift to charity. Lastly, the Torah addresses the need to consecrate both the donkey and the human unto God in one short breath and by this sequence (Exod 13:13; Num 18:15–16). Without a doubt, the donkey was highly respected in the life of the Israelites, in effect an inseparable part of the family, if not almost a "human" animal.

7. Alter, *Five Books of Moses*, 387.

The Ox and the Ass: The Only Two Animals of the Decalogue

The Ten Commandments—the Greek word "Decalogue" is more reflective of the Hebrew, meaning "words" or "utterings" rather than injunctions—as an iconic sacred writ was not only given for the sake of people but to benefit farm animals too; as such it is a harbinger of more biblical laws to come advocating for animal welfare. In the deuteronomic version of the Decalogue (5:14) that commands the cessation of all farm work on the Sabbath day, it is only the ox and the donkey that are individually singled out as distinct species side by side with the farmer's generic "livestock."

Indeed, in the one-heartbeat listing of the farmer, his children, and his slaves jointly with his farm animals, who together embody an integral unit that keeps the farm work going, both named animals precede even the alien hireling in the order of those who must be allowed to rest from work on the Sabbath. Also, when it comes to the prohibition against coveting (which concludes the Decalogue), it is a person's wife, bondman, handmaid, ox, and donkey who are cited again as similar entities—humans and animals alike—whom no one should obsessively desire, not even in one's mere fancies.

The Donkey Is Thieves' Favorite Stock

Alas, when Jacob's children raided Shechem following the massacre of its just-circumcised males by two of them, Shimon and Levi, "they looted the corpses and plundered the city." The Torah also spells out the livestock spoils—"their flocks and their herds, and their asses" (Gen 34:28);[8] the donkey, then, is the only farmstead animal that receives distinct attention as a species due to its import and, thus, being a favored animal for thieves.

When Moses defends his integrity before God in the wake of a serious rebellion by Dathan and Abiram against his purported overarching leadership, he says, "I have not taken one donkey from them, let alone harming any one of them" (Num 16:15 NOAB). Stealing a donkey would have been a serious embezzlement, with this animal being the sole example of farm animals "popular" with thieves. Similarly, to vouch for his incorruptibility when the Israelites clamored for a king to replace his prophetic leadership role, Samuel uses the same example (while adding the ox to the donkey) as an exceedingly desirable livestock that was likely to be targeted for being

8. Author's translation.

taken away from them by a despotic ruler: "Whose ox have I taken and whose donkey have I taken?" (1 Sam 12:3).[9] Indeed, Samuel warns the people that unlike him, a king would lay his eyes on and confiscate to himself their slaves "and the best of your young men, and your asses, and put them to his work" (8:16).[10] Evidently, the donkey was an esteemed animal meriting being mentioned by God's prophet without a pause with humans and their sons.

The Donkey in Other Torah Laws

Elsewhere, when the Torah discusses how to respond to a fellow whose finances go south, it urges an early supportive action to strengthen the struggling individual. Family and friends must intercede on his behalf as long as he is still on his feet, rather than procrastinate and see him collapse completely. The rabbis of yore resemble such a case with what should be done when too heavy a load was placed on a donkey threatening to crush it down; after all, helping the animal to its feet would be a much harder task than simply lightening its burden at the time of loading its back (or its harnessed cart). The obvious comparison of a human to a donkey as in this case attests to the similarities between both instances; thus, we may learn how to assist a needy person from the way we must help a distressed donkey.[11]

Yet, when such intervention did not happen and "you see the donkey of your nemesis sprawling helplessly under its burden, but you refrain from raising him, you must nevertheless help raise it" (Exod 23:5).[12] In other words, the suffering of the donkey is an essential concern that minimizes and overtakes a person's conflicting sentiments against the animal's owner. It is not about the estranged donkey's owner, but about the innocent animal that must be promptly helped, even if the owner is not present at the scene or is indifferent to his donkey's plight.

The entire biblical system of compassion toward domestic animals in similar adverse circumstances is predicated on this law. Inasmuch as the Torah prohibits punitive measures against a blameless child of a wrongdoing parent (or vice versa when the parent is innocent), so it does for the

9. Author's translation.

10. Author's translation.

11. "Sifra," Behar.

12. Author's translation.

animal; it should not suffer adverse consequences for its owner's sour relations with another man. Henceforth, the Torah, in a unique law throughout the ancient Near East, outlawed the yoking of any two animals (e.g., the ox and the donkey) of different sizes or weights to the same farming or agricultural tool; the smaller animal would be under stress and pain to keep pace with the bigger animal. Or, perhaps the bigger animal would have to work even harder due to the inability of the smaller animal to match the bigger one's output; either way, such a pairing is a verboten practice.

Other traditional commentators suggest that the ox's ability to chew on its cud would frustrate the non-regurgitating donkey upon seeing its fellow ostensibly nibbling, even as they pull together the plowshare. Additionally, animals like the ass and the ox must not be muzzled while laboring in a field lest they be prevented from snacking the agricultural produce while doing their work. According to the Talmud, thanks to the Torah's prohibition on muzzling these animals, human laborers at the same site were also entitled to eat whatever came to hand from the ripened and unharvested crop.[13]

Balaam's "Blindness" and His Clairvoyant Jenny

We have already seen how the biblical image of the donkey is generally a far cry from its contemporary stereotype that relegates foolhardiness and imprudent obstinacy to the animal. That the Bible rejects such a bias is evidenced, for instance, in the story of Balaam and his jenny (further discussed in chapter 29), for God "opened the jenny's mouth" (Num 22:28).[14] The only other mouth that the Bible informs us of being opened by God was the prophet Ezekiel's (3:27). God also assures Moses that he will be with his mouth and teach him what to say (Exod 3:12), which is close enough to what God did to the jenny. Thus, even as a she-donkey finds herself in the same company with two great prophets, the core lesson of that story might be then extracted to its essence with the insight of not calling an asinine person "an ass"; he should be called instead "Balaam."

Truly, it is Balaam's very life that his eagle-eyed jenny saved thrice by dodging three ramming collisions with "the angel of the Lord" (Num 22:27),[15] while Balaam, clueless about his jenny's conduct, wished to kill

13. M. B. Met. 7:2–3 and b. B. Met. 91b.

14. Author's translation.

15. Author's translation.

her with a sword as payback for her strange terrain maneuvers. In striking the jenny each time for her triple veering off, it was evident that it was the jenny, not the man who rode on her back, who proved herself to be a true clairvoyant, if not prophetic; Balaam's self-lauding as "the man of the open eye" (24:3 SB) only accentuated the chasm between him and his jenny.

In any event, God's angel sides with the jenny's when she complains to Balaam through the gift of speech that God gave her, as though she spoke for God, asking her master why he struck her (twice by his hand and then with "the stick"). In speaking truth to power, Balaam's jenny teaches us that it is necessary to protest a personal insult, not to mention a violent one, if you stand any chance of ending the abuse. The angel of God in his turn echoes the jenny's protestation, reprimanding Balaam's misconduct with the animal: "Why have you struck your jenny these three times. . . . Your way is contrary unto me" (22:32 NOAB); this divine voice made clear that in contrast to Balaam, God cares for animals; even when humans "hold sway over" animals, it is not a carte blanche to act cruelly to them. It is also this episode from which the Torah further derives its prohibition against hurting and distressing an animal.

Saul: From Losing Jennies to Finding a Kingship

Though Saul's family had a high socioeconomic status, his father Kish wanted to find his two valuable lost jennies. Significantly, Saul's prompt searching after them, accompanied by one of the servant lads, segues into his coronation as the first king of Israel on the third day of his quest for them. When his bread runs out, rather than return home empty-handed, Saul sets out to consult "the man of God" (the seer Samuel—1 Sam 9:6 JPS) concerning the animals' whereabouts, and gives him his last coin as a token gesture of gratitude for his help.

And before he anoints Saul as a royal ruler, Samuel brings up the matter of the jennies, informing Saul that they were already found, so Saul could dedicate his full attention now to his imminent regal status and the tasks ahead. Traditional commentaries point out God's role in the jennies' going astray—a common and pervasive occurrence—devised as a subterfuge to bring Saul to Samuel, so the seer would coronate the one who set out to search for his lost donkeys, even as the first king of Israel.

The Messiah Arrives on a Donkey

The top-ranking praise, however, that the Bible accords to the donkey is found in the book of Zechariah, the prophet who describes the messianic king who will enter Jerusalem "riding on an ass, even on a colt the foal of an ass" (Zech 9:9 JPS). Notably, both the first king (Saul) and the very last king of Israel, the messianic redeemer—"a shoot out of the stock of Jesse" (Isa 11:1 JPS), a Davidic bloodline scion—have a donkey that plays a significant role in their respective coronation narrative.

The simplicity of the donkey who will ride as one with the ultimate Davidic king, a donkey of an unimpressive size or strength but a mere colt born to one of the jennies, i.e., not a full-sized donkey, dovetails with Saul's humility at his coronation. It is at this peak moment that Saul exhibits his humbleness by seeing himself as a misfit for kingship being of "the least of all the families of the tribe of Benjamin" (1 Sam 9:21 JPS). He even "hid himself among the baggage" (10:22 JPS), being overwhelmed and unaffected by his divine election and anointment to be Israel's first king.

In this spirit, the Israelite army excluded the donkey from warfare tasks, unlike the Persian and Syrian armies' cavalry forces, which did assign a combat role to donkeys.[16] Thus, when it comes to the donkey-mounted messianic redeemer, whose foremost achievement would be revealed in universal harmony and well-being, the donkey, like the dove in the post-flood Noah narratives, is essentially a symbol of peace. No wonder, then, Jacob blessed his two sons, Judah (the leader among his brethren) and Issachar (the Torah scholar as the rabbis posited), by associating them with the donkey.

16. Got Questions, "Why Would a King"; Metcalfe, "1st Bioengineered Hybrid Animals."

CHAPTER 23

A Snake for a Blessing!

Contrary to common opinion, snakes are rarely aggressive. They're cowards. Humans are giant adversaries to snakes, so they do their best to avoid us.
—P. B. Whitaker and R. Shine

Joseph Encounters Snakes and Scorpions

The first biblical reference to snakes, other than the metaphoric serpent in the garden of Eden (discussed earlier in chapter 5), is found in effect in a commentary by Rashi about "the pit" that Joseph's brothers, out of spite and envy, heaved him into. Accordingly, though the pit was empty of water, it had snakes and scorpions; Joseph, however, never alluded to any such encounter.

According to the Talmud, one who fell into such a place is considered dead (unlike the case with one who fell into a lion's den as in chapter 20). The presumption is that pits and ditches that attract snakes to assemble therein are narrow; the person who fell in must have landed on snakes and been bitten instantly and fatally. In such a circumstance, the snakes bite, not because they are hungry—a human being is not their dinner anyway—but because of the immediate threat they sense to their safety. If the pit, the Talmud says, was somewhat spacious, allowing the snakes to spread about, or if they were burrowed safely without feeling alarmed by the person's seemingly hostile "landing" into their space, they might leave him alone. A person who fell into such a pit is not to be presumed dead.[1]

1. b. Ber. 33a; Yebam. 121a

By applying this talmudic logic, we may infer that Joseph's pit must have been broad enough to have allowed him to be dropped down without provoking any snake to bite him. Be that as it may, he was brought up alive from the pit, whether by his brothers or by Midianite merchants who passed by and snatched him from the pit without the brothers noticing them doing so.

Jacob Wishes for Dan to Be Like a Snake

The Bible refers next to snakes when Jacob on his deathbed blesses another son, Dan, wishing him to "be a snake on the road, as asp on the path, that bites the horse's heels and its rider topples backward" (Gen 49:17 ALT). Namely, Dan will form a good defensive line against an assaulting enemy. Although snakes can be icky and frightening, most snakes are non-offensive. This blessing presents the snake, not as an aggressor but as a defender. Indeed, though the snake is a quiet animal that does not intend to bite humans, it would only do so defensively when perceiving a serious threat to its safety.

Furthermore, the snake is also an emblem of healing and renewal; due to its periodic molting, which facilitates further growth of its scales, it removes parasites from some areas of the body. Native species can especially benefit the ecosystem in human habitations, where rattlesnakes play a crucial role in controlling rodent populations, thus helping to prevent crop damage and maintain a balanced ecosystem.

Is Humans' Innate Fear of Snakes Justified?

A 1999 major study that tracked encounters between humans and brown snakes (*Pseudonaja textilis*)—one of the most venomous snakes in Australia—revealed that "contrary to public opinion, the snakes were rarely aggressive," with less than 1 percent of such brushes proving to be offensive when the snake advanced toward a rapidly approaching human. "About half of the encounters resulted in the snake retreating, and on most occasions, they relied on crypsis," (i.e., environmental camouflage).

Initially "reluctant to bite," even when cornered and harassed, most brown snakes would give a warning before a strike, and even then "most strikes missed the target" with some "25% of strikes" being a bluff with the snake "closing its mouth and aborting the strike before reaching the antagonist." It is "estimated that only 15% of the strikes recorded had the potential to cause significant envenomation."[2]

Similarly, Neelim Kumar Khaire, India's foremost snake expert, while acknowledging people's extreme reaction when seeing snakes, says that 85 percent of snakes in India are non-venomous; being docile, snakes "will only attack when seriously provoked."[3] Globally, among the approximately 3,900 known species of snakes, only about 15 percent can kill or significantly wound a human. In the land of the Bible, out of 42 snake species, only 4 are life-endangering, which means that the vast majority of them are non-lethal to humans.[4]

That human primal fright of snakes—so overwhelming as to overpower the reality about them—is evidenced when Moses is seized by a great trepidation right after requesting magical signs from God on Mt. Sinai (before he left for Egypt to lead the Israelites out of Egyptian slavery). Seeing his staff transformed into a snake once he flung it to the ground, Moses instinctively "drew back from it" (Exod 4:3 NOAB), though the snake did not show any aggressive mien, let alone lunge at him. Had Moses not grasped it, even by its tail at God's command, the snake would have likely slithered away, as snakes are generally not combative.

The second-century CE talmudic Rabbi Shimon Bar Yochai taught, "The best of the snakes—crush its head!"[5] Rabbi Shimon sounds like he is second-guessing God's idea to create snakes and even his instruction to Noah to save all their species on the ark. Yet, Rabbi Shimon did not call upon his numerous students to go on a rampage and kill serpents, let alone their best species. The sage meant it allegorically about the pharaoh's servants who feared God's word about the imminent plague of hail and sheltered their horses in their houses (Exod 9:20).

Yet, that fear that led to the saving of the pharaoh's "best" horses was the very reason why he was able to pursue the Hebrew slaves at the Red Sea. As far as Rabbi Shimon was concerned, these horses should have been hit and perished by the heavy hail. Although Rabbi Shimon recognizes that some snakes can be good, he concurrently betrays his stereotype with his fear of them, not unlike Moses' when his staff turned into a serpent.

2. Whitaker et al., "Defensive Strike."

3. Maya, "Trapped with Deadly Snakes."

4. Wikipedia, "List of Dangerous Snakes"; Nitai; "Baaley khaim."

5. Midr. Tanḥ Beshalach 8; and Yal. 186:9.

The Israelites' Sole Encounter with Snakes

The massive plague of desert snakes that bit and killed numerous Israelites on their journey en route to their promised land, when they circumvented the land of Edom, was the comeuppance of the Israelites' griping about the quality of their foul bread and lack of water. This theological episode, rather than a natural phenomenon, will be discussed in chapter 30, as the snakes "acted" on God's behalf.

In contrast to this single episode when the Israelites had fatal encounters with biting snakes, Moses in his farewell address to his people reminds them of the gratitude they owed God for having led them safely "through the great and awesome wilderness of snake, fiery serpent, and scorpion" (Deut 8:15 STONE) without an adverse incident. For indeed, we hear of no further (or prior) lethal encounters involving snakes, other than those that God had unleashed and overwhelmed the Israelites with that one time.

Metaphorizing the Snake

The prophets Amos and Jeremiah prophesy of God assailing their people with biting snakes for their wrongdoing; yet, these two brief warnings were mere metaphors for a mighty nation, and in Jeremiah's case, he likely meant the Babylonians. Throughout the Bible, only these two prophets resorted to using the snake as a punitive symbol, and even then, they did so only once, which did not alter the fact of the human inherent dread of snakes.

David the psalmist, too, while mirroring the ubiquitous fright of snakes, compares "the wicked" who "speaks lies" to venomous serpents (Ps 58:3 NOAB) and "those who are violent, who plan evil things in their minds and stir up wars continually" to "vipers" for under their lips "is the venom of vipers" (Ps 140:1–3 NOAB). Still, the psalmist trusts that God would allow him to "tread upon the lion and asp," even to "trample under feet" on both of them triumphantly (91:13 JPS)—allusions to a deadly disease or attack by wicked forces.

And What About Scorpions?

In mid-November 2021, some 450 people were injured by scorpion stings in the wake of heavy thunder and hail storms in Aswan, Egypt, forcing swarms of scorpions into the streets and homes. Of the nearly two thousand different scorpion species worldwide, only around twenty-five species are considered seriously dangerous or potentially fatal to the very young, infirm, or elderly; it is estimated that scorpion stings account for approximately three thousand deaths a year worldwide.[6] One can, then, understand why Rehoboam, King Solomon's successor son, invoked the widespread fear of scorpions among his subjects. He did so when he callously (and foolishly) informed the protesting indignant Israelites that his taxation would increase exponentially in comparison to his father's, King Solomon: "I will add to your yoke; my father chastised you with whips but I will chastise you with scorpions" (1 Kgs 12:11),[7] a reference to an infamous instrument of scourging.

Upon Ezekiel's initiation as a prophet, God sought to reassure him ahead of his facing a hostile and rebellious constituency that was standing ready to sting the prophet from any possible corner; a serious and painful challenge, but not deadly. Hence, God's emboldening assurance: "Do not be afraid of them . . . though you live among scorpions" (2:6 NOAB)

6. Reptile Knowledge, "How Many People."

7. Author's translation.

CHAPTER 24

Who Is Afraid of a Bull?

The ox suffers, the cart complains.—VICTOR HUGO

Contemporary Fear of the Bull

The modern-day stereotype of an ox is that it is dangerous, dim-witted, and loutish; it could be reflected in a couple of incidents in recent decades that took place in the Queens borough of New York City. In June 1999, a terrified-to-its-wits bovine, or what the media called "a raging bull" escaped, if only temporarily, from its predicament into the streets.

The police thought little of the bull, named Roughrider, that absconded from a rodeo site, seeing the animal as an immediate threat to the lives of others. Roughrider, however, hurt no one while briefly roaming among a crowd of churchgoers, shoppers, and others watching it. Still, police officers shot it more than twenty times and killed it, as though it were the most wicked terrorist on earth. The police said that the shooting officers felt that they could not wait for the arrival of the emergency services unit with its shotguns and tranquilizer darts.[1]

In 2017, another bull (described by the media as "rogue" simply for wanting to live and giving it everything it had) ran off from a Queens slaughterhouse while being unloaded from a truck. This time, however, NYPD officers added insult to injury and sedated the bovine gratuitously before capturing it, so it soon died from an overdose of the tranquilizer.[2]

1. Kuntzman, "Cops Who Shot Bull."

2. Sandoval and Tracy, "Bull That Escaped Slaughterhouse."

In 2021, another bizarre scene took place in Nova Granada, Brazil, when a seven-hundred-pound bovine that broke free from its abattoir managed to escape to a nearby water park; after wandering around for a while, it found itself in a nearby, open-air swimming pool. Once there, the bovine climbed some stairs and reached the top of a water slide. It then slowly came down the winding path to a pool below. The bovine ended up as a family pet of the swimming pool's owner, who named it "Tobogã" ("sled").[3]

In 2024, a fourteen-hundred-pound debuting bucking bull named "Party Bus" escaped the arena at an Oregon rodeo event by leaping out of the ring over a six-foot-tall fence and into the sold-out fifty-five-hundred-seat arena, where two spectators sustained minor injuries from direct contact with it. Party Bus quickly made it to the rodeo grounds from where it careened through the concessions and then on to a parking lot where it charged a woman wearing a red shirt, flipping her high with its horns into the air before it trampled her, yet scarcely wounding her leg.

The bull then slammed into a table before running out back to the livestock holding pens, where the arena's pickup professionals quickly retained it, with the whole unruly behavior lasting thirty seconds. Rodeo organizers said it was the first time anyone could recall such a breach happening since their first event in 1940.[4] It seems that running loops around the arena trying to avoid a cowboy's lasso, while the crowd is waving their flashlights and singing along with the booming voice of Lee Greenwood's "God Bless the USA" was too much for Party Bus to take in stride before it snapped, as it had never been around many people.

While the bull's owner conceded that Party Bus made a mistake and did not intend to hurt anyone during its impromptu public "protestation" against being forced to perform as a startled entertainment bull, its station in life was incomparably better than those bulls transported to Pamplona, Spain, to take part in the annual Running of the Bulls during the eight-day-long San Fermín festival. At only five years old, bulls face a terrifying mob of people who chase them through the city's narrow streets. They often lose their footing around corners and crash into walls, sometimes breaking bones or injuring themselves in other ways. Repeatedly taunted in the subsequent "bullfights" in the bullring, where they are forced to run to

3. Fraga, "This Brazilian Cow."

4. Alund, "Rodeo Bull."

the point of exhaustion, the bulls are then stabbed with multiple weapons, enduring a slow and painful death.

The Biblical Man Has No Fear of the Bull

In contrast to modern times, the biblical man or woman did not fear an ox; the Torah's noting that an ox might strike out and gore humans to death notwithstanding. The Torah even commands a person in the position to do so to bring an ox (or an ass) that went astray back to the owner, even if the animal habitually ran off to other pastures, and yes, even if the owner happens to be the finder's antagonist. Furthermore, the Torah expects a person to return an ox to its owner, even if retrieving it would require considerable effort, as goading would be the only way to comply with this commandment governing the return of a lost item to its owner (Exod 23:4; Deut 22:1–3).

That there was no peril in handling an ox may be deduced from the basic idea that fulfilling a mitzvah (or a religious requirement) was not supposed to put its performer in harm's way (Lev 18:5). This reality may be further deduced from the prophet Samuel's farewell speech. As the "seer" Samuel prepared himself to retire as his people's religious leader, he worried lest his good name be forgotten by a new generation. Hence, he posed a rhetorical question to them: "Whose oxen have I taken?" (1 Sam 12:3 NOAB). In other words, stealing an ox would have been a cinch; it was not an animal that was difficult to handle, let alone fear.

Similarly, Job makes that case in his lamentation on the ubiquitous crime that goes unpunished; a cruel act that is seen in the possessing of a "widow's ox for a pledge" (Job 24:3 NOAB), namely, taken for a pawn to ensure that the poor woman would pay back her loan, even though without her ox she would be unable to plow her field to scratch her meager living. Such a widow, then, handled her ox single-handedly until her creditor came and led it away.

The Ox Symbolizes God's Might

Although the biblical ox was heavily used for farming (while being muzzle-free as the Torah requires), for hauling loads (yet, giving it full and refreshing rest on the Sabbath was compulsory), or for sacrifice and meat, it was held in high esteem, even admirably. Ezekiel includes the face of an ox (side by side with the face of a lion, an eagle, and a human) in his complex and detailed depiction of a mysterious chariot, functioning as God's throne, from which he beheld "the appearance of the likeness of the Presence of the Eternal" (1:28 PLAUT). Jacob, Isaiah, and the psalmist dub the ox poetically as "the Mighty One (or 'Champion') of Jacob" (Gen 49:24; Isa 49:26; 60:16; Ps 132:2, 5 JPS) or "of Israel" (Isa 1:24 JPS), thus comparing God's might to the prowess displayed by the bull.

The first Hebrew letter that starts the poetical word 'Abir (a bull) displays a resemblance of two horns; both in the archaic letter chart (where it looks somewhat like the letter K), and in its subsequent (third century BCE) overhauled (Aramaic-influenced Hebrew) format, א. With such images in mind, one could infer why the Israelites (per Exod 32:4, 8) chose an idolatrous golden horned bovine to worship during Moses' forty-day-long absence from the camp. David the psalmist suggests that the golden calf was shaped "in the likeness of an ox" (Ps 106:20 JPS) to represent God, or at the least Moses, who linked his people to God.

Why Did Jacob Refer to a Gelded Ox?

From his deathbed in Egypt at 147 years of age, Jacob denounces his two sons Shimon and Levi for "hamstringing an ox" (Gen 49:6 STONE) in the aftermath of their heinous massacre of all males in Shechem following the rape there of their sister Dina. But the Torah says nothing about Shimon and Levi gelding the bulls of the doomed town that they sacked. So, what could Jacob possibly mean?

The Rabbis interpret "they hamstrung an ox" to mean that Shimon and Levi uprooted "a line of converts,"[5] even as the male populace of Shechem willingly accepted and performed circumcision to be eligible for intermarrying with Jacob's clan. Thus, the Midrash has Jacob chastise his two blood-shedding sons for destroying a whole potential population of newcomers to his monotheistic faith. They are the hamstrung or gelded ox that Jacob refers to, who were massacred in perfidy because Shimon and Levi would not accept conversion to the religion of Israel, their father, for marriage; thus, they betrayed a disposition of ethnic purity.

For this atrocious crime, Jacob decrees for his two rogue sons that their future tribes will be dispersed with no independent existence among the eventual tribes that his other sons would evolve into. All in all, the

5. Midr. Ber. Rab. 98:5.

bull's image, even in this dismal episode, is positive if not honorific, as it metaphorically represents a whole line of would-be Israelites. Or, as C. M. Carmichael posits, the hamstrung ox is Jacob himself, who, in the wake of the wholesale massacre of Shechem's men that his two sons carried out, was exposed in his weakness, i.e., "hamstrung before his enemies" among the land's inhabitants.[6] Had his Canaanite neighbors retaliated and assaulted the heavily outnumbered clan of Jacob, it would have dealt disastrous consequences. Ergo, Jacob compared himself to an ox gelded by his two murderous sons.

Other Poetical Comparisons to the Ox

Balak, king of Moab, who feared that the mighty children of Israel would be encroaching on his land, compared them likewise to "the ox [who] nibbles the grass of the field" (Num 22:4 ALT). Hence, he desired to hire the non-Hebrew prophet Balaam to curse them. Though Balaam was compelled (albeit reluctantly) to heed the word of God, he, too, compared God to "the wild ox's [adorned by its lofty] antlers" (Num 23:22; 24:8 ALT).

It is highly likely that in his farewell address Moses compared Joshua upon ordaining him as his successor to a bull, even as he imparted to him from his own "majesty." Moses envisions here the great prowess that Joshua would display on the battlefield as befitting a powerful ox who gores with "the horns of a wild ox" (Deut 33:17).[7] Again, the bull or the ox—two words that the Bible uses alternatingly—has outstanding complimentary images ranging from God to the nation of Israel, or Jacob, if not a whole cohort of men seeking to embed themselves within his clan.

The Ox as a Legal Entity

While the Torah requires the execution by stoning of an ox that killed a human, it similarly metes out the same verdict to a human who murdered his fellow man (Exod 21:28–29; Gen 9:5–6). In both instances of the death penalty as rabbinic law has it—invoked against an ox or a human—it must be reached by a majority of twenty-three court judges who have heard two competent witnesses, even as the defendant, either the human or the

6. Carmichael, "Some Sayings," 435.

7. Author's translation.

animal, must be present for the pronouncement of the verdict.[8] Though not even a single case is cited in the Bible for such an action against an ox, the principle established here is that the ox was recognized as an individual, just like a human, fit to be adjudicated in a civil court.

The fact that the Bible does not require the death penalty for killing an ox does not stand at variance with the biblical definition of slaughtering one "as bloodshed" (or for that matter, of a sheep or a goat unless offered as a sacrifice to God on the altar). A violator of this protocol, like the prohibition against blood consumption, would be "cut off from the midst of his people"—perhaps by dying at a young age leaving no heirs (Lev 17:4 STONE). The prophet Isaiah doubles down on the severity in slaying an ox (for profane reasons) by saying, "He that butchered an ox" is as if "he slew a man" (66:3).[9]

Namely, Isaiah sounds a warning that the slaughtering of an ox, even as a mere *pro forma* sacrificial offering (with no personal contrition of guilt for wrongdoing, as Malbim comments), is tantamount to or would lead to the murder of a human being. The mere references to the slaughtering of an ox, like in the following instances, may likely attest to such killings, not as a casual matter or an afterthought but because they were noteworthy.

When an Ox Is Killed, Humans Are Next

When the Israelites "exchanged [God who was] their glory for the [gold] image of an ox" (Ps 106:20)[10]—as the psalmist calls the golden calf—and worshiped it with much hilarity, Moses first wrecked and burned the idolatrous image, thus he symbolically "butchered an ox." He shortly "gathered to him all the Sons of Levi"; following his order, they felled by the sword "some three thousand men" (Exod 32:28),[11] likely the ringleaders and the foremost frenzied homage-paying worshipers of that "ox" (or the golden calf).

This pattern of dispatching an ox that leads in short order to the slaying of people is evidenced again in the gory saga that takes place on Mt. Carmel, where Elijah the prophet faces off hundreds of his fellow Israelite pagan priests who served in the cult of the Canaanite idols Baal and

8. b. Sanh. 2a; 15b; 78a.

9. Author's translation.

10. Author's translation.

11. Author's translation.

Asherah. To make the theological statement that only God was the real deity, Elijah, with his militant followers, went on from sacrificing a bullock to slaying multitudes of people by the sword at the Kishon River (1 Kgs 18:33, 40).

Although Elijah ignored the commandment that restricted all types of offerings to "the place" that God designated "to cause His name to dwell there" (Deut 12:11),[12] which in Elijah's time was the Jerusalem Temple, God accepted that burnt offering of the bullock when a heavenly flame consumed it.

To be sure, God never instructs Elijah to commit this bloodbath, nor does God express approval, let alone contentment, at this mass slaughter. On the contrary, God decides in the aftermath of this atrocity that began with the slaughtering of an ox, and then led to the dispatch of numerous humans, to retire Elijah from his prophetic service and have him succeeded by Elisha ben Shafat.

Elisha, Elijah's successor in prophecy, opts to begin his new career by slaying his two oxen and boiling their flesh for a festive meal. Not long after taking over Elijah's prophetic tasks, he set two she-bears at a group of resentful children by invoking God's ineffable name, upon which the two animals dispatched the boys. (Since the bears acted in a non-normative pattern, this episode is covered in more detail in chapter 30.)

All in all, these three ostensibly unrelated incidents that lead from the slaughtering of bulls to the gratuitous slaying of many human lives make us wonder if that is what Isaiah meant when saying, "He that kills an ox is as if he slew a man."

12. Author's translation.

CHAPTER 25

The Big Bad Wolf: True or False?

For the strength of the Pack is the Wolf, and the strength of the Wolf is the Pack.—Rudyard Kipling

Jacob Likens Benjamin to a Wolf

The last of Jacob's sons to receive his blessing at his deathbed is his youngest, Benjamin, whom he wishes to be a "predatory wolf"; he surely meant it as a compliment—I, too, named my eldest son by this name (after my father). Indeed, the wolf is noted for its intelligence, thirst for freedom, and independence. At the same time, the wolf is a family-oriented animal and can associate easily, being loyal to its pack. Like many of us, wolves form friendships and maintain lifelong bonds; all examples for Benjamin to emulate.

No Danger to Humans

In September 2017, a female hiker was tragically torn apart and devoured in northern Greece; she was probably attacked by wolves while walking alone on a remote path. Still, this was an exceptional case in the country for lethal wolf attacks on humans. Rather, generally speaking, the wolf is fearful by nature of the unfamiliar and would hide away from humans.[1]

1. Kokkinidis, "Horrific Details Emerge."

Marcos Rodríguez Pantoja, in his true-life story of living with wolves, laments his inability to return to his adoptive wolf pack in Andalusia, among whom he spent twelve years (1954–1966) since he was eight years old. Pantoja, who had lost faith and trust in the humans he encountered in civilization, grieved the wolves' rejection of his efforts to rejoin them because he "smell[ed] like people."[2]

To be sure, the Bible does not allude even to a single case of a wolf attacking people. The Talmud cautions shepherds, however, that while a single person would find it rather easy to cope with a lone wolf that seeks to prey on his flock, he would not be able to deter a pack;[3] the wolf's preferred way to hunt is a masterfully coordinated group effort.

The Wolf as a Metaphor

Several biblical prophets chose to compare the "reckless," "unfaithful," and "transgressor" officials, judges, (false) prophets, and priests in Jerusalem to "roaring lions" and ravenous "wolves of the evening" who "do not leave a bone for the morning" (Zeph 3:3 DAV), or to "wolves tearing the prey" even as the city's princes destroy "lives to get dishonest gain" (Ezek 22:27 NOAB). To be sure, while Jerusalem's ruling class maliciously and systematically preyed by choice on their victimized subjects, they did so in contrast to the wolf, which does not kill its prey en masse, capriciously or maliciously, but for mere survival.

Nonetheless, by allegorically attributing to predatory animals the ills of Jerusalem's chiefs, these prophets continued to lay on animals the normative human evil and decadence, as though the honchos of Jerusalem accidentally or by sheer necessity slipped off and behaved meanly to emulate the emblematic vicious predator. Habakkuk describes the Chaldean cavalry approaching Jerusalem for conquest as "fiercer than the evening wolves" (1:8).[4] While the genuine predator must be so to break its day-long hunger, Chaldean riders outdid such hungry wolves in speed and ferocity.

2. Fahey, "Man Raised by Wolves."

3. M. B. Met. 7:9.

4. Author's translation.

Postscript

A myth of the Iroquois, some of whom had lived on the same lands where massive killing of wolves was taking place, presents a different approach to the problem of man and wolf that is foreign to today's realities. Accordingly, a council of the tribes was called to decide where to move on for the next hunting season. Unbeknownst to the council, wolves inhabited the place they chose to move to, thus generating a conflict of interest about hunting game. Indeed, repeated wolf attacks on their mutual prey whittled down considerably the Iroquois' share of that harvest.

A decision had to be made on whether to kill wolves or move away from these grounds. Killing the majestic wolf would diminish them as Iroquois: "It would make them the sort of people they did not want to be." And so, they moved on to avoid repeating their earlier mistake and decided that "in all future council meetings someone should be appointed to represent the wolf."[5]

5. Rowland, *Philosopher and the Wolf*, 4–5.

CHAPTER 26

Up, Down, Up: The Vicissitudes of the Dog's Image

Regarding hatred and persecution, men and dogs are alike.—S. Y. AGNON

Prologue

A young physician wrote to her rabbi requesting to hold a bat mitzvah (the iconic Jewish ceremony for youth upon becoming young adults) for her she-dog upon its turning twelve years old; (that request should have been made when the dog turned one year young to be compatible to age twelve in human years). There's a similar story about a person whose dog had just died who asked his rabbi to include the dog's name among the names of the community members who recently passed that are read out at the synagogue. Such requests speak volumes about the dog's status in our contemporary culture; surprisingly, even the Bible starts with a positive view of the dog before that image is marred, only to regain its positive image.

Genesis's Dogs in Rabbinic Teachings

We first meet the biblical dog in a rabbinic gloss informing us that the first shepherd in the Bible, Abel, had a dog that protected his flocks. After his brother Cain slew him, the dog faithfully protected the corpse from scavengers. According to the same midrash, God tasked the dog to henceforth accompany and shield Cain from anyone wishing to harm him for slaying

Abel. The dog, thus, became the very mark of protection that God gave Cain while showing him dedication and loyalty.[1]

In another midrash, the rabbis tell us further that when Jacob was shepherding Laban's flocks in Haran, he engaged dogs to guard them. Jacob's subsequent accumulation of wealth—for Laban and eventually for him too—the rabbis say is partially attributable to those dogs for they guarded the flocks from predators and minimized losses of livestock.[2] On his end, Job mentions his sheepdogs as being higher in status than those who mocked him in his ordeal; people unfit to be caretakers for his dogs. Why, engaging dogs in shepherding attested to their fairly high intelligence, while Job's scoffers could not even match it.

The Exodus Dogs: A Tribute and Reward

The dog makes its actual debut, however, on the stage of the Hebrew Bible—wherein it will henceforth be mentioned forty times—after Moses informs the pharaoh about the imminent tenth plague that would devastate all the land of Egypt and bring about a loud cry in every Egyptian household. That very night, as the Hebrew slaves began their exodus, not even one of Egypt's dogs, Moses communicated to the Pharaoh, would "snarl at any of the Israelites, at man or a livestock" (Exod 11:7 PLAUT), despite the dog's habitual pattern, as David the psalmist informs us, to howl at evening time (Ps 59:15), let alone in a tumultuous place.

In contrast, according to the midrash, when the tenth plague struck down Egypt's firstborn males, the resulting upheaval in Egyptian households triggered the dogs to bark, yet only on the Egyptian side.[3] All of that might tell us that even as the dog in Egypt enjoyed an unmistakably great status as a human's companion or pet in the royal palace and among the wealthy, many Egyptian commoners kept dogs in their yards for guarding, or at the least that dogs were permitted to roam at will close to the people's homes.

By not barking at the departing Israelites, Egypt's dogs enabled them to exit smoothly and, most importantly, honorably. Although the Israelites left "in haste" (Deut 16:3), the Egyptians were those rushing the Israelites to leave. Hence, due to the dogs' uncharacteristic reticence vis-à-vis the

1. Midr. Yal. Gen 4:38.

2. Midr. Ber. Rab. 73:11.

3. Midr. Shem. Rab. 31:9.

Israelites, they were able to be gone "with an upraised arm" (Exod 14:8 STONE). Hence, not long after the exodus the Israelites—who had taken with them "very much livestock" (12:38)[4]—were commanded how to dispose of the "flesh that is torn to pieces in the field—[that] you are not to eat; to the dogs, you are to throw it" (Exod 22:30 SB).

The rabbis say that it was God's will to symbolically recompense the dogs in Egypt for holding their tongues from barking despite the commotion about them (Exod 12:30), thus enabling a timely departure for the Israelites. Such flesh of ravened livestock would be a "payback" for shepherds' dogs, as "God does not deprive any deserving creature of its due reward."[5]

Naming Caleb for a Dog

Robert Alter sees the rewarding of sheepdogs with flesh torn by predators as "biblical contempt for canines," making them a "base receptacle for carrion."[6] However, such a low disposition to the dog would be incompatible with the fact that dogs are natural scavengers. And it would also be at variance with the name of one of the two highly praised Hebrew spies, Calev ("dog"), a name that might be a shortened form of *klb-el*, meaning "Dog of God,"[7] i.e., a foremost faithful and obedient servant; or as the Torah tells us, he "followed the Eternal fully."

Caleb, a man of an upstanding stature—indeed, the head of the tribe of Judah—was rewarded for his faith in God, a dog-like devotion to his master; it was featured in his bold public assertion of his full confidence in the Israelites' ability to capture the land of Canaan. Ten other tribal leaders who were Caleb's fellows on the scouting mission of the promised land incited the people to defy God's plan by returning to Egypt. While Moses pledged Hebron to Caleb as a reward to him for his bold stance and faith, Joshua, Moses' successor, delivered on Moses' oath promise forty years later; both men outlasted these many years of sojourning in the desert that God decreed in retribution for the people's defiance of his plan.

4. Author's translation.

5. Midr. Yal. Shmot, 247:187.

6. Alter, *Five Books of Moses*, 447.

7. Crawford, "Caleb the Dog," 24.

A Male Prostitute Is Called "a Dog"

The Torah itself (or the Pentateuch) has one more allusion to a dog when it rejects and prohibits bringing the earnings of a male prostitute, whom the Torah calls a "dog," as a monetary donation for the needs of God's sanctuary or for buying a sacrificial animal with it. However, a close-up reading of this text (Deut 23:19) reveals a comparison of a dog to a human being, albeit of a lowly yet licit occupation; neither male nor female whoring incurred a divine punishment, nor even a curse against providers of such services. It is significant, however, that even a whoring man wishes to support God's house, though God detests such an idea of a "religious" donation.

God's Model for Gideon's Commando

The next time the dog reemerges in the Bible is when God instructs the chieftain Gideon to designate out of his large army a downsized crack battalion to defeat the Midianite and Amalekite foes who terrorized the Israelites and destroyed their produce. This small striking unit would be chosen and assembled at the Spring of Harod when Gideon's numerous troops were to break their thirst at the brook. He "who laps up water with his tongue like a dog laps" (Judg 7:5–7),[8] God says to Gideon, would qualify to join his small special operations force; those who would bend their knees at the water would be discharged from it.

Unlike lions and tigers, who crouch and fold their forelegs while drinking, dogs do not stretch themselves flat on their belly or chest; if dogs did likewise it would make them vulnerable to predators in a visible and exposed location as a water source. Rather, the canine licks or dips its tongue in the water and retrieves it quickly, while being able to take off promptly when peril looms.

Such a dog-like posture symbolized agility and cleanliness; only three hundred of Gideon's warriors did not seek a leisurely way to cup water from the spring that would have them drop down their weapons to free both hands. Those troopers who imitated a drinking dog, thus drenching their thirst with small gulps, passed God's litmus test for boldness; it singled them out as combat-ready fighters. He who drank that way as the canine does, while drinking with one hand but holding on to his weapon with the

8. Author's translation.

other, was chosen for Gideon's special unit, poised to defeat the Amalekites and Midianites.

Declension in the Dog's Image

All in all, we have seen thus far a fair, if not favorable, image of the dog. But since dogs in Egypt were associated with the jackal-headed god Anubis, the god of mummification who helped deceased humans navigate their way to the afterlife,[9] the pagan association prevented the dog from having a bona fide enduring favorable standing in the Bible. Side by side with its positive view of the dog, the Bible would also inauspiciously (even pejoratively, though not contemptibly) relate dogs to an animal that might encounter physical violence by humans (which can happen today too).

Goliath as a Mirror

Indeed, the Bible starts to reveal its degraded disposition toward dogs, especially during the reigns of kings in Israel and Judah. We may first detect a significant omen of that in the sarcastic words of Goliath, the Philistine giant, upon seeing the young David ready to engage him in battle with no conventional weapon in the Valley of Elah: "Am I a dog that you come at me with sticks?" (1 Sam 17:43).[10]

In other words, dogs were customarily chased away or even struck by the shepherd's staff or stick; Job's lowliest hirelings had likely no qualms about using it. Other people used to clutch dogs by the ears and hurt them for no reason (Prov 26:17).

David and Others' Low Image of a Dog

David himself shared that poor image of the dog when calling out submissively from his hiding cave in the cliffs of the Ein-Gedi oasis to his pursuer, King Saul, who had a prize over his head: "After whom did the king of Israel set out to chase? After a dead dog? After a flea?" (1 Sam 24:14)[11]—the lowest ranking of all creatures. In resembling himself to a dead dog, David might

9. Jakada Tours Egypt, "Egyptian Dog God."

10. Author's translation.

11. Author's translation.

very well mirror in such an image his innocent yet abused and violated station in life that was akin to a dog's life.

Likewise, when David becomes king of united Israel, he promises kindness to Jonathan's son (and Saul's grandson) Mephibosheth, who immediately falls on the ground doing obeisance before David and asks: "What is your servant that you should look upon a dead dog such as I?" (2 Sam 9:8).[12] The Aramean commander Hazael also calls himself a "mere dog" in self-deprecation and incredulity when the prophet Elisha foresees that he will become a ruthless king toward the people of Israel (2 Kgs 8:13).[13] The prophet Isaiah doubles down on such lowly images, observing the dogs as slothful or "loving to slumber," and having "a mighty appetite" for "they never have enough" (56:10–11 JPS; NOAB). Subsisting on a meager dog's life is sardonically viewed by Qoheleth as "better [but only] than a dead lion" (Eccl 9:4 JPS).

The Dog as a Scavenger

Other biblical references describe the dog as an urban scavenger, even of human corpses, as when licking up the shed blood of the grapevine-grower Naboth after he was stoned to death in line with the nefarious scheme of Jezebel, wife of Ahab the king of Israel. Indeed, Elijah the prophet warns King Ahab that it will be his fate too, even at the same spot. And to emphasize the disdain associated with that scene, Elijah says to Ahab, "This is what the Lord has said: 'At the very site where the dogs licked up Naboth's blood, the dogs will lick up your blood, too" (1 Kgs 21:19).[14] By repeating twice within a short sentence the dogs' licking up the blood of the slain, Elijah magnified the revolting sense that such an action evokes.

As it transpired, however, after King Ahab was killed in a war against Aram, the dogs licked up the slain king's blood that stained his war chariot when it was washed off at the pool of Samaria. And to add insult (or salt) to injury the Bible notes that at the same time, the harlots were washing at the pool (22:38). In other words, the dog's low image was not worse than the low image of humans (albeit whores engaged in a licit occupation). Indeed, unlike the divining mediums or wizards, the presence of prostitutes was

12. Author's translation.
13. Author's translation.
14. Author's translation.

acceptable in Israelite communities, not unlike the presence of stray dogs. However, both were relegated to the farthest fringes of society.

A similar fate also met King Ahab's wife Jezebel; roaming dogs, presumably, ate up the bulk of her smashed body after she was toppled to her death by Jehu's men from the window of her house overlooking Naboth's perfidiously confiscated vineyard. When her remains were to be buried, only her skull, feet, and the palms of her hands were left for internment. To have dogs eat a dead human body was especially seen as a degrading comeuppance, as it practically meant that the deceased's body would not be buried.

Again, an Uptick in the Dog's Image

Nevertheless, though held in contempt, albeit never as a foolish animal, the dog continued to fulfill its traditional task as a guardian. David as the psalmist also expresses a likely good word for the dogs, whose presence among the human population indicated an acceptance to "prowl about the city" and howl in the evening—the only animal that could alert humans by barking at a possible danger (Ps 59:6).[15]

When Isaiah compares the chieftains of Israel or the people's false prophets to "mute dogs who would not bark" (Isa 56:10),[16] he does not only seek to admonish them for the malperformance of their leadership responsibilities. In dodging their duties, they stood in contrast to dogs who bark in the face of a looming danger, either in the city or on the field; a testament to the presence of gritty canines near humans as their protectors and property guards.

The Talmud Restores the Dog to the Positive Column

By the second century BCE, the dog had shed its biblical derogatory stereotypes, as we may deduce from the apocryphal Book of Tobit. The book tells us about the truly righteous Tobias who sets off on a long journey and as a matter of course has "his dog running with him"; a companion dog that delighted his owner by exhibiting "joy in fawning and wagging his tail" (Tob 11:9). The inclusion of this information about Tobit's companion

15. Author's translation.

16. Author's translation.

dog must attest to a societal norm of keeping a dog as a house pet, and not necessarily for merely guarding the house or deriving some immediate practical benefit by having it around.

The talmudic sage Eliezer ben Yaakov praises the "clever" dog as a paragon of dedication and faithfulness to the shepherd despite the scanty food it receives; nonetheless, it meticulously fulfills its tasks with its human master. The dog's staunch trust in its master is mirrored in the adage "the face of the generation is like the face of the dog."[17] This absolute loyalty is witnessed when a dog, running ahead of its master, turns to see where the master is heading at intersecting trails to follow his direction. Thus, the Talmud reams out at populist leaders who merely follow the whims of the populace; as it would be today by taking cues from the latest public opinion polls and TV ratings to choose their popular course of action.

The prominent talmudic Rabbi Eliezer even compared his wholesome learning from his masters to "a dog lapping from the sea."[18] A dog that licks water to its fill by taking small gulps until drenching fully its thirst, while doing so eagerly and excitedly—the image that inspired the talmudic scholar—conjures up the scene at the Spring of Harod, where God instructed Gideon how to choose his elite warriors. The contemporary giant talmudic scholar Adin Steinsaltz even suggested that "the dogs sustain the world through their prayers in the outdoors."[19]

Postscript

Though dog attacks on humans nowadays occur very commonly, they happen mostly in homes, not by stray dogs roaming the neighborhoods, or serving as guard dogs in grazing fields as in biblical days. And though tragically deaths from dog attacks occur, the Bible cites no dog attacks on humans.

In April 2020, while most Chinese folks weaned themselves from consuming dog flesh, the Chinese government resolved to reclassify dogs as "companion animals" instead of "livestock." By doing so, Beijing fell in line with the common practice in developed countries, including Hong Kong and Taiwan—not a small feat for a country that hosts a dog meat festival each June in the city of Yulin.

17. M. Sotah 9:15.

18. b. Sanḥ. 68a.

19. Tesler, "T'filot haklavim machazikot."

CHAPTER 27

Mind! The Mother and Her Child

Animals have personalities and minds and feelings.—Jane Goodall

Prologue

A short video I once watched featured a cattleman who passed by the pasture looking for new births. He noticed a cow that gave him a look, and then she started to walk away from him in a very certain direction. He continued to follow her for over a kilometer. Finally, she stopped where her big calf was caught in a Y-shaped tree branch. The cattleman helped the calf to free itself, and the two bovines repaired to the herd. I was left with the thought that a mother is a mother, whether a human or an animal.

Sensitivity to Animal Children

When Jacob returns to Canaan with his large family after living two decades in Haran, he is still agitated about encountering Esau, whose birthright he had "stolen" from their father Isaac. Jacob's fear was especially accentuated upon hearing that Esau was leading four hundred men to greet him. Hence, he petitions God: "I pray, save me from the hand of my brother, from the hand of Esau! For I fear him, lest he come and strike me down, the mother with the children" (Gen 32:12).[1] Jacob invokes again the same words that expressed concern, if not fear, for his offspring and their mothers when he

1. Author's translation.

described to Esau following their brief and amicable reunion his young and frail livestock as "the children."

Jacob did so to explain (albeit falsely) to his brother that he intended (he did not!) to accept his invitation and visit him in his new land of domicile (Se-ir, modern-day Aqaba), but his pace would be rather slow for "the children are tender, and the nursing flocks and cattle are upon me; if driven hard for a single day, then all the flocks will die" (33:13–14 STONE). Jacob thus compared his young flocks to his children, as though he were also their parent and not merely their shepherd.

Significantly, the Torah echoes verbatim the idiom "the mother with children"—by which Jacob referred to his young ones—in the case of a (pure or fit for food) mother bird whose nest was stumbled upon and discovered unintentionally with the nestlings (whether eggs or fledglings). In using the word "children" (literally "sons"—*ha-banim*) for the chicks in the nest, the Torah seeks in two long verses (Deut 22:6–7), dedicated to the cause of kindness to a mother bird, to avert her capture while she crouches over her nestlings. (Such birds could also be domesticated, like a hen or a goose that "rebelled" and flew the coop to live independently, even in a field or an orchard that belonged to her former owner.)

Importantly, the Torah neither wishes nor expects people to start and look for nests, if only to observe the commandment of sending off the mother bird; this commandment is relevant only when one finds such a nest by happenstance. At this juncture, the Torah forbids him to seize the nestlings, if even for a short moment, until he shoos away the dam to such a distance from where she would not be able to see him usurping her future generation. Hence, at this short time-out, the would-be expropriator might reconsider whether it is proper for him to interrupt the course of life; perhaps he might give up the idea and let the nestlings become what nature destined them for.

In effect, the commandment is not only to stay off the mother bird, for it implicitly instructs to refrain from harming the nestlings too, despite the ostensible permission to "take [them] for yourself." Both the fledglings and the eggs would have no value at one's dinner table; chicks have hardly any flesh, and fertilized eggs en route to hatching were inedible too, if only because of the presence of blood therein, which makes their consumption prohibited, as we first saw when God categorically prohibited Noah from consuming blood.

Kindness to Birds: An Elixir for Longevity

Poignantly, the person who sought to remove "the children" (the fledglings) from the nest would have to cope with the idea of killing "children" rather than "chicks." This word might sensitize him to the family dynamics in the nest, not unlike his own. Even if the would-be usurper callously chose, as he must do, to send away the mother bird to such a distance where she cannot see her nest being violated, it would certainly be an arduous, if not a challenging task, as the mother would not easily concede keeping an eye on the nest. For all practical matters, the prohibition of the Torah outlaws also the removal of the fledglings all together.

Maimonides, in his *Guide to the Perplexed*, explains why. To begin with, upon her eventual return to her violated nest, the mother bird would feel the pain of her loss; her agony over her lost children ought to be prevented. Moreover, "This commandment will cause a man to leave the whole nest untouched, because [the young or the eggs], which he is allowed to take, are, as a rule, unfit for food."[2]

The nineteenth-century Torah commentator Shadal explains that capturing the mother is verboten because her compassion for the nestlings compelled her to stay put to defend them rather than fly the coop for her safety. It would thus be an egregious heartlessness on the usurper's part if the brave bird's motherly instincts meant nothing to him as he went on and, with no moral inhibitions, captured her.[3] Shadal adds that by refraining from capturing the dam, the Torah teaches that no act of righteous behavior should be maliciously exploited. Hence, a potential marauder of a mother bird would internalize that such displayed grit for her fledglings was not a senseless attribute that backfired on her. He would see that parental compassion and sacrifice must be duly respected rather than be glibly ignored and abused; he would then keep his hands off the mother and her nest.[4]

If one does that and obeys this command that addresses the stumbled-on-nest, his reward would be that "it may go well with you and you may prolong (your) days" (v. 7).[5] It is an extremely rare promise of longevity for the Bible to make in tribute to motherhood; it is akin to a similar assurance in the Decalogue for those honoring their parents, which is right at the

2. Maimonides, *Guide to the Perplexed*, 3.48.8.

3. Leibowitz, *Gilyonot*, Mitzvat.

4. Luzzatto (Shadal), "Shadal on Deuteronomy," Deut 22:6.1.

5. Author's translation.

heart and the cornerstone of the Ten Commandments. Such a reward then pairs equally humans and birds alike.

On Bovine Motherhood

Like Jacob and the mother bird narrative, the Bible personalizes the herd's young by relating to it as "the son of cattle" (rather than just a "calf"). Isaiah similarly denotes the "children" of a cow and a bear by using the same word that describes human kids as well (11:7).[6] Job, too, refers to the little ones of the flocks as "their children" (21:11 NOAB) as does God in addressing him while relating to the young—but literally to the "children" or "sons" as in Hebrew—of the raven, (possibly) the ostrich, or the ibex (38:41; 39:3, 16 KRAUS), rather than to their "chicks" or "fawns." The Book of Proverbs also contributes to the same theme with "the vulture's sons" (30:17).[7]

This motif is also evident in the prophet Nathan's condemnation of King David for his nauseating adulterous affair with Bathsheba and for his attempts to cover it up, which led in lockstep to assigning her husband Uriah to the very frontline of a battle where he was sure to get killed. Nathan couches his accusatory words adroitly by telling the imperious monarch that it was he who acted like a certain wealthy man, who possessed numerous livestock but preferred to usurp the sole sheep of a poor man and slay it for a meal to honor a traveling guest at his home, rather than butcher a ewe from his very flocks.

Indeed, that one slain sheep, Nathan said to the king, was "brought up" by the poor man at home; "along with his sons, she ate of his skimpy bread and drank from his cup, she lay in his bosom being like a daughter to him" (2 Sam 12:1–4).[8] These words, Nathan must have properly reasoned, were sentimentally charged for David, reminiscent of the reverberating, loving, and kind words—what must have been now a cherished family heirloom—that Boaz, his paternal great grandfather, said to his great grandmother Ruth, a poor stranger, in his Bethlehem field: "My daughter . . . should you get thirsty, go to the jugs, and drink" and "partake of the bread" (Ruth 2:8, 14).[9]

6. Author's translation.

7. Author's translation.

8. Author's translation.

9. Author's translation.

The Bible thus compares animals with humans, seeing them as fellow co-creatures who deserve and receive recognition for their personhood, dignity, and respect. It is especially notable when it effectively equates the status of a mother animal and her young ones with the standing of a human mother. In so doing, the Bible invokes the same divine consideration and compassion due to both human and animal mothers alike.

Forbidding Cruel Practices Towards Mothers

The Torah tries to show a veritable degree of compassion to bovine mothers even within the realm of meat offerings. A newly born calf must not be slain for a sacrifice before it is at least eight days young, presumably to allow its mother a sense of motherhood, if not bonding, with her child. In sharp contrast to the practice in the contemporary industrial dairy farm, where the calf is callously removed from its mother soon after its birth to prevent any bonding between them, the Torah seems to recognize here the need of the mother bovine to nurture her child. It would be heartlessly cold to butcher the young of a bovine, or even a fowl before its mother experiences a measure of maternal nurturing. Allowing her to do that would earn such livestock farmers the unique accolade of "people of holiness" (Exod 22:30 STONE). Similarly, slaughtering them both on the same day on the altar would exhibit indifference to the motherly primal sentiments; it is prohibited too.

Maimonides avers that butchering a bovine child before its mother's eyes (as she is next in line)—even on the altar as an offering to God, or even when the two slayings were not to be performed by the same butcher—would be a very cruel infliction, for there is no difference between the emotional pain that a human suffers to that of an animal. Why, the "maternal love and her compassion for the child does not derive from the individual's wit,"[10] even as it is shared by most animals (birds included), just like humans experience these emotions.

Nixing the Mixing of Meat and Dairy

The Torah also proscribes thrice "You are not to boil a kid in the milk of its mother!" (Exod 23:19; 34:26; Deut 14:21 FOX), namely, the cooking of

10. Maimonides, *Guide to the Perplexed*, 3.48.7.

meat in dairy (rabbinic tradition also prohibits the eating of and trading in any such admixture). A classical commentator, Abraham Ibn Ezra, relates this prohibition to a symbolic show of sensitivity to the mother whose maternal milk and her offspring's flesh commingled into a culinary dish; it would constitute a morally disturbing situation.[11] In his German Bible translation of 1534, Martin Luther focused on the kid, which was still a suckling; it was too young to forfeit its life for a meal. Philo, too, viewed this practice with revulsion, calling it "a callous and perverse disposition that is irreverent and lacks all feeling of compassion."[12] Menahem Haran of the Hebrew University similarly detected a "rather deliberate" call here for "humane behavior, even amid [the] general jollity"[13] of a festival celebration featuring such food.

Other commentators see this prohibition as a harbinger that adumbrated the subsequent law prohibiting the taking of a mother bird along with her young (discussed above); its ultimate objective being "to tame cruel human instincts"[14] and distance the human from excessive gluttony that inheres the cooking of a baby animal in its maternal milk. Kook expands on the subject by asserting that the prohibition effectively reminds us that the maternal milk of a livestock animal has only one purpose: to nourish the tender child, "her beloved," just like the purpose of one's very mother's milk.

And yet the human usurps it for himself from the nursing mother. The destined fate of a kid is not to become food for any human, nor is such milk to be exploited as a spice and become a way to "slake one's despicable craving" in a "desirous stomach." Indeed, meat and milk are "so distant [from one another] and so revolting"[15] together—one ingredient symbolizes life, the other, death—as to be forbidden for any enjoyment from such an admixture.

Postscript

The same idea is found in India's ancient, traditional, and vast system of medicine, Ayurveda, which lists all eighteen antagonist or incompatible

11. Rothstein, "Figuring Out."
12. Mealy, "You Shall Not Boil," 38.
13. Schorch, "Do Not Cook."
14. Plaut, *Torah*, 533.
15. Kook, "Vision of Vegetarianism," 14.

food combinations (the *Viruddha ahara*) that interfere with the metabolic activity of the human body and poison it. One of these harmful food fusions is the concurrent consumption of meat and dairy.

The Significance of It All: The Story Behind the Story

As we have seen above, the Torah bars four insensitive or cruel practices to be wielded against mother animals:

- Sacrificing on the altar a calf younger than eight days old
- Concurrently eating meat and milk
- Same-day slaughter of parent and child
- Harming a mother bird (and effectively her nestlings too)

All four prohibitions, comments Robert Alter, deliver the "sense that the order of nature is violated when the destruction of life includes the biological producer and nurturer of life."[16] Indeed, Nachmanides discerns—in the cases of the same-day slaughter of parent and child, and of the bird's nest—a biblical grave concern with the resultant elimination of two generations: the "extinction of a whole species," or something akin to its "mass extermination." Yet, the overarching purpose, à la Nachmanides, of these biblical prohibitions is to ward off a person from developing "an evil heart" and to "teach us the value of compassion lest we become cruel"; if it is not contained and overcome, it would "expand further in a person's soul."[17]

Concrete Compassion

In Ucacha, Argentina, they replaced wooden light posts with concrete ones. But they cut parts of the wooden posts where woodpeckers nested to attach them firmly to the corresponding concrete post at the same height. And voilà, those nests were saved to honor the love and care of a mother bird for her nestlings.[18]

16. Alter, *Five Books of Moses*, 986.

17. Wikisource, "רמב"ן_על_דברים_כב_ו."

18. Varga, "When the Light Poles."

Breaking a myth: yes, it's totally "kosher" to refer to your pets or other animals that rely on you as "the children."

CHAPTER 28

What Can Animals Teach Us?

If having a soul means being able to feel love and loyalty and gratitude, then animals are better off than a lot of humans.—James Herriot, *All Creatures Great and Small*

In his reply to one of his rambling friends, Job sends them all to learn wisdom from "the animals and they will teach you, the birds of the air, and they will tell you . . . and the fish of the sea, and they will instruct you" (Job 12:7–8 KRAUS). Job mentions the river horse (hippopotamus), the strongest grass-eating land animal, which, despite its being a paragon of supreme strength, does not use it for preying on other animals for food. Rather, those animals that cohabit with it "frolic safely nearby" (40:20 KRAUS) in its presence; that could well apply to those sharing with the hippo the grazing land (but not to others venturing into what it considers as its "territorial water").

The river horse can teach us, then, as Job says—that being the strongest in the neighborhood is not a license to violently harm others, though it certainly could. Or, that "power is when we have every justification to kill, and we don't,"[1] which is what Oskar Schindler told Amon Goeth, the commandant of the Kraków-Płaszów concentration camp in German-occupied Poland.

According to the midrash, Adam and Eve, for instance, learned from a raven who had just buried a friend how to bury Abel after Cain killed him.[2]

1. Quotes, "Schindler's List."

2. Midr. Pirque R. El. 21:10.

Yochanan, a talmudic rabbi, also cites the cat as an animal that practices modesty when it answers nature's call and then covers its waste in privacy. The cat's conduct is consonant with a Torah commandment to use a spike to dig a hole to "cover up your excrement" (Deut 23:14 FOX). Yochanan also mentions the pigeon and the rooster as other models for imitation that could teach humans a thing or two about marital fidelity and conjugal intimacy respectively.[3] The Jewish daily prayer book features an early morning praise of God that one recites upon hearing a rooster's crow; the blessing expresses gratitude to God for giving roosters the discernment to distinguish between day and night, thus helping folks to wake up at an ideal (early) time to begin a person's daily labors.

A most popular talmudic tractate, 'Abot (Ethics of the Fathers), posits, "Be strong as a leopard and soar up as an eagle, run swiftly as a gazelle, and be brave as a lion."[4] But is it possible to be or do all of these things that these animals exhibit? Yes, say the commentators. For strength is exhibited when you ask your teacher, while overcoming shame, to explain again what was not understood, or by ignoring mockery launched at you for following God's commandments. Flying with lightness as the eagle does is done by reviewing your daily learning without allowing it to fatigue you. Imitating the swift deer can be achieved by running to do your God's will. And while imitating the bravery of the lion, the king of animals, one faces the daily challenges of life, like reigning over the strong appeal of following the luring of one's evil impulse.[5]

Animal Gratitude

Isaiah praises the "ox [who] knows its owner, and the ass [who knows] its master's stall," while lamenting that "Israel does not know, my people does not understand"; Israel then does not match the conduct of these two respected animals of the Bible. While the ox would never refuse to pull behind a plowshare, nor would the donkey demur to carry a load, tasks they constantly do without considering their self-interest, Israel did not want to hear of their duties and even worse to recognize God as their master (Isa 1:2–4 PLAUT). As Isaiah has it, these animals were superior to his people by exhibiting fidelity even in recognizing their benefactor.

3. b. 'Erub. 100b.

4. b. 'Abot 5:20.

5. Kehati, *Masechet Avot*, 124.

"The animal of the field, jackals and ostriches," Isaiah says, may well teach his countrymen how to honor their creator for providing "water in the desert, and rivers in the wilderness," though God does so primarily for the benefit of his people passing through them "so that they might declare My praise" (Isa 43:20).[6] But in reality, these and other animals who prowl those arid and sandy regions honor and thank God for watering these wastes plentifully, even as subsidiary beneficiaries.

Jeremiah, too, praises "the wild animals of the field" for their instinctive acumen that brought them "to serve" the Babylonian King, Nebuchadnezzar (Jer 27:6 NOAB). Unlike the feckless Judean King Zedekiah (early sixth century BCE), the animals knew, even if through a hidden impulse of nature that God implanted in them, that Nebuchadnezzar was their master. By contrast, how great must one's foolhardiness be, like King Zedekiah and his advisors, in not serving Nebuchadnezzar, unlike the very wildlife who did. For Jeremiah, the animals exhibited more intelligence than the rebellious Judean king who rose against Babylon, bringing calamity to his kingdom's subjects, family, and himself.

David the psalmist speaks similarly of the lions who understand that it is God that sustains them (Ps 104:21). Like people, David writes, so are "the animals and all livestock, creeping things and winged fowl," which similarly understand that they ought to hail and praise their creator (Pss 148; 150 JPS).

Tilling the Ground

Isaiah mentions again in one breath both the ass with the ox in the context of the earth that produces flourishingly, because they "till of the ground" (Isa 30:24 JPS). After God became the first tiller of the land by planting "a garden in Eden," he assigned Adam with this charge so he too would "till it and guard it." Adam would have the same mission following his expulsion from the garden and repatriation to the land where he was first formed (before God took and placed him in the garden). Back in the "real world" Adam would now have to sweat it out to produce food, indeed, to till the land laboriously while fending it off from "thorns and thistles," a role that Isaiah praises both the donkey and ox for fulfilling. Or, as the Book of Proverbs teaches, "The tiller of his land will be satiated with bread" (Prov 12:11;

6. Author's translation.

28:19).[7] The Bible portrays, then, both the human and the animal—the ass and the ox—as imitating God by engaging in the same very noble activity of land husbandry that began with God's planting of the garden.

The Ant: Teaching "Do Not Steal"

The Book of Proverbs sends off slothful persons to the ant—the tiniest, weakest, and lowest creature—to "consider its ways, and wise up" (Prov 6:6).[8] The Bible describes only King Solomon, the presumptive author of Proverbs, as wise; his future scion "from the stock of Jesse" will exclusively inherit "the spirit of wisdom" (Isa 11:1–2)[9] that God already implanted in ants.

Thus, while the Israelites are commanded to appoint "judges and officers" (Deut 16:18) in their cities, Proverbs tells us that ants get along with law and order better than humans do; they have such harmonious organization in their colonies that function well, without trace of such human systems of governance. Ants do not need police departments, a judicial system, courthouses, or prisons; yet, no crime is committed in their anthills. "Without having any chief, officer, or ruler, it prepares its food in the summer and gathers its sustenance in harvest" (Prov 6:7–8 NOAB).

The ants' famous summer diligence in gathering sustenance for the inclement winter season, Proverbs tells us, is based on their self-discipline; they do what they do instinctively without their queen, who is ensconced deep underground in the nest, supervising their work. Indeed, ants teach one another new skills, even as one ant shows another the route to a food source. The ants' wisdom is also displayed in their system of properly storing their seeds, grains, or lentils, protecting them from the rain or the dampness in the depth of the nest.

The talmudic sage Shimon ben Halfata says that the ant gathers grains from what is openly ownerless or forfeited, rather than stealing them. Once, the rabbi noticed an ant that dropped a seed it was hauling but continued to march on without realizing that she had lost it. Meanwhile, other ants, chanced by the lost seed, sniffed at it but moved on after smelling the scent of another ant.

7. Author's translation.

8. Author's translation.

9. Author's translation.

When the first ant realized its seed was gone, it traced its footsteps and found it exactly where it had fallen. Neither she nor the other ants would engage in embezzlement, not because of their fear of the law but simply in adherence to their inherent etiquette.[10] Or, as the talmudic sage Rabbi Yochanan has it: "Without the Torah, we would have learned . . . [about how not to] steal from an ant."[11] By distancing themselves from coveting, let alone from seizing that which belongs to others—two prohibitions of the Decalogue—ants do not require any officer to be appointed over them to either urge or compel them to carry out their summertime industrious labor.

The rabbis recognize other merits in the ants' celebrated toil, humility, and positive outlook on life worthy for humans to imitate. With her lifespan anywhere between one to three years—with males living only several weeks—the ant consumes one-half of a seed in a whole year, although the number of grains that each ant hauls and stores throughout her lifetime far exceeds her maximal consumption. Why does she do it? asks the sage Tanhuma. He explains this mystery in the ant's pondering a heavenly miracle that might extend her life beyond her allotted time; hence, she readies a bigger supply of seeds to sustain her in such a scenario, just in case.[12] And if it did not pan out, the grains will still feed future generations in her colony.

Such an explanation naturally conjures up for the rabbis of yore the ancient story from the second century CE about the Roman emperor Hadrian, who passed by an old man and inquired why he was planting a fruit tree that would take many years to yield its produce. The man replied that if he lucked out and was given a long life, he might as well enjoy the fruit, and if not, his children and grandchildren would, as will the generations that will follow them; why, he, too, found fruit trees that others planted before he was born.[13]

"The Episode of the Ant," a rabbinic parable about an encounter between King Solomon and an ant, the two whom the Bible recognizes for their wisdom, has the little creature chastising the monarch after he reminded her of his royal status. The ant retorted, "Take note that you came from a rancid drop of seminal fluid; do not be a swagger."[14] King Solomon

10. Midr. Dev. Rab. 5:2.

11. b. 'Erub. 100b.

12. Midr. Dev. Rab. 5:2.

13. Midr. Vaik. Rab. 25:5.

14. Project Ben Yehudah, *Ma'aseh Hanemalah.*

took to heart the ant's words and was embarrassed for himself and ashamed, thus reminding us that wisdom is equally found in all sizes.

Ants in the OR

According to *Current Biology*, scientists have discovered that ants in Florida perform life-saving surgery on their peers. They are only the second animal worldwide known to do this, along with humans. The researchers found that Florida carpenter ants (*Camponotus floridanus*) identify limb wounds on their nestmates and treat them with either cleaning or amputation.[15]

Migratory Birds: Teaching Timeliness

A person living in the land of the Bible, a unique air corridor connecting three continents for about 500 million fowls that usually fly in large flocks, does not need to be an accomplished bird watcher to witness their flight to and from Europe or Africa, carried out according to their biological clock. Rabbi Jack Riemer captured the spirit of such bird watching when he penned "On Turning," an inspirational reading for the High Holy Days that starts with the following observation:

> Now is the time for turning. . . . The birds are beginning to turn and are heading once more toward the South. The animals are beginning . . . to store their food for winter. For leaves, birds, and animals, turning comes instinctively. But for us, turning does not come so easily. It takes an act of will for us to make a turn. It means breaking old habits. It means admitting we have been wrong: and this is never easy.[16]

This passage is reminiscent of Jeremiah's prophetic words about birds and animals that to the prophet's chagrin the people of Israel were yet to learn from them and do likewise: "Even the stork in the sky knows her appointed seasons, and the dove, the swift, and the crane observe the time of their migration. But my people do not know the requirements of the Lord" (Jer 8:7).[17]

15. Frank, "Would-Dependent Leg Amputations."

16. Central Conference of American Rabbis, *Gates of Repentance*, 372.

17. Author's translation.

Jeremiah is dismayed and confounded by the contrasting comparison between his people to whom he prophesied and migratory birds. While the birds faithfully kept to their semi-annual winter–summer schedule, journeying for long distances thanks to their superb navigational aptitude, Israel had forgotten to return home to God's laws with no one "to blush." And while the itinerant birds act as if they know the laws of nature so they fly to their optimal weather to avoid adversity, Israel acts as though it does not know God's laws of retribution and reward.

Wings of One

Although wild geese are not mentioned in the Bible, they belong to the migratory avian species. What can humans learn from the flight that thousands of geese from Canada take to the southern part of the United States every autumn to escape the inclement cold winter and then again in the spring, back to the north?

These semi-annual airlifts are known for their V-shape flying pattern, with one alternating goose in the center leading its flock behind in two close lines. Avian observers have determined that by flying in this formation and pattern, each goose facilitates additional lifting power for its buddy behind by reducing its air resistance. The flock thus reaches its destination faster and with far less energy spent than if each goose flew the same distance alone.

When the lead goose gets tired, it drops out and takes its place as a follower at the rear of the formation, replaced by another member from the ranks. This pattern recurs numerous times during the long voyage to their destination. These tours of rotation are done while the birds communicate through loud honking. When a goose cannot continue the journey due to illness or injury, two other geese will drop out with their ailing fellow until it can continue to fly or die.[18] Flying alone, like racing without a team in the grueling Tour de France biking event, has only disadvantages reminiscent of Helen Keller's observation: "We live by each other and for each other. Alone we can do so little; together we can do so much."[19]

18. Peak Performance Center, "Teamwork."

19. American Foundation for the Blind, "Helen Keller Quotes."

The Eagle: It's All for the Children

Powerful lessons can be learned from the eagle too. Moses, in his last poem, invokes the image of the eagle (likely the golden eagle or the griffon vulture) as a model for humans on how to teach and protect their children. Indeed, the powerful eagle "arouses its nestlings [by] hovering over its young" (Deut 32: 11a STONE), waking them up with the movement of its wings outside the nest. Rather than abruptly, the large bird enters its nest with sensitivity to gently wake them up so they would leave the nest, albeit not against their will, leaving it up to them whether to come along and learn to fly.

For the greater majority of all fowls, flying means life. Beyond the physical aspect, the rabbis understood life to mean teaching one's child a craft or profession by which he (or she) would be able to make a decent living as an adult, akin to the eagle's teaching its eaglets how to live by mastering flight in record heights.

And by "spread[ing] out its wings" to take and carry its eaglets "aboard its wings," as Moses' poem notes (32:11b),[20] unlike some birds who under extenuating circumstances, if at all, haul gently their young ones by picking them up in the beak, the eagle carries its young "on the wings" (Exod 19:4 STONE). The Mechilta rabbi (whom Rashi quotes) understands the eagle's action as unique among all fowls; while the latter "carry their chicks between their legs [i.e., by their talons] in fear of the bird that soars up the highest above them, the eagle fears none of them but the man who is poised to shoot it down with an arrow. It is as though the eagle says to itself, 'let the arrow enter me rather than my child.'"[21]

The Eagle: Teaching Renewal

David the psalmist must have known of the severe molting or the shedding of their feathers that eagles undergo for two weeks at about five years of age only to be "renewed"; David wishes for God to similarly renew his spirit and redeem it "from the pit . . . [and be] renewed like the eagle's" (Ps 103:4–5 NOAB). Isaiah, anticipating that the Persian king Cyrus's forthcoming defeat and supersession of Babylon will herald a new era and revival for the exiles in Babylon, even their restoration to their homeland, invokes the renewal that the eagles (or vultures) undergo in their flight to instill hope

20. Author's translation.

21. Midr. Mech. Shem. 19:4.

among them. And he says, "But those who wait for the Lord shall renew their strength, they shall mount up with wings like eagles, they shall run and not be weary, they shall walk and not faint" (Isa 40:31 NOAB).

Isaiah thus alludes to the bird's wings, regaining their full strength as the day advances, when powerful gusts of rising air—wind thermals—lift them, replacing the chill of morning hours in which the birds rest upon the ground or rocky ledges. The eagle restores its strength daily with the warming up of the air as it restarts its circular flight that does not require active and protracted flapping of the wings, yet allows it to glide at ease once it reaches its desired altitude. From there on, repeating the same pattern of soaring to the next stream of hot air allows the bird to remain afloat with minimal waste of energy. Hence, Isaiah spurs on the Judean exiles by metaphorically comparing their forthcoming trek on foot to their homeland to the eagle's flight without getting tired, or by renewing their strength along the journey.

CHAPTER 29

Animals in the Service of God

At times it seems to me that it was not people who had saved me but animals, which I encountered in my way—AHARON APPELFELD

In Egypt, God employed frogs, lice, flies, and locusts en masse (through plagues) to disturb and annoy the Egyptians to coerce the pharaoh to let the Hebrew slaves go to the desert for a short religious holiday. Or, as the psalmist has it, "He sent among them swarms of flies, which devoured them, and frogs, which destroyed them" (Ps 78:45 NOAB). Or, as in Ps 105: "He spoke and there came swarms of flies and gnats in all their borders. . . . He spoke, and the locust came and the canker-worm without number" (105:31–34 JPS).

From "and I shall send the hornet-swarm before you and it will drive out [your enemies] before you" (Exod 23:28; Deut 7:20; Josh 24:12 STONE), it appears that God dispatched swarms of poisonous hornets to overwhelm and rout several Canaanite nations that the Israelites waged war against. Though the New Oxford Bible translation supersedes "hornets" with "the pestilence," this word is still associated with living creatures, for such endemic is known to be transmitted by fleas that slaked off the blood of plague-diseased rats.

This brings us to the calamity that befell the huge army of Sennacherib, the Assyrian king who laid siege to Jerusalem in 701 BCE. "That very night the angel of the Lord set out and struck down 185,000 in the camp of the Assyrians; when morning dawned, they were all dead bodies" (2 Kgs 19:35 NOAB). Neither this account nor its other rendition (in 2 Chr 32:21) tries to explain this mysterious catastrophe the Assyrians suffered while

Jerusalem was at their mercy. Stephen W. Caesar suggests with certainty the "septicemic plague" as the reason for the eerie downfall of Sennacherib's army "as it lay crowded around the relatively small city of Jerusalem. . . . Living cheek to jowl for an extended time, the Assyrian soldiers would have been particularly vulnerable [and prone to succumb] to the plague . . . since human remains and refuse attract rats, [and] unwashed human bodies attract fleas."[1] Hence, the colossal demise of the immense Assyrian camp might speculatively have been another case of God's recruiting from his living handiwork to do his bidding.

Balaam's Clairvoyant Jenny

Unbeknownst to Balaam, a non-Israelite prophet who was anxiously ready to jinx the Israelites at the behest of Balak, the king of Moab (see chapter 22), God recruited his jenny to undergo abuse by the hand of her master, whom he struck thrice for each of her deflections from his desired riding path. The jenny did so to avoid colliding with his messenger, who was invisible to Balaam but not to her. Indeed, though the jenny saved his life, the furious Balaam, who felt humiliated by his animal, dressed her down: "If I had a sword with me, I would kill you" (Num 22:29 PLAUT).

These words and their inner message evince why God commissioned the jenny: to convey a message to Balaam, a moral that would otherwise shun him even in his encounters with God. Balaam is thus made to understand the futility of any verbal cursing aimed at the Israelites and their detriment and defeat, a task that King Balak wished for him to assume. Despite his anger over the apparent disobedient shenanigans of his jenny, he could not have killed her just with his word, only by a sword which he regretted not having right then and there. And since Balaam could not talk his jenny to death, how much less could he do so to a whole people, when God had their back—and the jenny's to boot.

Moreover, the jenny showed him that while she could see God's messenger, he was compelled to confess—having only one "opened eye" (Num 24:3)[2]—his inability to see at all, either God's angel or word. Thus, instead of putting a curse on the Israelites, he did the very opposite despite his strong desire to earn a fortune by casting aspersions on that people. God uses, then, the jenny, whom he made to speak if only briefly, as an instrument

1. Caesar, *Annihilation*, 224.

2. Author's translation.

that would bring Balaam to botch up Balak's cursing design. Instead of imprecations that would fail to deliver—in as much as he could not damn his jenny to death even by his lofty speech—he could only offer sublime praise and blessings to the Israelites.

The Worm That Changed Jonah

After spending three gloomy days in the belly of a big fish that God had designated and readied to act as his emissary—a time during which Jonah overcame his previous absolute recalcitrance to prophesy to the Ninevites and warn them of God's catastrophic design for their city—the fish spewed out Jonah onto land. Though still troubled by his mission, the rebellious prophet was finally willing to go to Nineveh, when three days earlier he attempted to sail away from this assignment that God had appointed him to carry out. Jonah's wish to die in the turbulent sea, rather than warn off the Ninevites, was not fulfilled; by swallowing Jonah, the fish saved him from drowning against his own will. During those three days, Jonah came to realize that God wanted him alive, not dead, even as God wished the same for the Ninevites, provided that they reformed their morally debased, exclusively human ways.

Once Jonah entered the city gate of Nineveh, he was only willing to halfheartedly and minimally comply with God's commission. He thus warned its people laconically of their impending downfall; it was adequate and effective. Three days later, Jonah was still hoping that with "just a little bit of luck" he would watch in real-time how God wrecks Nineveh into oblivion, even from the comfort of his hut overlooking the city and in the shade of a gourd that sprang up overnight.

But God summoned another agent, a worm, whose mission was to nibble and decimate the shade-producing gourd. The worm God had called forth to his service had chewed up and devoured the gourd, so it quickly withered. God's action through the worm deeply agonized Jonah to his core and made him feel woefully sorry for himself.

It, however, provided God with the opportunity to make Jonah aware of his utter lack of compassion in his tormented soul for the would-be collateral obliteration of the large, innocent populace in Nineveh, including numerous animals—all destined to perish together, even with the city's penitent people. "You took pity on the gourd for which you did not labor, [God said to Jonah, yet, it] perished overnight. And I—shall I not take pity upon Nineveh . . . in which there are more than a hundred and twenty thousand persons who do not know their right hand from their left, and also many animals?" (Jonah 4:10–11 STONE).

Knowing that had likely softened Jonah's bitter disappointment, if not transformed the recalcitrant and reluctant prophet to witness to God's sparing of the whole huge city. Since Jonah did not respond to God's reproach, his silence should attest to conceding his total hostility or at least indifference to Nineveh's populace and stock.

Elijah's Ravens

To sustain the fugitive Elijah, God commanded the prophet to hide away from King Ahab of Israel at a creek by the Jordan River, after Elijah, in God's name, had declared the cessation of dew and rain (to mock the Canaanite god, Baal, who could not overturn Elijah's oath). God commanded the ravens to provide him bread and meat twice daily. These impure fowls, who possess self-awareness and can make decisions using their sense and reason to solve problems, are widely known to be cruel even to their children and to devour eggs and fledglings even of their own kind.

What possible divine roles could these ravens play here? The presence of ravens at Elijah's hideout would be a sensible indication for King Ahab's military patrols searching for his whereabouts to kill him, to skip over the site; Elijah was not likely to hide at such a defiled location of carcasses (per Ralbag).[3] Additionally, the kindness that such mean birds showed Elijah by their benevolence might serve him notice that he, too, should change his nature and be kinder to his people by ending his three-year-long cruel curse of drought and famine in the land (1 Kgs 17:1).

Perchance, seeing the ravens depriving vital food from their fledglings, if only to bring him his daily nourishment—we are not told that he ate of that religiously defiled carrion—might affect Elijah to show mercy upon his food-deprived people in as much as the ravens did so for him. The ravens then might have compelled him to wonder whether he would be willing to eat the food they brought him while his people experienced famine. Hence, God recruited ravens to act contrary to their nature and feed their scarce food to a stranger, who might take their hint and do likewise for his people towards whom he also felt estranged (as in 1 Kgs. 19:14).

3. Otzar HaTorah, 1 Kgs 17, n. 12.

CHAPTER 30

Lethal Animals: Only When Commanded by God

The snake does not bite, nor does the lion raven, unless it was whispered from above to do so.—RABBI ABBA BAR KAHANA

Venomous Snakes upon the Israelites

As the Israelites walked the long way around Edom, they began to protest bitterly to God and Moses for having neither satisfactory bread nor water, while they loathed the deficient bread—the manna that God had supplied them heretofore. In response to the people's grumbling, God sent "the viper-serpents"—not random snakes but such that were "suddenly and miraculously"[1] pre-poised to assail; the viper's natural choice to avoid, if possible, any contact with humans notwithstanding. Indeed, Moses reminds his people in his farewell speech that although God led them "through the great and dreadful wilderness, wherein were fiery serpents" (Deut 8:15 JPS), there were no other snake-related incidents.

But when the Israelites were going around the land of Edom, those serpents "bit the people, and many Israelites died" (Num 21:6);[2] this being the only instance in the Torah where a plague of deadly snake bites is reported, not to mention that it was particularly one instigated by God. It was also the first time in the Bible that God sent animals to kill humans besides

1. Alter, *Five Books of Moses*, 789.

2. Author's translation.

the quail, whose toxic flesh was voraciously eaten right after being captured by the Israelites, many of whom consequently perished.

This exceptional viper onslaught ceased only after Moses prayed to God on behalf of the people. Hence, even people who were bitten, yet did not succumb to the lethal burning venom, recovered when they looked at Moses' copper model of a serpent that he made at God's behest and placed on a pole.

"Bizarre" Lions Who Prey on People

In another incident, God employs an animal to kill a Judean "man of God" (thought to be the prophet Iddo), who was duped into accepting a hospitable invitation to break bread and drink water with an old false prophet of Beit El whom Iddo mistook to be a true one. In accepting this invitation Iddo violated God's prohibition of ever returning there. When Iddo got back on the road to Judea, riding on "the donkey" gifted to him by his host, "the lion" (not a random one) encountered him on that major road and struck him dead.

God pre-designated and assigned a role to play for both animals (1 Kgs 13:24). Though crushing Iddo's bones, the lion fulfilled a divine mission, but it had no interest in that human corpse as food. Even more so, a normative lion would not be oblivious to the presence nearby of conventional prey, yet the lion did not make any predatory advance on the donkey. Also, the donkey stood by stoically showing loyalty to its dead rider without attempting to disengage and distance itself from the lion, its would-be predator.

When the old false prophet who coaxed Iddo to defy God's word soon heard about what had happened to his guest, he hastened to the site, seeing both animals standing calmly by Iddo's corpse like loyal sentries. He loaded the body onto the donkey without fearing the lion at all and brought it to town for proper burial in the grave that he had prepared for himself. By exhibiting uncharacteristic exceptional behavior, both animals demonstrated instinctively their understanding of the role-playing assigned to them by their creator, in contrast to the prophet Iddo who defied God's ban on his return to Beit El.

In another mysterious case where God seems to be involved in designating animals to do his bidding, the refusal of one prophetical man to strike his fellow, though that would-be whacking was supposed to be sanctioned by God, results in "the lion" striking him, but not—as commonly understood—a deadly jolt, for the (Hebrew) text does not note that the outcome of that lion's strike was death (1 Kgs 20:37).

Deadly Onslaughts for Immoralities

Another similar episode occurred when the king of Assyria, Sargon II (late eighth century BCE), brought his subjects from Babylon and other provinces to colonize the largely empty cities of Samaria to replace the twenty-seven-thousand-plus Northern Israelite residents whom he had first exiled from their land.[3] And since the newcomers brought with them their own cultures and beliefs, they would not revere God, even as they served foreign gods and violated the ethical code of the land, all of which resulted in "God sending forth the lions" that slew "some of them." The colonists regarded their sufferings from the lions as a judgment from "the God of the land" (2 Kgs 17:25–26 NOAB).

Elisha's killer bears

In another highly unsettling episode, God seems to be behind the horrific death of numerous children from Na'aran who mocked Elisha shortly after he succeeded Elijah in prophecy. The children confronted Elisha in protest for depriving them of their meager income following his miraculous curing of the waters of a spring in nearby Jericho, perhaps adding other derisive slurs. Or they might have mocked him for his baldness (that contrasted with Elijah, who was hairy). Perhaps the children might have only meant to criticize Elisha for "shaving off" or rendering their source of earnings, like being hairless, which made them penniless.

Elisha responds to their vituperation by invoking God's ineffable name in a malediction of his own resulting in the immediate appearance on the scene of two she-bears who emerged from the forest and "mauled forty-two of the boys" (2 Kgs 2:24 NOAB). Some highly apologetic Bible commentators were able to find much fault with the children's disagreeable or offensive words they directed at Elisha and even justify the horrific

3. COJS, "Annals of Sargon II."

fate they met.[4] Others could not hide their grim disappointment or resign themselves to the prophet's ruthless, vengeful action.

Despite Elisha's otherwise laudable career, they considered his severe cursing a major failure in carrying out his prophetic duties. Consequently, the Talmud suggests that Elisha's illnesses that plagued him throughout his life were, in part, a punishment for his overreaction by siccing those bears on the children,[5] presumably even with God's willing collaboration.

This troubling episode stands in diametric contrast to the young shepherd boy, David, who told King Saul that he chased a bear that snatched a lamb from his flock, whacked it, and retrieved the prey; if the predator made a threatening move toward him, David would smite the bear and kill it. Normatively, then, two scores of teenagers of David's age, could defend themselves effectively and chase off two aggressive bears, unless this episode was divinely orchestrated and executed without any sense to make of it. Like in all other cases, the Bible does not mention any encounter between a bear and a human that ended with the latter's demise.

Daniel and the Lions

Daniel 6 is another iconic story that informs us about the lions who interfaced with Daniel, a leading young chamberlain from Judea serving the new king of Babylon, Darius, who reigned over Madai (or Medes) and Persia. Envied by his colleagues, they conspired to bring him down from his elevated status in the court, but came up empty—Daniel was above reproach. His nemeses resorted to their default attempt to mar his reputation by linking his religiosity to insubordination against the king. Indeed, Daniel "of Judea" was soon discovered "red-handed" praying to his God rather than to Darius, a violation of a new rule that banned prayer or petitioning to anyone but the king. Offenders were to be thrown into the royal lions' den.

Devoid of any other recourse—the king's law is the law—Darius authorized Daniel's verdict. However, before he was taken to the lions' lair, Darius, hoping in his heart for a divine miracle, said to him, "May your God, whom you faithfully serve, deliver you!" (Dan 6:17 NOAB). The chamberlains, however, suspected that the king would try to save Daniel stealthily from the lions, only to explain away his would-be mysterious "disappearance" by arguing that he managed to extricate himself. To avert

4. Bible Hub, "2 Kings 2:24 Commentaries."

5. b. B. Met. 87a.

it, they sealed the top of the den to foil any attempt to extract Daniel from the pit without making it crystal clear.

Mourning for Daniel's imminent demise, King Darius retired to his palace and fasted while abstaining from other ordinarily pleasing activities. That night, he could not fall asleep. With the first light of morning, King Darius hurried to the den while still hoping against all odds that Daniel miraculously survived. And from the top of the den, he sadly called out, "Daniel, the servant of the living God. Has your God . . . been able to spare you from the lions?"

And Daniel answered, "My God sent His angel and he closed the lions' mouths for they did not harm me thanks to a merit that He has found in me, even as I did not wrong you" (Dan 6:23).[6] The king immediately ordered to bring Daniel up and out of the den, and he was found to be intact "because he had trusted in his God." To be sure, both King Darius and Daniel firmly believed that God stood behind Daniel's survival.

Nevertheless, this biblical episode only concludes when the king orders all chamberlains who had conspired against Daniel, their sons, and their wives, to be cast into the den. Before they reached its bottom, the lions ravened them all. The lions' simultaneous preying on the chamberlains and their kin, rather than sufficing with a sole individual among them to satiate their hunger is uncanny and a supernatural imposition on the story; a story that also runs contrary to God's law (per Deut 24:16) because innocent family members must be spared from the fate of the relative who was sentenced to die. In contrast to God's direct involvement in protecting Daniel in the lions' den, he is not associated with these deaths.

Being a Copy Is Deadly

The supernatural magnitude of the inexplicable survival of Daniel did not replicate itself again in 1991 when a very popular Nigerian "prophet," Daniel Abodunrin, was devoured by lions in a zoological garden at the University of Ibadan while attempting to recreate the story of his biblical namesake, Daniel. Whether permitted entry by the cage keepers or sneaking into the lions' cage, the Nigerian, with a Bible under his armpit, approached the walled area of the cage while reciting Bible verses, speaking in tongues, and calling unto the "God of Daniel" to perform the same wonders à la Daniel

6. Author's translation.

6. But as the "prophet" moved closer to the lions, they killed him and fed on his remains.[7]

Who Is "an Evil Animal"?

The term "an evil animal" (as in the Hebrew text) reappears in Lev 26:6 when God assures the Israelites that if they obey his laws, he will "grant peace in the land, and . . . make an evil animal cease out of the land,"[8] i.e., the existence of such an animal as a threat to the people's well-being depended on God's will. God could then manipulate the animal's behavior vis-à-vis humans and render it "evil" even though no animal heretofore was called or described as such.

Indeed, when God continues to warn off the people that if they do not hark to him he "will send-loose against you the animal of the field,"[9] God avoids repeating the word "evil"; still, the "animal of the field" could only wreak havoc on the Israelites at God's behest. Hence, the idea of an evil animal that harms humans—even killing them—becomes a biblical reality only when such animals do God's bidding as his commissioned messengers.

As we further unpack that biblical reference to an "evil animal" we come to see that God's "punchline" in that verse, the one that repeats the same message by using different words—"and a sword will not cross your land" (v. 6 PLAUT)—equates the animal with a sword, essentially meaning an external human enemy and war. "An evil animal," as we may recall, was a pair of words first concocted and used by Joseph's brothers in their conspiracy to cover up his would-be assassination.

But as it transpired, they attributed his selling off as a slave or mysterious disappearance from the pit to such a bogus animal. In other words, that fabricated "evil animal" was merely the brothers' intended action with which they poised to become such an animal. Jacob's spontaneous response upon seeing Joseph's blood-smeared coat did not necessarily exclude his pondering whether the "evil animal" that ravened on Joseph was one of his sons who slew him, with the rest of them being collaborative accomplices.

Ezekiel similarly refers to "an evil animal" (as in Hebrew, but commonly translated as "wild animals" as in 14:15; 34:25) that God would send throughout the land. The animal that Ezekiel invokes in his rebukes

7. David, "Miracle Turned Tragedy."

8. Author's translation.

9. Author's translation.

is a metaphoric punitive tool at the disposal of God against Jerusalem. The four mighty nations (Babylon, Madai or Medes in Central Asia, Persia, and Edom), which would wage wars against Judah, were symbolically tantamount to that "evil animal" in addition to famine and pestilence that would visit upon her at God's timely discretion.

Likewise, Ezekiel's fellow contemporary prophet, Jeremiah, mentions the dogs, the fowls of heaven, and the animals of the earth as those who would serve God by devouring and destroying Judea (15:3). These allegorical visions were ultimately realized when Judah was crushed fiercely by a human agent of God—the Babylonians. Jeremiah describes vividly in Lamentations the egregious level of their ruthlessness that they exacted on Jerusalem.

Though acting at God's behest, the Babylonians' degree of viciousness was a vintage of their own choice: "They have ravished the women in Zion, the maidens in the cities of Judah. Princes are hung up by their hands" (Lam 5:11–12;[10] or impaled on a stake, or their corpses exposed after execution for degradation as *The New Oxford Annotated Bible* comments). That the Babylonians chose that level of cruelty without God's acquiescence may be inferred from Jeremiah's petitioning to "pay them back for their deeds, O Lord, according to the work of their hands! Give them anguish of heart; your curse be on them! Pursue them in wrath and destroy them from under the Lord's heavens" (Lam 3:64–66 NOAB). The Babylonians proved to be Judea's evil conquerors in 586 BCE; they stood not on four legs, but on two, their hideousness being exclusively human.

10. Cohen, *Five Meggilloth.*

CHAPTER 31

Isaiah's Vision: Back to the Future

Until we extend our circle of compassion to all living things, humanity will not find peace.—ALBERT SCHWEITZER

Humans: The Apex Predator

While animals, albeit rarely, can be agents of mayhem and death when recruited by God to act in contrast to their normative behavior, the Bible also presents us with a vision of absolute harmony and amity among all creatures. En route to its fulfillment, the Bible (and the rabbis) sends us to animals to learn values and moral behavior such as gratitude, personal change, renewal, refraining from harming others, avoiding embezzlement of our fellows, and maintaining self-imposed discipline over our actions. Yet, we humans continue to believe that our race is superior to other species; why, God singled out our kind to be stamped with "his image" (Gen 1:27).

Nonetheless, humans have been veritably and invariably the super predator upon the earth, whose level and scope of ferocity and destructiveness of other lives—human and animal alike—has remained unmatched before and after the killer flood. The fact that the Torah singles out only in the seventh generation since the creation of Adam one *Hanokh* who alone "walked in accord with God," and then once again, Noah, in the tenth generation who also walked alone "in accord with God," effectively concedes the other generations' "great evildoing . . . [whose] heart's planning was only evil all the day" (Genesis 6:5).[1] But the would-be corrective killer flood did not change a single thing, so this grim reality continued, even as God conceded anew in its aftermath that the impulse of the human's heart is evil from his youth.

To be sure, the foremost killers of humans are, by far, other fellow humans. Humans have always been eminently capable of treating their kind like prey, not to mention other species. Though humans (as well as wolves, lions, and spotted hyenas) murder adults of their respective species, humans conspicuously stand out by preying upon their very kind and other kinds alike.

By contrast, the Bible neither calls any animal species "malicious" nor "savage," nor does it condemn predatory animals' modus operandi by such words. Nevertheless, we brazenly and commonly use our pat response to heinous human actions by calling them "inhuman," "beastly," "brutal," and "reflective of the laws of the jungle," thus associating them with wild animalistic behavior. Indeed, the Book of Genesis shows us graphically, even from the very beginning of the Bible, the ubiquitous prevalence of evil, malice, bloodshed, violence, abuse, bullying, discrimination, and criminality that humans can and are willing to commit.

Only when humanity is able to admit and recognize these embedded characteristics, with which it is permeated, will we have a chance to climb up from the moral nadir in which we have wallowed since Cain slew Abel, and Noah whimsically slaughtered fellow animal flood survivors. In doing so, humanity will make a good case for its eligibility to see Isaiah's prophecy, as envisioned in Isa 11, making headway towards its realization.

Returning to the Past

Isaiah prophesies a vision of a mended world by heralding peace among nations and within people, between humans and nonhuman living beings, and within the animal kingdom encompassing all species. The envisioned return to such harmonious relations, as it was back then when God brought all creation's living beings to Adam to name his fellow earthlings, or for that matter, when pairs from all extant species came to Noah's ark to preserve their kind, is then both a worthy and a feasible prospect. And it deserves, therefore, a renewed comeback. Isaiah thus declares: "They will not hurt

1. Author's translation.

or destroy" (11:9 NOAB), envisioning an age when neither humans nor animals regard one another—or their fellows—as quarry or menace.

This prophecy resonates both in Ezekiel and Job, while Hosea, too, envisions the sealing of "a covenant . . . on that day with the animal of the field and the bird of the heavens and the creeping thing of the ground" (2:20 DAV). This pact will not only retire the people's ubiquitous fear for their physical safety from the animal kingdom but for their crops too.

Thus, the human-animal (and intra-animal) amity—that prevailed from the fifth day of creation until the post-deluge Noah—will be renewed and return to its pristine camaraderie. The reinstituted rapport will hence upend the current state of "red in tooth and claw" (a phrase coined by English poet Alfred Tennyson). Animal sustenance will then revert to plants only (even as it was on Noah's ark); so, it is not an esoteric idea that had not been actualized before. Hence, past carnivorous animals (e.g., the bear) will no longer prey on others (e.g., the cow), returning to graze hay likewise. Indeed, it will be a return by choice, rather than by a divine edict to abstain from eating the flesh of one another, back to the "Golden Age"[2] of harmony and peace encompassing all creatures.

The scenario of "And a calf, and a lion and a fatling together and a little child is leading them" (Isa 11:6 STONE) demonstrates that such animals will not merely live side by side, but rather in unity to double down on their reestablished kindred friendship. Placing the predator amid two prey animals adds to the sense of the quarry animals' well-being. Bible scholar Yair Zakovich points out that this vision of a new order, where the circle is closed when the future returns to the past of creation's first ten generations, will feature even a gentler version of the original state of affairs. Humanity was charged back then with dominating the animal kingdom; such mastery of animals would shift from adults to children, a much gentler relationship.[3]

As to predatory and prey animals, the leopard will be the one to "seek that closeness to highlight their mutual tranquility and peace."[4] Notably, when only two animals are mentioned in one breath—as in "And a lion will eat hay like cattle" (v. 7 STONE)—by having the lion as the subject, like the wolf and the leopard with each being the erstwhile killing animal, the prophet intimates that it will be the predators' initiative to change their

2. Frankel, "Va-yetse," 212.

3. Zakovitch, "Gan eden."

4. Frankel, "Va-yetse," 209.

current nature. And it is they who "will come to their weaker counterparts" to lower their previous powerful status and equalize it to the station of those they used to scarf down on. Thus, they will "reform themselves repentantly by disarming their very hunting activity, and by ending once and for all their carnivorous conduct,"[5] as Bible scholar Leah Frankel acutely observes.

When Isaiah prophesies "their children [i.e., the cow's and the bear's] shall lie down together" (v. 7 STONE), he places the (Hebrew) word "together" first to impart the sense of a given, or from the outset. As we saw before, in using the (Hebrew) word for "their children"—not "their cubs" or "their calves" but "their children," the same word that is used for human kids—Isaiah further implies that the peaceful camaraderie of the two mothers, "the cow and the [she-] bear" will not only be a temporary phase for this very generation, but one that is bequeathed from mother to child from one generation to the next.

Like "a pet animal designated to entertain toddlers"[6] the "new" snake—as in Isaiah's vision—will neither be seen nor heard outside its hole. And although a defenseless "nursing baby" or "weaned infant" (v. 8) will actively play at the opening of a deadly snake's lair, there will be no fear of a hostile encounter, despite the age-old human–snake enmity. Children will be safe in the company of snakes as "the danger [for either player] will be succeeded by eternal calmness."[7]

Recognizing His Error: Rabbi Yehudah the Prince

Possibly, the Talmud, too, chose to double down on Isaiah's vision of the end of meat eating by telling the story of an esteemed talmudic rabbi, Yehudah HaNasi (the "prince"). So important was this story for the ancient rabbis that they included it also in the sacred literature (i.e., *Bereshit Rabbah*, *Yalkut Shimoni*, and in the Jerusalem Talmud to boot). The story traces Rabbi Yehudah's suffering to the following incident: One day, a calf was led to slaughter. The animal, sensing its imminent doom, fled to Rabbi Yehudah. It hung its head on the corner of his garment and wept. (A calf has feelings; not only does it know when it is led to its demise, but it also wants to live, and hence seeks compassion wherever it might be found—perchance, a sympathetic preeminent rabbi.)

5. Frankel, "Va-yetse," 210.

6. Zakovitch and Shinan, *Lo kach*, 29.

7. Frankel, "Va-yetse," 211.

But the sage callously—seemingly citing from a studious and stern protocol—told the hapless calf, which tried to meet the rabbi's eyes: "Go! You were created for this purpose" (i.e., to have your flesh as food for humans). These decisive and unambiguous words that the sage blurted at the terrified calf exposed him as a person who believed that he could speak for God in this matter, unaware that his words to the calf did not necessarily represent God's stance. At that moment, heaven decreed, "Since Rabbi Yehudah failed to show compassion to the calf, the Rabbi should suffer painful dental afflictions himself."

Rabbi Yehudah's response to the calf was wrong. The slaughterhouse was not the calf's proper or natural last address. The scholarly rabbi who was very likely engaged in learning the Torah when the poor calf ran to him seeking sympathy and protection, if not God's succor, should have known better what the Torah teaches about eating meat. Indeed, there was an essential moral flaw in killing animals for food. And even when the Torah does permit eating meat (like the permission to enslave other humans, albeit committing the master to a strict code of conduct), it does not permit cruelty to animals or even to ignore their predicament.

Yet, the sage was disengaged from the painful realities of the imperfect world where he lived, just like ours today, a world where one like him must study the Torah while a calf must be slain to become gratuitous food. "C'est la vie," said the preeminent Torah scholar to the doomed animal, reminding it that this world has its order and there is no need to seek to change it. When mere abstract study failed him, Rabbi Yehudah's prolonged, excruciating comeuppance sensitized and connected him not only to the long-ago-butchered calf but to the ongoing abuse and suffering of other sentient animals.

Rabbi Yehudah was only healed and relieved from his agony thirteen years later when he asked his maidservant not to harm small rodents she discovered in the house and allow them to remain there, for "God's compassion extends to all of His creations" (Ps 145:9); Hence, the talmudic rabbis posit that as heaven saw Rabbi Yehudah's compassion, "They [the 'royal we'] said: 'Since he has pity, we will have mercy on him.'"[8]

Dispatching the rodents in his house as the maidservant was contemplating doing would have been a normative thing to do, as Bible professor Yael Shemesh writes. By telling her to let them stay in the house, Rabbi Yehudah acted in an exceptional way, contrary to housekeeping standards.

8. b. B. Met. 85a.

And while thirteen years earlier he neither could nor would hear the calf's weeping voice and offer his empathy, if not custody when acutely needed, the rabbi was able to hear now in his soul the rodents' presumed voiceless weep for compassion. "It is quite possible that this new stance came in response to the horrific ordeals that descended on him and purified his soul, leading Rabbi Yehudah to identify with the plights of others, even of young rodents."[9]

In choosing to include this story in the Talmud (and elsewhere) the rabbis taught that people, especially eminent Torah scholars, were not created solely to serve humans and their delectations. Moreover, even a genuinely admired scholar must not stiffen and harden his heart vis-à-vis other ensouled creatures who wish to avoid pain and escape death.

The significance of this story is not only in the grand attention that the rabbis have given to the awareness of animal suffering but also in suggesting that a total transformation of attitude accompanied by a new behavioral reality is possible, even as we wonder whether Isaiah's vision of all species' goodwill could ever transpire. Rabbi Yehudah evinces greatness in his ability to recognize his mistake and change his thinking by repenting for his pitiless attitude toward the calf.

His revamped stance symbolizes Isaiah's vision of a dramatic change in the relationship between predatory and prey animals alongside humans and animals, and it is not a far-fetched illusion or fantasy. Despite God's concession that "the impulse of the human heart is evil from youth," this proclivity is not a determinant of the human DNA; ergo, it may change course one day. For that reason, Isaiah's vision for a new tomorrow—even at the end times when a new era of post-history shall commence—is a valid concept worthy of realization.

Done but Incomplete

After all tomorrow is another day
—SCARLET O'HARA, *GONE WITH THE WIND*

9. Shemesh, "Rabbi Yehuda."

Bibliography

"11 Allies Condemn Nazi War on Jews; United Nations Issue Joint Declaration of Protest on 'Cold-Blooded Extermination.'" *New York Times*, Dec. 18, 1942. https://www.nytimes.com/1942/12/18/archives/11-allies-condemn-nazi-war-on-jews-united-nations-issue-joint.html.

Abarbanel, Isaac. "Abarbanel on Torah." Sefaria. https://www.sefaria.org/Abarbanel_on_Torah?tab=contents.

Adams, Cecil. "Was Born Free Author Joy Adamson Killed by a Lion—or Murdered?" Straight Dope, Mar. 28, 1985. https://www.straightdope.com/21341599/was-em-born-free-em-author-joy-adamson-killed-by-a-lion-or-murdered.

Aelian. *On the Characteristics of Animals*. Translated by A. F. Scholfield. Vol. 2. Loeb Classical Library. Cambridge: Harvard University Press 1959.

Ahmed, Suhail. "12 Most Dangerous Creatures in North America." Animals Around the Globe, Aug. 18, 2025. https://www.animalsaroundtheglobe.com/12-most-dangerous-creatures-in-north-america-4-302436/.

Albo, Joseph. *Sefer HaIkkarim* (*Book of Principles*). Philadelphia: Jewish Publications Society of America, 1929.

Alchetron. "Gustav Wagner." Sept. 20, 2024. https://alchetron.com/Gustav-Wagner.

Aleichem, Shalom. *Chayei Adam* (*The Life of a Person*). Translated by I. D. Berkovitch. Tel Aviv: Dvir, 1968.

Alund, Natalie Nesya. "Rodeo Bull Named 'Party Bus' Jumps Fence and Charges Spectators, Injuring 3." *USA Today*, June 9, 2024. https://www.usatoday.com/story/sports/2024/06/10/sisters-rodeo-bull-escapes-jumps-fence-videos/74042097007/.

American Foundation for the Blind. "Helen Keller Quotes on Progress." https://afb.org/about-afb/history/helen-keller/helen-keller-quotes/helen-keller-quotes-progress.

American Humane Society. "Facts About the Link Between Violence to People and Violence to Animals." https://www.animalhumanesociety.org/sites/default/files/media/files/2017-07/TheLinkBetweenViolence.pdf.

Amichai, Yehuda. *The Selected Poetry of Yehuda Amichai*. Translated by Chana Bloch and Stephen Mitchell. Oakland: University of California Press, 2013.

Answers. "What Happens to Males When a Pride Is Taken Over by a New Dominant Male Lion? Feb. 6, 2025. https://www.answers.com/biology/What-happens-to-males-when-a-pride-is-taken-over-by-a-new-dominant-male-lion.

———. "What Percentage of All Animals Are Carnivores?" May 25, 2024. https://qa.answers.com/natural-sciences/What_percentage_of_all_animals_are_carnivores.

Archaeology Newsroom. "Team Discovers 12,000-Year-Old Flutes Made from Bird Bones." Archaeology, June 12, 2023. https://www.archaeology.wiki/blog/2023/06/12/team-discovers-12000-year-old-flutes-made-from-bird-bones/.

Ashkenazi, Bini, et al. "Netanyahu achrei khisool Sinwar." *Walla*, Oct. 17, 2024. https://news.walla.co.il/item/3698561.

Associated Press. "George Adamson, 83, Husband of 'Born Free' Author, Slain by Bandits: 'Brave Man' Died Trying to Help Aides Under Attack." *Los Angeles Times*, Aug. 21, 1989. https://www.latimes.com/archives/la-xpm-1989-08-21-mn-798-story.html.

———. "Thousands of 'Nuisance Alligators' Are Killed Each Year." WTSP, Dec. 4, 2022. https://www.wtsp.com/article/life/animals/thousands-nuisance-alligators-killed-each-year/67-e1dfb58e-02ac-4f57-beb8-f0510e1a7a76.

AZ Quotes. "Albert Camus Quotes." https://www.azquotes.com/author/2398-Albert_Camus.

———. "Mark Twain Quotes." https://www.azquotes.com/author/14883-Mark_Twain.

———. "Robert Frost." https://www.azquotes.com/quote/920256.

"Bal Tashchit – Achrayoot sevivatit." Sefaria. https://www.sefaria.org/sheets/217934.1?lang=bi.

BBC. "Coronavirus: Wild Animals Enjoy Freedom of a Quieter World." Apr. 28, 2020. https://www.bbc.com/news/world-52459487.

———. "Juliane Koepcke: How I Survived a Plane Crash." Mar. 24, 2012. https://www.bbc.com/news/magazine-17476615.

Beddoes, Zanny Minton. "*The Economist* Interviews Volodymyr Zelensky." *The Economist*, Dec. 31, 2023. 3:12. https://www.youtube.com/watch?v=I4ZRw96TP8Q&t=4s.

Ben Asher, Jacob. *Baal HaTurim Chumash—Devarim*. Translated by Jacob Mermelstein. New York: Mesorah, 2004.

Berkowitz, Adam Eliyahu. "Mount Ebal: The Lost Altar Scientists Refuse to Find." Israel365News, Dec. 25, 2018. https://israel365news.com/327997/mount-ebal-lost-altar/.

Bible Hub. "2 Kings 2:24 Commentaries." https://biblehub.com/commentaries/2_kings/2-24.htm.

———. "2 Samuel 23:20 Commentaries." https://biblehub.com/commentaries/2_samuel/23-20.htm.

Bible Outlines. "Numbers 19:1-22—Laws of Cleansing—Dealing with Defilement from Death." https://www.bibleoutlines.com/numbers-191-22-laws-on-cleansing-dealing-with-defilement-from-death/.

The Blinkist Team. "Top 10 Albert Camus Quotes to Inspire Existential Reflection." Blinkist Magazine, Nov. 29, 2023. https://www.blinkist.com/magazine/posts/top-albert-camus-quotes-inspire-existential-reflection.

Block, Kitty, and Sara Amundson. "China's Recognition of Dogs as Companion Animals Bodes Well for Its Animal Welfare Future." Humane World for Animals, Apr. 10, 2020. https://www.humaneworld.org/en/blog/chinas-recognition-dogs-companion-animals-bodes-well-its-animal-welfare-future.

Bodeen, Christopher. "Animal Rights Activists Target China Dog Meat Festival. AP, April 4, 2016. https://apnews.com/general-news-international-news-74172cdb55fc49f5a84d422b4fdaaa75.

Bond, Anthony. "How to Steal a Lion's Lunch." *Daily Mail*, July 9, 2012. https://www.dailymail.co.uk/news/article-2171236/Three-men-risk-lives-steal-dead-wildebeest-15-bloodthirsty-lions.html.

Bradford, Alina. "Carnivores: Facts About Meat Eaters." Live Science, Dec. 4, 2018. https://www.livescience.com/53466-carnivore.html.

Brainy Quote. "Ross Perot." https://www.brainyquote.com/quotes/ross_perot_10943.

Braslavi, Yossef. "Arayot b'Midbar T'koa b'sefer Amos." *Beit Mikra: Journal for the Study of the Bible and Its World* 32 (1968) 56–64. https://www.daat.ac.il/daat/vl/betmikra/betmikra006.pdf.

———. "Ha-isha'ag Aryeh baya'ar veteref ein lo?" *Beit Mikra: Journal for the Study of the Bible and Its World* 30 (1967) 12–16. http://www.jstor.org/stable/23502702.

Breier, Idan. "Between the Bible, the Midrash, Philosophy, and Kabbalah: Ethics and Animals in the Writings of the Maharal of Prague." *Journal of Animal Ethics* 10 (Fall 2020) 135–60.

Britannica Online. "Nanjing Massacre." Apr. 22, 2025. https://www.britannica.com/event/Nanjing-Massacre.

———. "Rwanda Genocide of 1994." Sept. 24, 2025. https://www.britannica.com/event/Rwanda-genocide-of-1994.

Brown, Emilio. "The Mighty Mouths of Hippos: Two Feet Wide and Deadly." A–Z Animals, July 15, 2025. https://a-z-animals.com/animals/hippopotamus/what-is-a-hippos-bite-force/.

Burkhead, Lynn. "Oregon Bowhunter Fatally Gored by Charging Elk." Bowhunter, Aug. 31, 2020. https://www.bowhunter.com/editorial/oregon-bowhunter-fatally-gored-by-charging-elk/383987.

Burin, Ofer. "Elohim mefarmet et haolam." Knowledge Production, Oct. 27, 2019. http://www.יעד.com/27/10/2019/אלהים-מפרמט-את-העולם-עופר-בורין.

Caesar, Stephen W. "The Annihilation of Sennacherib's Army: A Case of Septicemic Plague?" *Jewish Bible Quarterly* 45 (2017) 222–26.

Carmichael, Calum M. "Some Sayings in Genesis 49." *Journal of Biblical Literature* 88 (1969) 435–44.

Caspani, Maria. "Mountain Lion Kills Man, Injures Brother in Rare California Fatal Attack." Reuters, Mar. 24, 2024. https://www.reuters.com/world/us/mountain-lion-kills-man-injures-brother-rare-california-fatal-attack-2024-03-24/.

Center for International and Security Studies at Maryland. "Deaths in Wars and Conflicts in the 20th Century." University of Maryland School of Public Policy, June 20, 2006. https://cissm.umd.edu/research-impact/publications/deaths-wars-and-conflicts-20th-century#:~:text=%2D%20An%20itemized%20total%20sum%20of,of%20this%20sum%20are%20provided.

Central Conference of American Rabbis. *Gates of Repentance*. New York: CCAR, 1978.

Chizkuni. *Perushei HaTorah*. Jerusalem: Mossad HaRav Kook, 1982.

Citatis. "Andrew Linzey Quotes." https://citatis.com/a27977/174b21/.

Cohen, A. T*he Five Megilloth*. 9th ed. Soncinco Books of the Bible. London: Soncino, 1970.

———. *Joshua and Judges*. 5th ed. Soncino Books of the Bible. London: Soncino, 1967.

Cohen, Matt. "Thousands of 'Nuisance Alligators' Are Killed Each Year." *Tampa Bay Times*, Dec. 2, 2022.

COJS. "The Annals of Sargon II, c. 722 BCE." https://cojs.org/the_annals_of_sargon_ii-_c-_722_bce/.

Connor, J. Burgin, et al. "How Many Species of Mammals Are There? *Journal of Mammalogy* 99 (2018) 1–14.

Crane, Jonathan K., ed. *Beastly Morality: Animals as Ethical Agents*. New York: Columbia University Press, 2016.

Crawford, John S. "Caleb the Dog: How a Biblical Good Guy Got a Bad Name." *Bible Review* 20 (2004) 20–27. https://library.biblicalarchaeology.org/article/caleb-the-dog/.

C-Span. "Secretary Blinken Remarks at the U.N. on the Israel-Hamas War." Oct. 24, 2023. https://www.c-span.org/program/public-affairs-event/secretary-blinken-remarks-at-the-unon-the-israel-hamas-war/634119.

David, Samuel. "Miracle Turned Tragedy: All You Need to Know About '1991 Incident' Involving Pastor Daniel and Lions of Ibadan Zoo." Within Nigeria, Sept. 24, 2021. https://www.withinnigeria.com/news/2021/09/24/story-of-how-pastor-daniel-was-torn-apart-and-eaten-by-lions-at-ibadan-zoo-in-1991/.

Davies, Brooke. "Man Survives Month Lost in Amazon by Eating Bugs and Drinking Rainwater from Shoe." Metro, Mar. 2, 2023. https://metro.co.uk/2023/03/02/bolivian-man-survives-month-lost-in-amazon-rainforest-18373004/.

Davis, Margaret. "Man in Uganda Beats Lion With Bare Hands In Bloody Battle Before Feasting on the Beast for Dinner." The Science Times, Apr. 11, 2022. https://www.sciencetimes.com/articles/37101/20220411/man-uganda-wrestled-ferocious-lion-leaving-severely-injured-killing-beast.htm.

Dentelsky, Avi. "Adam uvehemah (Man and Livestock): 'Al behemot keh-mayatsgot et ha'adam b'khamah misipoorey hamikra." PhD diss., Ariel University, 2017.

Department for Environment, Food, and Rural Affairs. "Lobsters, Octopus, and Crabs Recognized as Sentient Beings." Gov.uk. Nov. 19, 2021. https://www.gov.uk/government/news/lobsters-octopus-and-crabs-recognised-as-sentient-beings?utm_medium=email&utm_campaign=govuk-notifications&utm_source=994c7ffd-9c00-4347-9563-bc9a0754ecad&utm_content=immediately.

Derworiz, Colette. "Bear That Killed 2 People in Banff National Park Was Old, Had Bad Teeth: Officials." Global News, Oct. 3, 2023. https://globalnews.ca/news/10002378/banff-bear-attack-description-grizzly/.

Dohm, Michelle. "Dressed-Up Donkey Discovered at Religious Burial Site." Plos Blogs, EveryONE, Mar. 8, 2013. https://everyone.plos.org/2013/03/08/dressed-up-donkey-discovered-at-religious-burial-site/.

Dr. McDougall's Health and Medical Center. "Extreme Nutrition: The Diet of Eskimos." *It's the Food: The McDougall Newsletter* 14 (2015).

Dunham, Will. "Moroccan Cave Yields Oldest Clues About Advent of Human Clothing." Reuters, Sept. 16, 2021. https://www.reuters.com/lifestyle/science/moroccan-cave-yields-oldest-clues-about-advent-human-clothing-2021-09-16/.

Dunn, Rob. "Human Ancestors Were Nearly All Vegetarians." *Scientific American*, July 23, 2012. https://www.scientificamerican.com/blog/guest-blog/human-ancestors-were-nearly-all-vegetarians/.

Eberhardt, Davin. "15 Most Dangerous Animals in North America." Nature of Home, Aug. 14, 2024. https://thenatureofhome.com/most-dangerous-animals-in-north-america/.

Eichner, Itamar. "Netanyahu: Anachnu b'ma'arachah al havtachat kiyoomenu." Ynet, Oct. 9, 2023. https://www.ynet.co.il/news/article/hkevtt1111a.

Enviroliteracy Team. "Are Snakes Aggressive to Humans?" Environmental Literacy Council, Mar. 21, 2025. https://enviroliteracy.org/animals/are-snakes-aggressive-to-humans/.

———. "Could Lions Go Extinct?" Environmental Literacy Council, Mar. 5, 2025. https://enviroliteracy.org/could-lions-go-extinct/.

———. "How Many Species Have Gone Extinct in the Last 100 Years?" Environmental Literacy Council, Apr. 19, 2025.

———. "Where Is the Deadliest Mosquito Located?" Environment Literacy Council, Mar. 17, 2025. https://enviroliteracy.org/animals/where-is-the-deadliest-mosquito-located/.

Faguy, Ana. "Where Does America's New Secretary of State Stand on Key World Issues?" BBC News, Jan. 20, 2025. https://www.bbc.com/news/articles/cvg5kzk42xdo.

Fahey, Ryan. "Man Raised by Wolves in a Cave Admits He's Disappointed with Human Life." *Mirror*, Aug. 16, 2023. https://www.mirror.co.uk/news/world-news/man-raised-wolves-cave-admits-30705458.

Fairstein, Linda. Endorsement of *The Evil That Men Do: FBI Profiler Roy Hazelwood's Journey into the Minds of Sexual Predators*, by Stephen G. Michaud and Roy Hazelwood.

Farber, Zev. "The Mitzvah of Covering the Blood of Wild Animals." The Torah. https://www.thetorah.com/article/the-mitzvah-of-covering-the-blood-of-wild-animals.

"Fatal Dog Attacks in the U.S." Fatal Dog Attacks, Oct. 28, 2025. https://www.fataldogattacks.org/.

Feld, Ed, ed. *Day of Atonement Mahzor Lev Shalem*. New York: The Rabbinical Assembly, 2019.

Florida Fish and Wildlife Conservation Commission. "Statewide Nuisance Alligator Program." https://myfwc.com/wildlifehabitats/wildlife/alligator/snap/.

Flyn, Cal. *Islands of Abandonment: Nature Rebounding the Post-Human Landscape*. New York: Viking, 2021.

Fox, Michael V. *The JPS Bible Commentary: Ecclesiastes*. Philadelphia: The Jewish Publication Society, 2004.

Fraga, Kaleena. "This Brazilian Cow Escaped Slaughter and Headed Straight for an Amusement Park." ATI. https://allthatsinteresting.com/toboga-escaped-cow.

Frank, Eric T., et al. "Wound-Dependent Leg Amputations to Combat Infections in an Ant Society." *Current Biology* 34 (2024) 3273–3278.e3. https://www.cell.com/current-biology/fulltext/S0960-9822(24)00805-4.

Frankel, Leah. "Va-yetse Khoter mi-Geza Yishai." Prakim ba-Mikra. https://www.daat.ac.il/daat/vl/frenkelprakimbamikra/frenkelprakimbamikra06.pdf.

Frankel, Viktor E. *Man's Search for Meaning*. Boston: Beacon, 2006.

Gallagher, Tim. "The Hero Who Convinced His Fellow Ornithologists of the Obvious: Stop Shooting Rare Birds and Watch Them Instead." *Smithsonian Magazine*, Dec. 2024. https://www.smithsonianmag.com/science-nature/hero-convinced-fellow-ornithologists-obvious-stop-shooting-birds-watch-them-instead-180985445/.

Gabbelby, Peter F. "The Evidence Is Mounting: Humans Were Responsible for the Extinction of Large Mammals." Science Daily, July 2, 2024. https://www.sciencedaily.com/releases/2024/07/240701131808.htm.

Gantz, Benny. "בני גנץ—Benny Gantz's Post." https://www.facebook.com/share/p/1725SUjBdx/.

Ganzfried, Shlomo. *Kitzur Shulchan Arukh* (*Code of Jewish Law*). Translated by Eliyahu Touger. New York: Moznaim, 1991.

Gates of Repentance. *The New Union Prayerbook for the Days of Awe*. New York: CCAR, 1978.

Gender Security Project. "CRSV: The Circassian Genocide." https://www.gendersecurityproject.com/crsv-observatory-cases/circassian-genocide.

Gilmour, Michael. *Eden's Other Residents: The Bible and Animals*. Eugene, OR: Cascade, 2014.

Ginindza, Bulelwa. "How I Fought Leopard and Won." *Daily Sun*, July 25, 2022. https://www.snl24.com/dailysun/news/fight-with-a-leopard-i-punched-it-until-it-fell-20220725.

Gleiser, Marcelo. "How Darwin Felt About Slavery." *Orbiter*, Feb. 21, 2019. https://orbitermag.com/how-darwin-felt-about-slavery/.

Got Questions. "Why Would a King Ride a Donkey Instead of a Warhorse (Zechariah 9:9-10)?" https://www.gotquestions.org/king-ride-donkey.html.

Grazing Facts. "Wildlife Killing." Center for Biological Diversity, https://grazingfacts.com/wildlife-killing.

Greenberg, Yitz. "Covenant: Parashat Noach 5781." Sefaria. https://www.sefaria.org/sheets/268963?lang=bi.

Griffing, Alex. "Blinken Recalls How Hamas Gunmen Brutally Tortured and Murdered a Family of Four in Israel and Then 'Sat Down and Had a Meal.'" Mediaite, Oct. 31, 2023. https://www.mediaite.com/news/blinken-recalls-how-hamas-gunmen-brutally-tortured-and-murdered-a-family-of-four-in-israel-and-then-sat-down-and-had-a-meal/.

Grosser, Stefanie, et al. "Invader or Resident? Ancient DNA Reveals Rapid Species Turnover in New Zealand little Penguins." *Proceedings of the Royal Society B: Biological Sciences* 283 (2016) 1–8. https://royalsocietypublishing.org/doi/epdf/10.1098/rspb.2015.2879.

Hacham, Amos. *Sefer Iyov*. 3rd ed. Jerusalem: Mossad Harav Kook, 1976.

Hakmon, Alon. "O-nes v'hit'aleloot achzarit." *Maariv*, Nov. 8, 2023. https://www.maariv.co.il/news/law/Article-1050786.

Handwerk, Brian. "Elephants Attack as Humans Turn Up the Pressure." *National Geographic*, June 3, 2005. https://www.nationalgeographic.com/animals/article/news-elephants-attack-humans-pressure.

Harari, Yuval Noah. *Unstoppable Us: How Humans Took over the World*. Vol. 1. New York: Bright Matter, 2022.

Harman, Terry. "Why a Lamb Was Chosen for Passover? Exodus 12:1-14." The Tabernacle Man, Aug. 18, 2025. https://www.thetabernacleman.com/post/why-a-lamb-was-chosen-for-passover-exodus-12-1-14-by-dr-terry-harman.

Hebenstreit, Yitzhak. *Sefer Kivrot HaTa'avah he torat hatsimchoni*. Edited by Moshe Nachmani. Jerusalem: Hai Roee, 2017.

Hellmans, Alexander. "What Did Ancient Egyptians Really Eat?" Live Science, May 8, 2014. https://www.livescience.com/45450-what-did-ancient-egyptians-really-eat.html.

Hooper, Ben. "Steer Spared Slaughter After Water Slide Adventure in Brazil." UPI, Nov. 10, 2021. https://www.upi.com/Odd_News/2021/11/10/brazil-escaped-steer-takes-water-slide-Nova-Granada-Brazil/5071636575247/.

Human Rights Watch. "I Can't Erase All the Blood from My Mind." July 17, 2024. https://www.hrw.org/report/2024/07/17/i-cant-erase-all-the-blood-from-my-mind/palestinian-armed-groups-october-7.

———. "Iraq: ISIS Escapees Describe Systematic Rape, Yezidi Survivors in Need of Urgent Care." Apr. 14, 2015. https://www.hrw.org/news/2015/04/14/iraq-isis-escapees-describe-systematic-rape.

———. "October 7 Crimes Against Humanity, War Crimes by Hamas-Led Groups." July 17, 2024. https://www.hrw.org/news/2024/07/17/october-7-crimes-against-humanity-war-crimes-hamas-led-groups.

Ibn Ezra, Abraham. "Ibn Ezra on Genesis." Sefaria. https://www.sefaria.org/Ibn_Ezra_on_Genesis?tab=contents.

Ifergan, Shimon. "Dayarim b'Eilat divkhu." Mako, Aug. 30, 2022. https://www.mako.co.il/men-men_news/Article-f8f14e5059ee281027.htm.

International Wolf Center. "Are Wolves Dangerous to Humans?" https://wolf.org/wolf-info/factsvsfiction/are-wolves-dangerous-to-humans/.

Jakada Tours Egypt. "Egyptian Dog God: Anubis the Friend of the Dead in Ancient Egypt." July 25, 2025. https://jakadatoursegypt.com/egyptian-dog-god/.

JDN News. "Nesi hamedinah." Oct. 8, 2023. https://www.jdn.co.il/news/2049275.

Jewish Virtual Library. "Jewish Concepts: The Seven Noachide Laws." https://www.jewishvirtuallibrary.org/the-seven-noachide-laws.

Josephus. *Against Apion*. Book 2. https://www.earlyjewishwritings.com/text/josephus/apion2.html.

———. *The Wars of the Jews*. Book 1. https://www.earlyjewishwritings.com/text/josephus/war1.html.

Kaplan, Mordechai, M. *Questions Jews Ask: Reconstructionist Answers*. New York: Reconstructionist, 1956.

Karo, Yossef. *Shulchan Aruch: Code of Jewish Law*. Translated by Eliyahu Touger and Uri Kaploun. New York: Kehot, 2004.

Keeley, Matt. "More People Die Taking Selfies Than by Shark Attacks." *Newsweek*, June 28, 2019. https://www.newsweek.com/selfies-deadlier-shark-attacks-1446363.

Kehati, Pinchas. *Masechet Avot*. Jerusalem: Kontres Yomi, 1983.

Kikar HaShabbat. "B'ma'amad kore'a lev." Mar. 13, 2011. https://www.kikar.co.il/israel-news/64478.

Klimek, Chris. "Are Wild Animals Really Just Like Us?" *Smithsonian Magazine*, Sept. 21, 2023. https://www.smithsonianmag.com/science-nature/are-wild-animals-really-just-like-us-180982939/.

Kli Yakar. "Kli Yakar on Deuteronomy." Sefaria. https://www.sefaria.org/Kli_Yakar_on_Deuteronomy?tab=contents.

Kokkinidis, Tasos. "Horrific Details Emerge as Coroner Finds British Hiker Eaten by Wolves in Greece." *Greek Reporter*, Sept. 28, 2017. https://greekreporter.com/2017/09/28/horrific-details-emerge-as-coroner-finds-british-hiker-eaten-by-wolves-in-greece/.

Kook, Abraham Isaac Hacohen. "A Vision of Vegetarianism and Peace." Edited by David Cohen. Translated by Jonathan Rubenstein. Unpublished thesis. https://archive.org/details/AVisionOfVegetarianismAndPeace/mode/2up.

Korte, Gregory, and Alan Gomez. "Trump Ramps Up Rhetoric on Undocumented Immigrants: 'These Aren't People, These Are Animals.'" *USA Today*, May 16, 2018. https://www.usatoday.com/story/news/politics/2018/05/16/trump-immigrants-animals-mexico-democrats-sanctuary-cities/617252002/.

Kraus, Yair. "Toshavey gvul hatsafon punoo, hachayot yotsot vehateva pore'ach." Ynet, Feb. 5, 2024. https://www.ynet.co.il/environment-science/article/byxa6ra9t.

Kuntzman, Gersh. "Cops Who Shot Bull Get Set for Grilling." *New York Post*, June 22, 1999. https://nypost.com/1999/06/22/cops-who-shot-bull-get-set-for-grilling/.

Kuta, Sarah. "What Wild Animals Were Really Doing During Covid-19 Lockdowns." *Smithsonian Magazine*, June 9, 2023. https://www.smithsonianmag.com/smart-news/what-wild-animals-were-really-doing-during-covid-19-lockdowns-180982351/.

Landau, Ezekiel (Noda BiYehudah). "Noda BiYehudah II." Sefaria. https://www.sefaria.org/Noda_BiYehudah_II.

Learish, Jessica. "The 20 Deadliest Animals on Earth, Ranked." CBS News, Aug. 29, 2018. https://www.cbsnews.com/pictures/the-20-deadliest-animals-on-earth-ranked/.

Leibowitz, Nechamah. *Gilyonot*. Sefaria. https://www.sefaria.org/collections/%D7%92%D7%99%D7%9C%D7%99%D7%95%D7%A0%D7%95%D7%AA-%D7%A0%D7%97%D7%9E%D7%94?tab=sheets.

Leibowitz, Yeshayahu. *Seven Years of Discourses on the Weekly Torah Reading*. Jerusalem: Kether, 2003.

Libquotes. "Charles Darwin Quote." https://libquotes.com/charles-darwin/quote/lbz8e2e.

Liles, Jordan. "Trump's 'Animals' Remark Referred to Migrants Who Entered the US Illegally and Were Charged with Murder." Snopes, Sept. 18, 2024. https://www.snopes.com/news/2024/09/18/trump-illegal-migrants-animals-murderers/.

Lillis, Kathy, and Alex Marquardt. "US Intelligence Suggests Sinwar Believes Hamas Has Upper Hand in Negotiations with Israel, Officials Say." CNN, June 11, 2024. https://www.cnn.com/2024/06/11/politics/us-intelligence-sinwar-gaza/index.html.

Linzey, Andrew. *Creatures of the Same God: Explorations in Animal Theology*. Woodstock, NY: Lantern, 2009.

Lunney, Joan K., et al. "Importance of the Pig as a Human Biomedical Model." *Science Translational Medicine* 13 (2021) 1–19. https://www.science.org/doi/10.1126/scitranslmed.abd5758.

Luntschitz, Shlomo Ephraim ben Aaron (Klia Yakar). *Kli Yakar on Deuteronomy*. Sefaria. https://www.sefaria.org/Kli_Yakar_on_Deuteronomy.

Luzzatto, Samuel David (Shadal). *Shadal on Deuteronomy*. Sefaria.org. https://www.sefaria.org/Shadal_on_Deuteronomy.

Magramo, Kathleen. "Struggling Pig Kills Butcher at Slaughterhouse in Hong Kong." CNN World, Jan. 21, 2023. https://edition.cnn.com/2023/01/21/asia/hong-kong-pig-kills-butcher-intl-hnk.

Maimonides. *The Guide to the Perplexed*. Translated by Lenn E. Goodman and Phillip I. Lieberman. Palo Alto: Stanford University Press, 2024.

———. *Mishneh Torah: Code of Jewish Law*. Houston: EitzEchad, 2024.

Malbim, "Malbim on Tanakh." Sefaria. https://www.sefaria.org/topics/malbim?sort=Relevance&tab=notable-sources.

Mariotti, François. "Animal and Plant Protein, Sources, and Cardio Metabolic Health." *Advances in Nutrition* 10 (2019) S351–66.

Martel, Yann. *Life of Pi*. Boston: Mariner, 2003.

Matthews, Melissa. "Humans Kill 100 Million Sharks Every Year, but That's About to Change." *Newsweek*, Nov. 3, 2017. https://www.newsweek.com/humans-kill-100000-sharks-every-year-thats-about-change-700854.

Maya. "A Man Once Spent 72 Hours Trapped with Deadly Snakes to Prove They're Friendly." Life of Us, July 26, 2021. https://lifeofus.net/blog/a-man-once-spent-72-hours-trapped-with-deadly-snakes-to-prove-theyre-friendly/.

Mealy, J. Webb. "You Shall Not Boil a Kid in Its Mother's Milk (Exod. 23:19b; Exod. 34:26b; Deut. 14:21b): A Figure of Speech?" *Biblical Interpretation* 20 (2012) 35–72.

Mendoza, Jordan. "Here Are the Deadliest Wild Animals in North America and States with the Most Fatal Attacks." USA Today, Sept. 20, 2021. https://www.usatoday.com/story/news/nation/2021/09/20/deadliest-animals-north-america/8353918002/.

Metcalfe, Tom. "1st Bioengineered Hybrid Animals Discovered—in Ancient Mesopotamia." Live Science, Jan. 14, 2022. https://www.livescience.com/hybrid-kungas-discovered-mesopotamia.

Michlelet Herzog. "Shiloh'ach ha-ken: Leket Mekorot." Da'at limoodei yahadut varuach. https://www.daat.ac.il/daat/tanach/tora/shiluah-2.htm.

Migiro, Katy. "Despite Murderous Attacks, Tanzania's 'Witches' Fight for Land." Reuters, Mar. 21, 2017. https://www.reuters.com/article/world/despite-murderous-attacks-tanzanias-witches-fight-for-land-idUSKBN16S2HT/.

Mikkelson, David. "Does This Photograph Show a Saved Whale Saying 'Thanks'?" Snopes, Apr. 24, 2006. https://www.snopes.com/fact-check/saved-whale-says-thanks/.

Miller, Norman. "The Animals That Detect Disasters." BBC, February 14, 2022. https://www.bbc.com/future/article/20220211-the-animals-that-predict-disasters.

Mishan, Ligaya. "What Does the End of Beef Mean for Our Sense of Self?" *New York Times Magazine*, Mar. 6, 2022. https://www.nytimes.com/2022/03/03/t-magazine/meat-beef-vegetarianism-veganism.html.

Myhrvold, Nathan. "Lions: Africa's Magnificent Predators." Edge, July 31, 2007. https://www.edge.org/conversation/nathan_myhrvold-lions-africas-magnificent-predators.

National Geographic. "The Development of Agriculture." https://education.nationalgeographic.org/resource/development-agriculture/.

National Park Service. "What Happened to the Bison?" https://www.nps.gov/articles/000/what-happened-to-the-bison.htm."

NDTV. "Bureaucrat's 'Behave Like Animals' Advice to Tourists. What It Means." Jan. 10, 2024. https://www.ndtv.com/offbeat/behave-like-animals-bureaucrats-advice-for-tourists-4837819.

Neath, Amelia. "California Man, 34, Was Supposed to Go on a 3-Hour Hike. He Was Found 10 Days Later Covered in Mud." *The Independent*, June 24, 2024. https://www.the-independent.com/news/world/americas/california-hiker-found-santa-cruz-b2567678.html.

Newsflare. "Man Kills Rogue Leopard with Bare Hands to Protect Wife and Daughter." Feb. 23, 2021. https://www.newsflare.com/video/412289/man-kills-rogue-leopard-with-bare-hands-to-protect-wife-and-daughter.

Ng, Kate. "Mother and Three Children Survive 34 Days in Peruvian Jungle by 'Eating Berries.'" *The Independent*, Jan. 28, 2020. https://www.the-independent.com/news/world/americas/peru-mother-children-survive-jungle-berries-a9305541.html.

Nied, Michael. "Girl, 14, Dies After Being Attacked by Lion in Home in Kenya." *People*, Apr. 21, 2025. https://people.com/14-year-old-girl-killed-by-lion-kenya-11718666.

Nitai. "Baaley khaim." https://www.nitaim.com/post/בעלי-חיים-ארסיים/.

Nitnaware, Himanshu. "Ancient Humans May Have Hunted 150 Large Animal Species to Extinction over 50,000 Years, Suggests Study." Down to Earth, July 21, 2024. https://www.downtoearth.org.in/science-technology/ancient-humans-may-have-hunted-150-large-animal-species-to-extinction-over-50000-years-suggests-study.

Noone, Gregory P., et al. "Russian Use of Rape as a Weapon of War in Ukraine." Public International Law and Policy Group. https://www.

publicinternationallawandpolicygroup.org/lawyering-justice-blog/2025/6/25/the-use-of-rape-as-a-weapon-of-war-in-ukraine.

Otzar HaTorah. “Melachim Alef, Perek yud zain.” https://www.otzar.org.il/
בית-מדרש/אוצר-המקרא-על-התנך/אוצר-המקרא-לספרי-הנביאים/מלכים-א/פרקים-י-יט/מלכים-א-פרק-יז.

Pallotta, Nicole. “China Reclassifies Dogs from ‘Livestock’ to ‘Companion Animals.’” Animal Legal Defense Fund, May 20, 2020. https://aldf.org/article/china-reclassifies-dogs-from-livestock-to-companion-animals/.

The Peak Performance Center. “Teamwork: Lessons in Nature. Five Facts About Geese.” https://thepeakperformancecenter.com/development-series/skill-builder/interpersonal/teambuilding-2/facts-geese/.

Pearce, Fred. “Poaching Causes Hippo Population Crash.” New Scientist, Aug. 29, 2003. https://www.newscientist.com/article/dn4109-poaching-causes-hippo-population-crash/.

Penteriani, Vincenzo, et al. “Human Behaviour Can Trigger Large Carnivore Attacks in Developed Countries.” *Scientific Reports*, Feb. 3, 2016. https://www.nature.com/articles/srep20552.

Pester, Patrick. “How Would Earth Be Different If Modern Humans Never Existed?” Live Science, Nov. 9, 2021. https://www.livescience.com/what-if-humans-never-existed-on-earth.

———. “Humans are Practically Defenseless. Why Don’t Wild Animals Attack Humans More Often?” Live Science, July 12, 2021. https://www.livescience.com/https://www.livescience.com/why-wild-animals-dont-attack-humans.html

Petfood Industry. “UK Pet Food Association Recognizes Plant Based as Healthy for Pets.” Feb. 6, 2023. https://www.petfoodindustry.com/news-newsletters/pet-food-press-releases/press-release/15469509/uk-pet-food-association-recognizes-plant-based-as-healthy-for-pets.

Philo. “The Midrash of Philo.” Sefaria. https://www.sefaria.org/The_Midrash_of_Philo.

Philosiblog. “All Cruelty Springs from Weakness.” Apr. 6, 2013. https://philosiblog.com/2013/04/06/all-cruelty-springs-from-weakness/.

Physicians Committee for Responsible Medicine. “Cancer: Reducing Cancer Risk With a Plant-Based Diet.” https://www.pcrm.org/health-topics/cancer.

Pinfield, Tom. “Addressing the Snakebite Challenge—Progress Towards the 2030 Roadmap.” The Royal Society of Tropical Medicine and Hygiene, Jan. 29, 2025. https://www.rstmh.org/news-blog/blogs/addressing-the-snakebite-challenge-progress-towards-the-2030-roadmap.

Poncet, Lisa. “Suckers for Learning: Why Octopuses Are So Intelligent.” The Conversation, July 6, 2021. https://theconversation.com/suckers-for-learning-why-octopuses-are-so-intelligent-162122.

Predator Defense. “Cougars at Risk.” https://www.predatordefense.org/cougars.htm.

Project Ben Yehudah. *Ma’aseh Hanemalah* (*The Ant’s Deed*). https://benyehuda.org/read/26144.

Propper, David. “A Rare Cougar Attack in 2023 on an 8-Year-Old Boy in the Olympic National Park in Washington State.” *New York Post*, July 30, 2023. https://nypost.com/2023/07/30/cougar-attacks-8-year-old-boy-at-olympic-national-park/.

Quotation, “Quote by Harriet Tubman.” https://quotation.io/quote/never-wound-snake-kill.

Quotes. “Schindler’s List.” https://www.quotes.net/mquote/82961.

Rabbi Kaganoff. “Mixed Breeds.” https://rabbikaganoff.com/mixed-breeds/.

Recker, Jane. "Scotland Issues Formal Apology to Thousands Accused of Witchcraft." *Smithsonian Magazine*, Apr. 5, 2022. https://www.smithsonianmag.com/smart-news/scotland-issues-formal-apology-to-thousands-accused-of-witchcraft-180979869/

Reed, Steve B. "Animal Phobia—Fear of Animals—Zoophobia." Psychotherapy Center. https://psychotherapy-center.com/counseling-issues/ovecoming-anxiety/phobias/animal-phobia/.

Reptile Knowledge. "How Many People Have Died from a Scorpion Sting?" https://www.reptileknowledge.com/reptile-pedia/how-many-people-have-died-from-a-scorpion-sting.

Richards, Bailey. "Mother Orca Still Carrying Dead Calf After 11 Days—Over 6 Years After Her First 'Tour of Grief' with Different Baby." *People Magazine*, Jan. 13, 2025. https://people.com/orca-whale-mom-still-carrying-dead-calf-after-11-days-8773627.

Richards, Jennie. "Charles Darwin—The Lower Animals, Like Man, Feel Pleasure and Pain, Happiness and Misery." Humane Decisions, Apr. 30, 2016. https://humanedecisions.com/charles-darwin-the-lower-animals-like-man-feel-pleasure-and-pain-happiness-and-misery/.

Richi, Evelyne Battaglia, et al. "Health Risks Associated with Meat Consumption: A Review of Epidemiological Studies." *International Journal for Vitamin and Nutrition Research* 85 (2015) 70–78.

Rinpoche, Patrul. *Words of My Perfect Teacher.* Translated by Padmakara Translation Group. Boston: Shambhala, 1998.

Ritchie, Hannah. "Wild Mammals Make up Only a Few Percent of the World's Mammals." Our World in Data, Dec. 15, 2022. https://ourworldindata.org/wild-mammals-birds-biomass.

Rothstein, Gideon. "Figuring Out the Torah's Presentation, Figuring Out Where Copilot Goes Wrong." Torah Musings, Feb. 20, 2025. https://www.torahmusings.com/2025/02/figuring-out-the-torahs-presentation-figuring-out-where-copilot-goes-wrong/.

Rowland, Mark. *Philosopher and the Wolf.* New York: Pegasus, 2009.

Sadiq, Muhammad. "What Happens When Animals Migrate Through War Zones?" Animals Around the Globe, Oct. 1, 2025. https://www.animalsaroundtheglobe.com/what-happens-when-animals-migrate-through-war-zones-3-335830/.

Saligumba, Maria Faith. "The Jaguar's Disappearing Lands: The Effects of Habitat Loss and Hunting." Discover Wild Science, Oct. 18, 2025. https://discoverwildscience.com/the-jaguars-disappearing-lands-the-effects-of-habitat-loss-and-hunting-3-279419/.

Sandoval, Edgar, and Thomas Tracy. "Bull That Escaped Slaughterhouse Dies After Being Tranquilized in Queens Backyard." *New York Daily News,* Apr. 6, 2018. https://www.nydailynews.com/2017/02/21/bull-that-escaped-slaughterhouse-dies-after-being-tranquilized-in-queens-backyard/.

Schaller, George B. *The Serengeti Lion: A Study of Predator-Prey Relations.* Chicago: University of Chicago Press, 1972.

Schorch, Stefan. "Do Not Cook a Kid Still Suckling in Its Mother's Milk." The Torah. https://www.thetorah.com/article/do-not-cook-a-kid-still-suckling-its-mothers-milk.

"Sefer HaChinukh." Sefaria. https://www.sefaria.org/Sefer_HaChinukh.

Shemesh, Yael. "Rabbi Yehudah HaNasi lomed." https://anonymous.org.il/art392.html_Anonymous.org.il.

Shrader, Adrian M. "Ecology: Humans Are Scarier Than Lions." *Current Biology* 33 (2023) R1144–62. https://www.cell.com/action/showPdf?pii=S0960-9822%2823%2901308-8.

"Sifra." Sefaria. https://www.sefaria.org/Sifra?tab=contents.

Sinclair, Henry. "What Eats a Hippo? 5 Hippo Predators." Wild Explained, July 9, 2022. https://wildexplained.com/blog/what-eats-a-hippo/#google_vignette.

———. "Why Do Lions Roar? Reasons Behind the Iconic Sound." Wild Explained, Mar. 23, 2023. https://wildexplained.com/blog/why-do-lions-roar/.

Slifkin, Natan. *Man and Beast: Our Relationships with Animals in Jewish Law and Thought.* New York: Yashar, 2006.

Smith, Patrick. "How 4 Children Survived 40 Days in the Amazon Jungle After a Plane Crash." NBC News, June 13, 2023. https://www.nbcnews.com/news/world/how-4-children-survived-40-days-jungle-plane-crash-amazon-colombia-rcna88791.

Soloveitchik, Joseph, B., and Michael S. Berger, eds. *The Emergence of Ethical Man.* New York: Ktav, 2005.

Solzhenitsyn, Alexander. *Prussian Nights: A Poem.* Translated by Robert Conquest. New York: Farrar, Straus, and Giroux, 1977.

Sommerlad, Joe. "How Many People Are Killed by Alligators in the US Each Year?" *The Independent*, Feb. 21, 2023. https://www.the-independent.com/news/world/americas/alligator-attacks-deaths-florida-louisiana-b2286682.html.

Spitzer, Maya. "'Desert Kites' Were Key to Survival 5,000 Years Ago." The Jerusalem Post, March 2, 2009. https://www.jpost.com/health-and-sci-tech/science-and-environment/desert-kites-were-key-to-survival-5000-years-ago.

Staff Writer. "In Pictures: How German Women Suffered Largest Mass Rape in History by Soviets." Al Arabiya English, May 20, 2020. https://english.alarabiya.net/features/2018/03/11/PICTURES-The-largest-mass-rape-in-history.

Stav, Avraham. "Kasher parveh: haTsimchonoot hee lo rak'hazon hatimchnoot v'hashalom' shel HaRav Kook." *Makor Rishon*, Sept. 9, 2022. https://www.makorrishon.co.il/culture/522895/.

Stone, Ken. *Reading the Hebrew Bible with Animal Studies.* Redwood City: Stanford University Press, 2017.

Sweetney, Don. "Coyotes Prowl Empty San Francisco Streets as Coronavirus Locks Down City." *Sacramento Bee*, Apr. 21, 2020. https://www.sacbee.com/news/coronavirus/article241616581.html.

Tesler, Yitzhak. "T'filot haklavim machazikot." Ynet, Sept. 12, 2022. https://www.ynet.co.il/judaism/article/bkzcborgi.

Thompson, Helen. "Why Some Mammals Kill Babies of Their Own Kind." *Smithsonian Magazine*, Nov. 13, 2014. https://www.smithsonianmag.com/science-nature/why-some-mammals-kill-babies-own-kind-180953318/.

———. "Yes, Lions Will Hunt Humans if Given the Chance." Smithsonian Magazine, June 5, 2015. https://www.smithsonianmag.com/smart-news/why-lion-killing-tourist-south-africa-isnt-surprising-180955512/.

Tributsch, Helmuth. *When the Snakes Awake: Animals and Earthquake Prediction.* Cambridge: MIT Press, 1984.

Tsavo National Park. "The Story of the Man-Eating Lions of Tsavo." https://www.tsavonationalparkkenya.com/the-story-of-the-man-eating-lions-of-tsavo/.

University of Wyoming. "UW Professor's Research Challenges Hunter-Gatherer Narrative." Jan. 24, 2024. https://www.uwyo.edu/news/2024/01/uw-professors-research-challenges-hunter-gatherer-narrative.html#:~:text=The%20oft%2Dused%20description%20of,a%20University%20of%20Wyoming%20archaeologist.

Urness, Zach. "Oregon's First Fatal Cougar Attack in the Wild Claims Hiker Near Mount Hood." *Statesman Journal*, Sept. 11, 2018. https://www.statesmanjournal.com/story/news/2018/09/11/oregons-first-ever-fatal-cougar-attack-reported-near-mount-hood/1272976002/.

Vaaitz, Carmit Sapir. "Im nihyeh tovim el hateva." *Maariv*, Nov. 13, 2021. https://www.maariv.co.il/journalists/Article-876653.

Varga, Tamás. "When the Light Poles in a Small Town Were Replaced, They Saved the Woodpeckers' Home." Earthly Mission. https://earthlymission.com/woodpeckers-home-nests-saved-light-poles-replaced-argentina-town-ucacha/.

Way, Kenneth C. "Assessing Sacred Asses: Bronze Age Donkey Burials in the Near East." *Levant: The Journal of the Council for British Research in the Levant* 42 (2010) 210–25. https://www.tandfonline.com/doi/abs/10.1179/175638010X12797246583852.

Wellbank, Lauren. "Hippos Are Known for Being Aggressive—Are They Actually All That Bad?" Green Matters, July 9, 2024. https://www.greenmatters.com/travel/why-are-hippos-so-aggressive.

Western Wildlife Outreach. "Grizzly Bear History." https://westernwildlife.org/history/.

What's Up New Brunswick. "From Janis Mirynech." https://www.facebook.com/WhatsUpNewBrunswick/posts/361214003160503/.

Whitaker, P. B., et al. "The Defensive Strike of the Eastern Brownsnake, *Pseudonaja textilis* (Elapidae)." *Functional Ecology* 14 (2000) 25–31.

Wikipedia. "Aurochs." https://en.wikipedia.org/wiki/Aurochs.

———. "Bosnian War." https://en.wikipedia.org/wiki/Bosnian_War.

———. "Gustav Wagner." https://en.wikipedia.org/wiki/Gustav_Wagner.

———. "Hunting Success." https://en.wikipedia.org/wiki/Hunting_success.

———. "Jungle Justice." https://en.wikipedia.org/wiki/Jungle_justice.

———. "List of Animals Deadliest to Humans." https://en.wikipedia.org/wiki/List_of_animals_deadliest_to_humans.

———. "List of Dangerous Snakes." https://en.wikipedia.org/wiki/List_of_dangerous_snakes.

———. "List of Fatal Bear Attacks in North America." https://en.wikipedia.org/wiki/List_of_fatal_bear_attacks_in_North_America.

———. "Mongol Incursions in the Holy Roman Empire." https://en.wikipedia.org/wiki/Mongol_incursions_in_the_Holy_Roman_Empire.

———. "Passive Rewilding." https://en.wikipedia.org/wiki/Passive_rewilding.

———. "Sack of Aleppo (1400)." https://en.wikipedia.org/wiki/Sack_of_Aleppo_(1400).

———. "Soviet War Crimes." https://en.wikipedia.org/wiki/Soviet_war_crimes.

———. "War Crimes in the Russo-Ukranian War (2022–Present)." https://en.wikipedia.org/wiki/War_crimes_in_the_Russo-Ukrainian_war_(2022%E2%80%93present).

Wikisource. "רמב"ן_על_דברים_כב_ו." https://he.wikisource.org/wiki/רמב"ן_על_דברים_כב_ו

Williams, Leoma. "11 Gruesome Cannibal Animals: Discover the Surprising Creatures That Feast on Their Own Kind." Discover Wildlife, July 16, 2025. https://www.discoverwildlife.com/animal-facts/cannibal-animals-creatures-that-eat-their-own-kind.

Williams, Ted. "Despite Criticism, the Last of the Rattlesnake Roundups Hang On." Yale Environment 360, June 4, 2024. https://e360.yale.edu/features/rattlesnake-roundups.

Wilmshurst, Janet. "Human Effects on the Environment." Te Ara Encyclopedia of New Zealand. https://teara.govt.nz/en/human-effects-on-the-environment/print.

World Health Organization. *Global Status Report on Road Safety 2023*. https://www.who.int/teams/social-determinants-of-health/safety-and-mobility/global-status-report-on-road-safety-2023.

———. "Homicide: WHO Global Health Estimates (2019 Update)." https://apps.who.int/violence-info/homicide/.

———. "Snake-Bite Envenoming." Sept. 12, 2023. https://www.who.int/news-room/fact-sheets/detail/snakebite-envenoming.

———. "Vector-Borne Diseases." Sept. 26, 2024. https://www.who.int/news-room/fact-sheets/detail/vector-borne-diseases.

World Population Review. "Wolf Population by State, April 2025." https://worldpopulationreview.com/state-rankings/wolf-population-by-state.

Zakovitch, Yair. "Gan eden b'har hakodesh birushalaim." https://www.lib.cet.ac.il/pages//item.asp?item=12689.

Zakovitch, Yair, and Avigdor Shinan. *Lo kach katoov baTanach*. Tel Aviv: Yediot Sfarim, 2004.

Zielinski, Sarah. "Humans Steal Food from Lions." *Smithsonian Magazine*, July 28, 2009. https://www.smithsonianmag.com/science-nature/humans-steal-food-from-lions-14896586/.

Zlotowitz, Meir, trans. *Genesis*. Vol. 1. New York, Mesorah, 1977.

Zoological Gardens in Jerusalem. "Persian Fallow Deer." https://www.jerusalemzoo.org.il/animals-en/persian-fallow-deer.